10 Days in December

...where dreams meet reality...

Dream.
Explore.
Discover.
—*Mark Twain*

Where were you in 1978?
Eleanor

a memoir by
Eleanor Deckert

BOOK 1

◆ FriesenPress

Suite 300 - 990 Fort St
Victoria, BC, Canada, V8V 3K2
www.friesenpress.com

Cover Design By: DADEM Studios
www.dademstudios.com

Graphics: Kevin Deckert
Photo Credits:
Author Portrait: Kevin Deckert
Young Eleanor photo taken by my Dad
Cabin: Fran McRae
To protect privacy, names in this memoir have been changed.

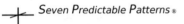 *Seven Predictable Patterns* ®

www.eleanordeckert.com

ISBN
978-1-4602-6503-1 (Hardcover)
978-1-4602-6504-8 (Paperback)
978-1-4602-6505-5 (eBook)

1. *Biography & Autobiography, Personal Memoirs*
2. *Family & Relationships, Ethics & Morals*
3. *Self-Help, Green Lifestyle*

Distributed to the trade by The Ingram Book Company

DEDICATION

To the Reader:
As I share my thoughts and feelings, memories and plans, what I fear and laugh about, hear and see, learn and wonder, love and dread, and even the tunes I am humming, please remember this: not one step of this Journey, not one hour of this experience, not one word of this book would have been possible without the on-going provision and encouragement from my kind, loyal, patient, strong, trustworthy, skillful, dedicated husband, Kevin.
"Thank-you" is written in between every line.

ഇ ✿ ഌ
...I was a stranger and you took me in...
Frances Mae Hulton McNabb McRae
February 5, 1927 – June 6, 2016
ഇ ✿ ഌ

ACKNOWLEDGEMENTS

Thanks to my Mother and Father for the myriad and various experiences you provided. Thank-you, Mother for playing the piano. Thank-you, Daddy, for singing to us at bedtime. Thanks to my siblings, cousins, friends, classmates and neighbours for your part in my growing up. Thanks to Kevin's extended family for shaping his formative years.

Thanks to my teachers and pastors for your patience with all of my questions. Thanks to Liz, Lauren, Lori, Dulce, Trevor and Lynne, Ian and Frea, Tim and Aleda, and Greg for believing us when we spoke of our log cabin dreams.

Thanks to my chapter readers: Riis, Andreas, David, Kathryn, Susan, Alice, Elaine, Sandy, Aarti, Roger and Lauren. Thanks to Lori, Liz, Uncle Peter and Fran for reading the whole manuscript. Thanks to Lynne Frizzle and Gord Dubois for their time and effort to proofread. Thanks to my Project Manager at FriesenPress, Pip Wallace, for the extra four months of encouraging emails while I took a detour mid-project through cancer treatments.

Thanks to Editor, Keith McNeill of the North Thompson Times, for patiently coaching me while I write news and views and local history for the paper for nearly 30 years .

Thanks to Dean Nicholson MA in Counselling Psychology, Kathy Green MSW, RSW and Professor Howard Hotson for their careful reading and insightful comments.

Thanks to Dan Deckert of DADEM studios for the front cover and web page design.

A special thanks to Fran and Archie, Jim and Cheryl for opening their homes to us 37 years ago and including us in their family ever since.

The original manuscript was a gift to my Mother on her 80th birthday.

The finished book is a gift from Kevin and I to our children.

FOREWORD

Who, as a child or teenager, has not dreamed of going off on a grand adventure, fighting for one's beliefs, exploring uncharted territories? Eleanor Deckert's *10 Days in December* recounts the real life adventure that Eleanor and her husband, Kevin, undertook in the mid-70's. Recounting the first 10 days they spent in their hand-build cabin in the middle of the wilderness of British Columbia, Canada, like a modern 'Roughing it in the Bush.'

But Eleanor's story is more than a story of physical survival. Throughout the narrative she weaves back and forth in time, reflecting on how her childhood experiences of family, education and church community, informed her world-view, personality and hinted at the paths she would take. And the choices were not easy. Raised in a church community which on the one hand provided a great sense of security and belonging, but which on the other hand told her she would never be able to follow her calling to be a minister of God's word, Eleanor left her home with her husband to find a way to follow her dream of being self-sufficient, family-focused and of service to the Lord.

It is a credit to Eleanor's writing that she does not minimize the angst, anxiety and self-doubt she experienced during those first 10 days. Rather, she takes us through all of the emotional, physical and spiritual highs and lows that she experiences, before coming to a place where she is able to affirm her decisions, her faith and her sense of belonging, despite the hardships endured. As a result, *10 Days in December* offers lessons for all who seek to live a more authentic life.

Dean Nicholson M.A. in Counselling Psychology

Table of Contents

Photographs to illustrate each chapter can be found
on the author's web page www.eleanordeckert.com

Chapter 1
December 21, 1978
Thursday

I expect to pass through this world but once.
Any good therefore that I can do,
or any kindness that I can show to any fellow creature,
let me do it now for I shall not pass this way again.
—*William Penn*

"I thought you were going to be in by winter?"

That raised eyebrow. That mocking tone. That taunting posture. That laughing eye. That smirking smile. She spoke aloud what the others were thinking.

Their doubt feeds my self-doubt. And I have plenty of those sounds in my head already.

For a brief moment at 2:00pm each day, the morning cook, foot weary and finished, the evening cook, bracing herself for the task ahead, sit sipping coffee together at the staff table while they exchange information about the progress in the kitchen and what's left on the to-do list. For a brief moment each day everything is correctly full or empty, chilled or simmering, clean and ready, the dishwasher silenced, the orange upholstered booths unoccupied, the sunlight like a finale streams boldly through the wall of windows. For a brief moment each day the morning waitress, cheerfully hurrying to meet her sweetheart and I, the evening waitress, new, fumbling, a misfit, pass each other into and away from the multitasking quick-step of serving customers.

And so, today, while the eyes of my more experienced co-workers question and their ears await my response what else can I do but blush.

I struggle to compose a civil answer. How many times have I been in this place, awkward, not fitting in? When my siblings play tricks. When the kids on the school bus name-call. When a neighbour kid laughs at my tears. When classmates fill my boots with snow. I resort to being super polite, extra bright smile, stiffly straight posture, clear diction. Good manners and rules are my security. 'Nice.' I want to be 'nice.'

I don't get why some people tease. I never know if it means playful friendly jokes, deliberately mean or just plain rude. So, I hide behind my 'never break the rules' mannerisms. I want them to like me so I try even harder to be 'good.'

Why does it matter to me what 'they' think of me? Why am I so easily shaken?

I had a blissful and secure childhood. In my teens I was sheltered while living in a Church community for ten years. Everyone had a half acre. Everyone had a big house with three or four bedrooms, a living room, a family room and a garage.

Everyone was white. Everyone spoke English. Everyone had a good education and a reliable income. Everyone was married and had children who went to the Church school. Everyone lived by the same morals, dress code and expected conduct. Everyone worshiped the same God on Sunday in the same way at the same time in the same place.

It was easy to get the message that 'different' was 'dangerous.' Yet, somehow, I thought that God was bigger than that. It seemed sensible to me that a Creator made and therefore could see and hear and love people of all colours, languages and creeds. And somehow I thought that such a Being expected me, not to remain in the shelter, but to reach out to the many possibilities and variations and alternatives of 'other,' too.

I have come to a very different part of the world now, but I believe that the Good Lord put me in this place at this time with these people for a reason. I believe that each one of them can teach me something I could not have learned if I had stayed living in the limitations of the Church community's culture. And, perhaps I can bring something good and true, something bright and worthwhile to this new place and people, too.

It's not easy or comfortable, though. Everything about the people here is new and unfamiliar to me. Conversely, I suppose that everything about me seems different and alien to them. But then, I am used to feeling like a foreigner. As a child, when our family moved west, I was from the east. When we moved south, I was from the north. When we moved to Canada, I was from the USA. Now I am in rural Canada and, clearly, I am from the city.

'In by winter?' If the first snowfall is the mark measuring the start of winter, then my co-workers see me as a failure or perhaps, lazy, a liar, a fraud.

These women, waiting for my reply, all know each other. Some have lived their whole lives here in the mountains of

British Columbia. They are satisfied with life as it is and hear my big plans with a measure of disbelief. These women see me as The New Girl. The City Girl who thinks she knows so much. The Girl who went to college. The Girl with the fancy vocabulary. The Girl who might know about Mozart and Monet, but doesn't know a thing about…well…anything a practical person would know how to do! In school I had ballet training and was a straight 'A' student. Now I am clumsy and continuously make mistakes.

"Eleanor?" the evening cook prompts me out of my daydreams.

My feet are locked to the floor. My posture rigid. My heart aches. Blinking my eyes, I blockade the stinging tears. It seems as though they join the ranks of others who have laughed at my values, at my dreams, at my world view, at my core. Time seems to stand still while my mind races to compose a respectable answer.

"Yes, we have been aiming to be in by winter," I reply, steadying my voice and I hope my face. "Today is the first day of winter, December 21. You know. The Solstice. Longest night. Shortest day. We are actually ready. We will move in tomorrow morning so we can unpack and set things up."

Darlene turns her back to me and shares her facial expression with the others at the staff table. They nudge each other and murmur while I step away and tie on my apron to begin the evening shift as waitress.

I glance in the mirror to check my appearance before I begin to meet the public. After all, since I came in out of the cold and shed my parka, hood and wool pants it is possible that my clothing is in disarray. Yes, my long, brown braids are still smooth. No, my brown uniform has not wrinkled, nor the orange collar flipped inside out. I tie my brown suede shoes on over my pantyhose, glad to be rid of the heavy winter boots.

Without make-up, there is nothing to touch-up, but out of habit, I clean my glasses.

How I wish I could confide in any one of these women. I wish I could hear about each person's childhood, thoughts, goals. We each have a story. I wish I could convey to even one of them the enormous sense of wonder of being led by the Lord, brought together in marriage, guided in decisions, protected during our travels and the many moments when obstacles were overcome and our needs provided for. From the first day that Kevin and I met four years ago, through to our arrival at Avola four months ago, our confidence has increased as our dreams become reality through our accomplishments.

Little did they know that the differences between us are part of the mission that was keeping me here. My life in the city was very predictable. This wilderness of trees and rivers and mountains, wide and empty and cold was not the only thing I had come to experience. This rural place and people were my attempt at entering a foreign culture. Work and fun, 'his' and 'hers' roles, family dynamics, status symbols, holiday customs, even the way words are used here is different from my upbringing.

A little discomfort between one culture and another is to be expected.

As my husband and I searched across Canada and chose a place to live, we were also seeking a rural town too small to have its own church. Perhaps by offering instruction and kindness to the children, we would be able to impact whole families as well. Besides the rugged 'Back-to-Nature' lifestyle which had become popular in the 1970's, starting a Sunday School is also my mission. It is a calling I have been preparing for since I was a very young child.

"What are your plans? Where will you live?" inquisitive neighbours and well-meaning elders had asked when Kevin and I had announced our engagement two years ago.

"We are going out west," I replied with determination in the face of their surprise. Yes, we would leave the familiar southern Ontario land of plenty and head out to the untamed wilds of British Columbia, Canada. Yes, we would leave behind the city with all the variety of cultural experience, theatre, music, sports, university, careers, friends, the Church and libraries, museums, shopping and endless learning. We would say good-bye to extended family, beloved congregation and Pastor, childhood friends and familiar places. Leaving behind well-known places where every need is met, we would go far away to a place where the very essentials of life would be a struggle.

Why?

The reasons for such a monumental decision tumble and vie for predominance. It would take a whole book to explain it. But one thing is obvious.

Mountains.

I have always known I would return to the mountains. From my earliest childhood in Pennsylvania, Daddy and Mother described to their four children the Colorado mountains he loved, the land and three-room cabin he owned there, envisioning a time when our family would live there. Young President John F. Kennedy was newly in office. It was a time when young families in America believed in hope, in personal goals, in a bright future which was possible with just a little effort. A golden era for the whole country was just within reach.

I remember the drive west, always west, towards the hot afternoon sun. I remember the crayons melting where my brothers and sister and I played on top of the boxes and bedding in the back of the Ford station wagon. I remember the long hours of flat land stretching golden and unchanging with the irregular ridge of the Rockies up ahead. Gradually Pikes Peak became a clear distinct shape and finally, there they were: the *purple mountains majesty* filling the eyes and lifting the heart.

For five years our home in Colorado was the centre of the universe that shaped my mind. Daddy had bought 52 acres of land from his Uncle Allan. It was a little valley with a rough gravel road up the middle. 'Talcot Gulch' was the name on the map but 'Hummingbird Hollow' was the name my Mother gave it when my siblings and I tumbled out to enjoy the walk up the driveway that August dawn in 1962, sleepy-heads rubbing our eyes and breathing in the fresh early morning chill.

Ponderosa pine were towering matriarchs. Aspen groves, spear grass, yucca, prickly pear cactus, sage brush, somehow found nourishment in the dry, red, gravelly soil. The precious rain also brought wild roses, wild onion, Indian paint brush, choke cherry bushes, the fragile blue columbine, fuzzy pink anemone and very rare white Sego lilies to bloom.

We first lived in old Uncle Allan's three-room cabin which was just down from the dilapidated cabin Daddy had lived in as a boy. The front porch offered a splendid view of mule deer or elk in the wild grasses, the tip of Pikes Peak just clearing the hill. When Daddy took us exploring we found diggings where prospectors not so long ago had hoped to find a second Cripple Creek. But only the sparkling 'Fool's Gold' was abundant.

Our cabin was built of rough studding, slab siding on the outside, building paper on the inside, crumpled newspaper and cardboard egg cartons were the crude insulation. One bare light bulb illuminated each room, turned on with a pull string. Mother had a wood cook stove in the kitchen and a white enamel sink, big enough for us kids to sit in for a bath. The outhouse was just over the hill. Daddy brought five-gallon tin cans of water home from a spring for Mother to use for cooking, drinking, washing and sink baths. The wood heating stove in the middle room was fed by the pine firewood that we all helped Daddy carry and stack. Unskilled in practical matters himself, he rented a chain saw and took it back whenever the cutting teeth got dull.

The third room was a bed room shared by Mother and Daddy's big bed, a bunk bed for my sister, Julie and I. My brothers were twins. A cot for Andrew in the bedroom and another cot in the living room for James caused jealousy at Christmas time. "But, James will get to see Santa when he comes down the chimney!"

Rex, our black lab, and Tommy, our fluffy black and white cat, curled up beside the wood heater stove while Mother read to us every night before tucking us into our beds. Stacks of library books were enjoyed. 'Mike Mulligan and the Steam Shovel' encouraged us to keep on trying. 'The Duchess Bakes a Cake' brought billows of laughter as the illustrations showed the cake rising higher and higher. 'Charlie Up and the Snip Snap Boys' was a world made of paper cut-outs. 'Flicka, Ricka and Dicka' were three sisters and 'Snip, Snap and Snur' were three brothers who got into mischief in their neighbourhoods. All of Bill Peet's amazing illustrated books stretched our imaginations while delivering a life lesson. After the storybook, Daddy would sing to us while we drifted off to sleep. He knew hymns and sea chanties, Gilbert and Sullivan and cowboy songs, Rogers and Hammerstein and opera. Although our cabin was in a remote location, my parents filled their children with an education of outings, a variety of experiences and fine culture.

Daddy was a professor at the Colorado College. He had been to school there in the early 1950's and this campus had always been his dream career location. In the summer of 1954, he had brought his young bride to Hummingbird Hollow on their honeymoon. Now that a position was open at the College, he could begin living his dream: to raise his own family where he had grown up.

Mother walked to the school bus with me wearing dresses she stitched for me to wear. While I was gone, a well drilling rig came, belching up cool mud, seeking to provide indoor running water. Later Daddy bought a house-trailer to install alongside the cabin because it was equipped with indoor plumbing in the kitchen and bathroom. Since there was not enough water in the well, Mother still had to go to the laundromat.

When the bright gold coins of the aspen leaves had faded and November's frost silvered the trees every morning, a dreadful day came. Daddy came home from teaching, just as the day became dark, slouched in a chair with his brief case still in his hand, his overcoat still weighting him down, his shoulders heaving, his hands covering his face. He wept. Mother came, asking, comforting, "What is it?" that could bring such deeply felt and agonizingly expressed sobs, moans, stammering incoherent sounds.

"The President has been shot!"

"Who will take care of us now?" I silently screamed. My young heart beat so hard it hurt. My Daddy's raw emotion met my eager patriotism. I felt shaken and afraid. We had no TV to see the grim Dallas event, Mrs. Kennedy's pink coat splattered with blood, their children standing so small, the entire country shocked. Immediately began the collection of unanswered questions echoing down the decades.

We attended Sunday services at the congregational 'Church in the Wildwood' and our family participated in the warm sense of community with annual events, meals together, choir, Sunday School, skating parties on the Green Mountain Falls lake.

The next year Daddy negotiated with a local architect, Bill Page, to build a one of a kind house worthy of the magnificent beauty of the view of Pikes Peak. Photos were featured in the 'American Home,' a nationally distributed architecture magazine. The year after that our youngest sister, Carole, arrived and the family was complete.

Sunday night Mother brought supper upstairs so we could watch 'Lassie' and 'Walt Disney' in black and white, our only glimpse of television.

At last Daddy could step into the golden future he had long enjoyed imagining.

When I was in Grade Three, my teacher read aloud Laura Ingalls Wilder's 'Little House in the Big Woods' to the class. On the very last page Laura muses, "This is now. It can never be a long time ago." When I realized that Laura was then about seven years old, the very same age I was, I began to deliberately notice the experiences and details of our family's life. I had a double motive. From that time on, I began to store up and remember my own life so that I could write it down for others to know about the time I was living in because eventually it would also be 'a long time ago.' Also, I wanted to reproduce these family customs in the future so that my own dream would one day become a reality: husband, home, music, books, outdoor pretend play, Christmas and birthday traditions, Sunday School, Cub Scouts and Brownies, choir, bake sales, community loyalties, annual events, small town living, all to take place on a large mountain property for lots and lots of children to romp, explore, build forts and feast on experiences in nature.

Suddenly, we left Colorado and moved to Florida. "Why are we moving, Daddy?" bewildered young faces asked. "Here, I am an Assistant Professor. At the university in Florida I will be a Full Professor," he explained. "If I can demonstrate that I am wanted elsewhere, perhaps they will offer me a better position here and we can return," I heard him explain to Mother. All of the children were disappointed. No amount of swimming could replace the fun we had had in our mountain home. Snow! Skating! Sledding! In Grade Six, I would often stare out the Florida school windows and daydream.

We lived in the suburbs near the school and swimming pool and went to orchards to pick oranges, tangerines and grapefruit. The ice-cream truck tinkled by in the afternoon. After we cleaned our rooms on Saturday morning, cartoons on TV filled the hot afternoon. With a buddy we were allowed to ride bicycles along level roads to the library. I read all of Laura Ingalls Wilder's books. I asked my Mother about one part. "Why did Laura's Mother tell her that 'Jeeze' and 'heck' were naughty things to say?" Mother explained to me that these and also 'darn, shoot, gosh' and others are thinly disguised cuss words. I pledged to remove those words from my speech.

The Vietnam War was surging, invading homes through the television, overtaking conversations, tearing families apart, sending those opposed to prison or fleeing to Canada. Racial tensions were spilling into riots. Miss America strutted across the stage for her crown while other women shouted and burned their bras in the street. Air plane hijackings made the news. Conflict and violence seemed to be the language of the time.

In less than a year we relocated to Ontario. In the mid-to-late 1960's, Canadian universities were seeking to improve their faculty and course offerings, hoping to attract and keep young, talented, ambitious minds in the country and stop losing them to the United States in what was called 'the Brain Drain.' Skilled workers, scientists, entertainers, talent were lured to the USA by fatter pay, more publicity, glamour and 'Big Names.' Daddy had a three-part reason to agree to the position. One: the university paid for our move. Two: he was offered tenure and soon the position of Chairman of the Department. Three: the Church community and school located near the University of Waterloo seemed an ideal place to raise his family.

In June of 1969, a moving van came for our furniture and boxes for the long drive from Florida to Canada. We slept on the floor until the date of our air plane flight. Mother timed it so that we could watch the first Moon Landing on TV before we left the United States. "One small step for man. One giant leap for mankind."

Mother made activity bags to occupy each of my siblings during the long day. I hid my anxiety about the air plane by tending to my youngest sister, making sure she was comfortable and amused.

Canada had a Queen on all of the money!

The farmland and opportunities in Canada were a benefit, but from the first I began to think to myself, "If I marry an American, I will live in the mountains of Colorado. If I marry a Canadian, I will live in the mountains of British Columbia or Alberta."

Ontario was a cornucopia of farmland producing orchards, cornfields, vegetables, livestock and an abundant culture of back yard gardeners. I bit into my first sun-ripened tomato, pulled a pippin from the branches of an apple tree on my way to school, pushed the wide, deeply green leaves back to search for a cucumber. In neither the dry, high elevation of Colorado, nor the hot, humid low lands of Florida had I ever before known the generosity of the earth, the sweetness of corn from the 'you-pick' field, the spectrum of ways to use apples when you have trees and trees to gather from.

As for my future dreams: I wanted the mountains *and* the farm...but first I would need to find a husband who would be able to bring the physical strength, know-how and steady, reliable courage to accomplish such a lifelong task.

How I met and wed Kevin is its own story. But the dream of the West is woven into the fabric of my life from a very young age.

I was so determined about a western home that I postponed answering Kevin's proposal of marriage until he bought a 30-day Greyhound bus pass and travelled to Colorado, up through Idaho to Seattle, into Vancouver, up the Caribou to Dawson Creek and Fort St. John, out to the Pacific coast and finally returned to Ontario.

And so, at the age of 20, "Yes," he said about the mountains. "Yes," I said about the marriage.

The ink was barely dry on our marriage license when we loaded up our red and white Volkswagen van and drove westward.

North, first and around the Great Lakes. Our first overnight campground was called 'The Whispering Pines.' In my mind, the Canadian Shield transformed from a coloured area of a map on the pages in a book to the three-dimensional reality of a vast, untamed world of lakes and rocks, moose and moss, water ways and trails. Unimaginably difficult to penetrate, I realized how much geography shapes history. And history became meaningful to me as I tried to picture the First Nations peoples' knowledge, the European fur traders, the Black Robed priests, surveyors and map makers trying to untangle the routes, avoid dangers and find necessary resources.

Then, West. Like walking through an open doorway, we plunged out of the dense woods and onto the flat-land, blue-sky, wide-open prairie. That night a hail storm was loudly pounding on the roof of the van which made it impossible to sleep as we lay in wonder at the forces of Nature.

How vast, how richly crop-filled, how much the prairies are *not* what we are seeking. Yet, I could think of the gladness of settlers who left behind hunger and political pressures in Europe to come to make a new life. I could imagine the loneliness of the women. Some were used to multi-generation farming families with well-developed cultural traditions and close family ties. Some had left fine city elegance, factory-made luxuries, education, entertainment, ancestral homes. How would they cope with living here without such essentials as schools and churches and doctors? My heart ached as I tried to imagine the grief of the displaced Native Peoples of the plains who lost their livelihood and boundaryless view of the world as the trappers, map makers, the railroad and settlers made claims to the land.

We paused to wait for mail, worked for a friend-of-a-friend in Cranbrook, BC, then entered the part of the Canadian map that we had been so eager to explore. First along the south. No. This rugged mining area did not match the picture I had in my imagination. Keep driving. Avoiding the Fraser Valley, the populated coast, the fiords and islands, we entered the north-south Okanagan Valley. Providing fruit to the world, this amazing geography was hard to comprehend. Sage brush climbing up every hillside. Irrigation bringing the valley bottom soil to life. Orchards tightly packed. Cherries, apricots, peaches, plums, pears, grapes and apples blossom and bear fruit as far as the eye could see. Who knew there were so many kinds of apples? Braeburn, Jonagold, Pink Lady, Honey Crisp, to name a few. Previously, I had only munched on Macintosh, Spartan, and red and yellow Delicious which had always been in my 'Mary Poppins' school lunch bag. Pressed against the highway, encircling the houses, invading the towns, fruit trees in rows and rows were marching up and down every gully and ridge. It had its own beauty, but, no. This was not the view I wanted out of my window. We kept driving.

The hub-like city of Kamloops was named with a word from the local Native People's language meaning 'Meeting-of-the-Waters.' Northwest from there was our next attempt at searching for the ideal location to begin our homestead. The Cariboo Country turned out to be ideal for cattle ranches. Wide, low grassy hills are uninterrupted by fences or towns. Gold Rush! Barkerville's gold brought a rapid population growth in the mid-1800's. Later logging and ranches, highways, rail and tourists stabilized the area. Nope, this was not 'it.'

We came to another hub, Prince George, and turned due west, towards the Pacific coast. The greenery changed from grass to thick forest, waterfalls trickling, spilling, swooshing into the ever-widening river. It was a landscape of deep, narrow valleys, snow-capped peaks, home to bald eagles, salmon, bear, elk, caribou. It was a feast for the eyes, but not enough deep soil, nor enough sunshine and too much rain for a self-sufficient garden.

We reached the Pacific Ocean at Prince Rupert. I phoned Kevin's mother. "We're 40 miles from Alaska!" She nearly dropped the phone! At our campsite I felt like a miniature human. The fern fronds were higher than my head. I ventured into the cedar forest, like a cathedral, arched and solemn, like light filtered through green stained glass, so silent with mossy carpets muffling every sound. The spongy moss was so deep, covering every rock and slope, so green, so many kinds, drawing life from every fallen log. What was this thorned, knobby branch supporting enormous maple-leaf-shaped leaves? 'Devil's Club' is the perfect name for such a violent plant, threatening the traveller with a nasty rash irritated by the sticky sap, spreading into any sun-lit space beneath the high rain-forest canopy.

Thank Goodness our only engine repair became necessary while we were near the resources and skills found in a town. While awaiting replacement parts for our VW van, we enjoyed a welcome pause to renew and review our mission. Certainly there were others in British Columbia seeking the 'Back-to-the-Land' lifestyle? But how could we find each other? We had seen posters in health food stores and laundromats from like-minded folks. And then we struck gold. While in the southern part of BC, we had purchased both the last copy of the August issue and newly unwrapped, first day on the shelf September issue of the 'Natural Life' magazine. Look! We saw the advertisement we had sent in! Perhaps, by some finely focused act of Providence, matched with our searching, somewhere in these pages there just might be the answer to our quest.

"We are serious minded, hard working young people: no drugs, no cloudy philosophies: Eleanor and myself, Kevin. We need to find land with or near other self-supporting families in British Columbia. We presently live in the city in Southern Ontario. So we need to contact any and all we can. If you can help us, Please write: K Deckert"[1]

Those magazines were better than a gold mine, packed full of information on gardening and chainsaws, goats and wood splitters, cordwood and homeschooling, natural birth and home remedies, pickles and jam, bread and cheese, solar and wind power, composting and chickens. Addresses, advertisements, recommended books, names of equipment and products...it was all there. We felt a surge of encouragement from people who were actually accomplishing with muscles and sweat what we were as yet still reaching towards. All Canadian content, the magazine was crammed full of essential things we needed to learn so that we could provide for our future family.

Would our dream homestead location be so very hard to find? Ontario and other parts of eastern USA and Canada, were so obviously an excellent choice, yet in these places precious fertile land was definitely starting to be crowded out by cities and industrial pollution. Beloved Colorado and the mighty mountainous regions of both the USA and Canada were harshly arid with gravel-like nutrient-poor soils and high altitude bringing early winter and late spring. The orchards in the Okanagan were abundantly ideal, but so very tightly packed. Would it be possible to find soil, climate, rainfall, a view, a small population density and no industrial pollution?

I noticed three advertisements that named places we would soon be passing through as we returned to Prince George, searched along the Yellowhead Highway looping south past Jasper, back towards Kamloops. I circled the information on the magazine pages to check out along the way. Burns Lake had a food co-op. Dunster had a farm-school. And I noticed a letter to the editor in the magazine that was a mirror image of our own advertisement. We said, "Here we come. Where is there good land?" And the other letter said, "There is good land here. Come and see." It was from a couple named Fran and Archie McRae of Avola, BC.

"We are a retired couple who have found the perfect location for gardening and small town living. Many abandoned homesteads here were once fruitful. The climate, soil and resources are the kind that the 'Back-to-Basics' young people are seeking. This 'alternative lifestyle' was so recently everyone's economy."

Kevin and I felt a new surge of hopeful energy as we pulled away from our campsite which had been home for a week in the rain.

"I feel like I am pushing the van!" I announced. "Or running underneath like Fred Flintstone!" I laughed.

"It's all downhill" Kevin replied with a silly smile as if the north-south, top-to-bottom page of the map indicated a speedier gravity-tugging coasting down towards the south.

So, back along the same highway, past Prince George then along the Yellowhead Highway Route to consider the last possibility before we adjust our thinking and go look in Alberta where the prairie meets the mountain range.

At last, now we are seeing the kind of landscape I have been so hungry for since I moved away from Colorado! Peaks meet wide, grassy valley floor. The little town of Valemount looks so much like the town of Aspen, Colorado, with a crown-like circle of mountains providing uplifting views.

"We might come back here if Avola doesn't work out," I suggested. There was a little grocery store, café, a few small churches, an elementary school and a high school. "I can just imagine walking in with my guitar and teaching Sunday School," I pointed to a little brown non-denominational church across the train tracks.

"Looks like there would be places where I could get a job," Kevin noticed. "Logging, sawmill, railroad, highway, ranches, mechanics all work here."

An hour later, the next sign of human habitation was a much smaller town named Blue River which also reminded me of Aspen and Breckenridge, Colorado. "Looks like they can turn snow into money," Kevin observed as helicopters were just beginning to be used to realize the economic potential of ski tourism.

Crossing the bridge spanning the wide, clear river, all at once, here we are! With exactly $40 left in all the world, we arrived in Avola, BC. We asked directions from the teenager manning the pumps at the solitary gas station. With the tiny population on a first name basis, we soon found the way along a dusty dirt road.

As we approached, along both sides of the road we could see abandoned homesteads.

"Look, Kevin! It's a sign that what we are looking for is possible!" I was bursting with excitement at the sight of grey, rotting log structures, tilted roofs, crooked fence posts, abandoned barns.

"It was all here a few decades ago." Kevin added. "It looks like it's none too easy. If hard working resourceful people tried to live here and succeeded, but at some point turned their backs and walked away, we will have to find out why."

On a sunny slope a gateway sign read 'Brooksong' and we had a sense that we had been led to this destination. We pulled up alongside an old log house and a young woman with two clinging toddlers stepped out on the porch.

"The letter said 'retired,'" I whispered to Kevin.

He stepped to face the woman and politely asked, "We are looking for Fran and Archie McRae."

And in her cautious, country-wise not exactly suspicious, yet, still guarded manner she replied, "I'll tell you where they are if you'll tell me who you are."

Although none of us recognized it at the time, this meeting with Cheryl was the beginning of a lifelong friendship.

Fran and Archie had recently found exactly what we were also looking for. This handsome, original log house was well built using fire-killed cedar. It was where they planned to retire, garden and enjoy the view. However, with nine children between them, one after another, the young adults had followed, finding work in the nearby sawmill and railroad. So, the older couple kindly allowed the young folks to squeeze into the log house's rooms and rafters while they lived in the house-trailer just a few steps away. The young woman with the little boy and girl were part of the family beginning another generation.

As soon as we explained how we came to knock on their door, we were immediately welcomed and indeed, adopted by the authors of the letter in the magazine. From the start, we were generously mentored, sheltered, encouraged and fed. It seemed that 'just a few more' for dinner was a way of life for this amazingly kind couple.

A waitress job at the highway truck stop was the only available income. $2.57 per hour was the minimum wage. And so, four days after arriving, I started to waitress at my first full-time job with Gloria, Cecile, Jennie, Georgina, and Darlene. Local loggers and railroaders, long haul truck drivers and leisurely tourists are the clientele.

Darlene is 18, engaged to Ed, 23. She moved here six years ago, with a Native mother and Irish red-head father. Her many brothers and sisters, both older and younger, have found their way into the logging industry. She is blond, petite and very sure of herself. She manages the friendly banter from the men as though it was an enjoyable game of ping-pong. She knows her way around the restaurant and knows the other women. She eagerly awaits her fiancé who comes in a big red 4X4 pick-up truck to drive her home after work. Once I asked about her up-coming marriage. As a newlywed, I had hoped we could become friends, confide in each other and enjoy the planning and hopes and little ups and downs of the relationship as the big day approaches. But, no. She has sisters and her high school friends. She needs neither my input nor connection.

Gloria is tall and thin, fast paced and blunt. She ties her white apron twice around her thin frame and moves with angular gestures. She sharply rings the bell and calls, "Order up!" when she lifts the plates of hot food to the shelf under the heat lamps. She corrects my methods, telling me which side to bring the plates to and take away from the customer. She comments on the length of time it takes me to answer each customer's request. She notices if the ashtrays are not spotlessly clean. She takes the money at the cash register to keep customers from waiting if I am elsewhere. She complains if the coffee pot runs dry. Her role as cook is busy enough. There should be no need for her to take my place. But I can't seem to keep up the pace. I feel inadequate and ashamed.

One soggy day Kevin stood to wait for me near the front door. Tired and dirty from working to build our cabin, he was withdrawn, not wanting to track mud on my newly mopped floor. He does not enjoy small talk. He gestured to me that he was waiting. I gestured to him that I was nearly done. Gloria made her own negative interpretation of his silence. "I wouldn't put up with that," she said to me, frowning.

Another time when Kevin came to pick me up on a sunny autumn afternoon, she asked me, "Aren't you afraid of him?"

I couldn't begin to guess why she said that. Kevin is big and tall, muscular with dark hair and beard. He is quiet and standoffish, but in no way portrays anything violent, angry or dangerous. Not until I listened to the women talking and learned more about the life of these western mountain families could I understand. She meant, "Aren't you afraid that he will hit you?" Was this the reality for any of the other women? Had they felt the blow, push or slap from the men they are married to? No, I am silently thankful, I could never imagine that nor have I ever experienced anything close to that.

Cecile is a motherly, experienced, no nonsense daytime cook. She can multitask in the oven, on the grill and still have the soup up on time and baking ready. She has five children with her Native husband. She has previously cooked for logging camps. Their family has been moving about the province as new logging areas open up, bring in many men, then close down as the hillsides are scalped. She might be baking for 250 men: bread, pies, cookies and muffins, tarts, and her famous matrimonial cake. She might have meat, casseroles, soups and a vat of mashed potatoes to prepare.

Since the sawmill in Avola was shut down two years ago, the town has become suddenly smaller. Only the eight railroad workers' families and a few who depend on the forest industry remain. With a population of 125, there are still road builders, fallers, skidder and loader operators and truckers who carry the massive cedar, fir, spruce, hemlock and pine logs to the mill 25 miles south in Vavenby.

I like working with Cecile. Her Native ancestry, her years cooking at the logging camps, her husband's travels and her five children's daily pranks make for lots to talk about during quiet moments or while I am in the kitchen preparing the salads, desserts or working at the dishwasher.

Jennie, also of Native ancestry, is a cheerful, smiling, community minded, Catholic woman. She works now and then at the restaurant. She can cook or waitress. Her husband is out in the bush for days and weeks at a time. Her only son is at home until kindergarten starts next year. She babysits for Cecile's youngest children and loves to be in and out and around the neighbourhood. She often tells humorous real life stories and always sees the sunny side of life.

Georgina is an older lady. Because I felt left out and small when I first came, not really trained in or given a chance to learn in a step-by-step way, rather I felt left to sink-or-swim, I made a special effort when she came, to show her everything. "Here is where the supplies are kept. This is the time to start cleanup. Let me show you how the boss wants things to be set up." Well! Here she was, an experienced cook with already many years at this restaurant. She had been away for the summer. I was treating her like a simple minded child! How embarrassing.

This week I am on evening shift 2:00-10:00. I'd better get started.

The sun is setting behind the high mountain wall. Slowly, but surely, the sky will be pitch dark in two hours. Last summer, when we first arrived, the sky began to be light at 3:00am and full darkness was not until after 10:00pm. Now the reverse is true. At this northern latitude, daylight barely begins at 7:30am. The mountains I love so much block the sun's rays in this narrow north-south valley until 10:00am. Direct sunshine lasts barely four hours until just before 2:00pm. By 4:00pm darkness will cover everything. It is hard to comprehend the reality of living with these limitations although every child's science book explains how the northern latitudes have less and less sun light in the winter and longer hours in the summer. Interesting to read about. Uncomfortable to experience.

My glasses steam up as I lift the lid on the hot steam table to stir the soup. Cecile makes the soup in the morning and it looks very welcoming, noodles, beef, vegetables, brown broth. But, my vegetarian needs will have to be met some other way. The salad in the cooler needs to be refreshed so I carry the bowl back to the kitchen and prepare the lettuce, carrots and tomatoes. The dessert today is peach cobbler. Cecile saved some for me. Darlene always leaves everything very clean and all the dishes done so I am ready for the first customers.

Big, new 4-wheel drive pickup trucks pull up. The women step inside. School will be out in an hour and the Moms like to come in for coffee before they go get their kids. They can see the grey log one room schoolhouse, built in 1939, across the street and down the hill. Gathering to gossip, these logger's wives leave their shiny-clean trucks running in the cold. It's not a waste of fuel, it's a status symbol to signal their more-than-enough income. They share plans for the Christmas holidays. Many have extended family right in town. Others will travel as far as Saskatchewan or Edmonton to see relatives.

An ancient rock slide tumbled down the notch made by Avola Creek, delivering rocky fill. This apron-like feature along the beautiful riverbank is the only place for 25 miles in either direction that is neither too steep, nor too swampy, thus an ideal place to build a town. The roads in the town of Avola are laid out in a simple figure-8. The railroad runs along the river bank. The highway is cut into a higher ridge. The town is built between them. There are about 40 houses and house-trailers with cats and dogs, horses and chickens, workmen and their women and children, elders and toddlers. The 20 bed motel, gas station and restaurant were built just ten years ago when the paved highway came through in 1969.

Cheryl parks, turning off the engine of her five-year-old GMC 'Jimmy' and comes noisily in with her two shy preschoolers. Her winter coat is not zipped closed and her tummy is beginning to show the third child growing inside her since summer. She doesn't buy anything. She brought eggs to sell. She knows that the women gather here at this time of day and she can relay a message or gain information she would miss if she stayed away. Her husband will get off work on the railroad in a few minutes. She came in from the farm to pick him up. The logger wives don't care much for the railroad wives. But Cheryl's cheery voice and peppy manner pushes past the limitations others set and she finds a way to mingle.

Today they are talking about the Christmas concert the children put on for the community last night. I missed it. I knew about it because 'Santa' came to the restaurant to get 'his' outfit checked out, beard adjusted and a pep talk from the staff before entering the scene. The menfolk have apparently made a disappointing Santa in the last few years, requiring a little too much 'liquid courage.' So, this year one of the Moms offered to give it a try.

The restaurant was very quiet last night because everyone was at the Community Hall just down the hill. Built with logs in 1937 by the same Scandinavian brothers who built the school house, this hub plays an important role in the social life of the people, especially throughout the long winter months. Dances, weddings, funerals, dinners, floor hockey, film night and the annual Christmas Concert draw people together for homemade fun. Whether you have children or grandchildren or no children at all: nobody wants to miss going to the town Christmas Concert. Traditionally put on by the elementary school pupils, the evening will include both culture and humour, contrasting reverent hymns and ridiculous rhymes, festive decorations and practical parkas, kindergarten recitations and tumbling routines by the older students make a variety show for all to enjoy. Sometimes an accordion, violin or guitar will appear. The teenagers might hold back, elbowing each other, commenting, leaning against the wall, or they might surprise everyone and join in with a skit or air band complete with props and costumes.

After the entertainment, wide-eyed little ones get their pictures taken with Santa who delivers a gift and a bag of candy to every child. Then there is a sing-along and cocoa and cookies for everyone. It is the highlight of the year. The two teachers prepare the entertainment. The 26 school students glow in the attention they get from the townsfolk. The Ladies Auxiliary group secretly plans fund raisers for the gifts and asks the grocery store for donations of oranges and candy canes.

A wave of heartbreaking loneliness crashes inside me as I overhear the cheerful talk of these women who 'belong.' I will share Christmas with no family. Not this year. For the first time in my life I will be away from home. I will have to be an adult and not a child anymore.

Next year, I hope to get to know the people here better, perhaps by volunteering in the elementary school. Then I will bring my guitar and offer to teach Christmas hymns and prepare a Nativity Scene for the Christmas Concert so the people can be reminded of the sacred reason for the season.

Across the snowy field, the teacher steps out on the top step and rings the brass school bell. The women leave. Cups in the dishwasher. Tables wiped. The room is empty.

At 4:15 the school bus arrives with the high school students. Clearwater Secondary School is an hour's drive to the south. On this shortest day of the year, students boarded the bus at 7:30 this morning in the pitch dark. As daylight gradually returned, they arrived at the business centre of Clearwater, a town of perhaps 2,000 people. Less than 300 students in four grades are taught by some 20 teachers. In contrast to the parents, few of whom have completed high school, the university educated teachers try to bring history, culture, literature, science and life skills to the young people who live in this long, narrow valley.

Ten years ago, there was only a dirt highway linking nine tiny villages along this 100 mile^2 stretch, with a population totaling perhaps 4,000 people. The students from the furthest three villages could not make the trip daily, so they stayed in dormitories or roomed in a distant city or dropped out. In 1969, (while I watched the Moon Landing in Florida) the bridge crossing the wide river near Avola was complete. It was the last link of the paved highway to close the gap. For the first time, the high school students could commute to school and return home on the same day. But the cost of this ten-hour school-day, including four hours of riding on the bus, resulted in the disappointing inability to participate in after school activities. There is an alarmingly high dropout rate. There is an alarmingly high rate of teen pregnancy. At ever younger ages there is tobacco, alcohol and marijuana use. The students have such a short time in the dark winter evening to complete their chores, do homework and prepare to return the next day. Opportunity and strain are difficult to balance.

Only five years ago the entire town of Avola was powered by a huge generator housed on a cement slab in the centre of town. At 10:00 at night it was shut off and people went back to kerosene lamps in their homes. No 'youth spending too much screen time' here. Recently, three TV channels have become available with fuzzy sound and blurry reception. If snow covers the mountaintop rebroadcasting antenna, everyone waits all day for neighbours to snowmobile about fifteen miles up the mountain to break off the ice and sweep off the snow, returning to view an especially important sporting event or favourite weekly show.

The nine teens who live in Avola are siblings or cousins, half-brothers or stepsisters. Some are friends since childhood, others have just arrived. These boys and girls, hovering between childhood and adulthood feel 'out' while in school with the town kids and 'in' while here stomping off the snow, jostling for position and carrying mugs of hot chocolate, coffee, tea, or cans of pop from the cooler to the same booth they always inhabit for a few minutes before walking home.

Today one of the boys who works on the weekends, stands at the cash register and takes the money each student digs out of their purse or pocket. Other days they might sit and wait for me to serve them. They seem to like to confuse me. They share sideways glances when I approach. When I turn to fetch their order, I can hear muttered comments followed by a burst of laughter. I am glad they cannot see me blush. They certainly are not comfortable with me nearby, nor I with them, although barely three years separate us.

Having slept most of the way home on the school bus, sharing cast off comforters and borrowed blankets that were stashed in the overhead racks, they have perked up and their renewed energy is sometimes more than the restaurant can comfortably hold. Today, they sprawl and stay longer. It was their last day of classes. For the next twelve days they are home for Christmas. No homework to face. Just snow, time and whatever their family has planned for the holidays.

I have work to do at the counter near their table. The heavy pan of soup on the steam table is nearly empty. I need to remove it, scrub, and replace it with fresh soup for the supper-time guests.

While I work, I can hear their voices but not understand their conversation. So much of teenagers' communication is conveyed through body language. Or sarcastic comments. Or clipped replies. Or variations of cuss words. Or jokes. Or teasing. You have to be part of the group to have any idea what is happening between the individuals.

One curly headed boy lights up a cigarette dangling from his lip. His gestures are followed by the younger boy. Yet something in his face is somehow sad. Alcohol is a big factor in some households. I don't know, but they all know how this will play out over the next few days and nights.

The girl sitting close beside her boy friend, eyes heavily outlined, casts sideways glances at the others, checking that her role is secure. One girl is too loud, too bold, her laughter is high pitched.

A boy with thick, straight black hair never speaks. His eyes downcast, flicking ash, stirring coffee, watching the others with a permanent side-ways grin.

"My parents are going to town tomorrow. They'll be gone all day. Come over." The boy with the blond sister invites.

Enthusiasm, shifting postures, eyes meet, heads nod, something to look forward to. Fun times. Good to belong to a group. Turn up the music. Laugh.

"I can get my Old Man's snowmobile. Let's pull toboggans up to the steep hill?" the tallest boy suggests. More nods.

"Maybe get the key to the hall for some floor hockey after?" the loud girl wants attention. A shrugged shoulder. A gesture of 'maybe, maybe not.' But no eye contact. Hope towards a plan, but not too much. Only if they can get an adult to supervise.

I learned to skate in an arena. I learned to swim in a chlorinated pool with a life-guard. I have been chaperoned at every boy-girl event I attended. I wonder what it is like for these kids to grow up here? What will it be like for my own children to grow up here?

They move to leave. The cold pours in through the open doorway.

The teens left spills, drips and dribbles, crumpled serviettes, sticky spoons. Their ashtray holds crushed cigarette butts, although some of the students are quite young.

This time they did not pull any pranks. Sometimes there are surprises. Sooner or later every waitress gets the unscrewed pepper lid, the upside-down sugar, the stacked creamers, the missing salt shaker.

Cleanup. Reset the sugar, salt, pepper, ketchup, napkin dispenser. Dump the ashtray. Bring a new, clean glass ashtray.

It is a rhythm I have learned in these four months. Calm repetition between the hurry-scurry of serving.

Travellers come in off the highway. I realign my friendly exterior, smile and bring menus, offering 'Today's Special' and pointing to the washrooms.

Besides the usual menu, there are also two features for Today's Specials: Salisbury Steak, potatoes (baked, mashed, French fries), peas and carrots, peach cobbler or white cake. Or spaghetti and meat sauce, garlic toast, green salad, white cake or peach cobbler.

The family unbundles their coats and settles in. "Where are you headed today?" I start the polite, predictable small talk every waitress uses to begin the encounter. "We left Edmonton this morning and hope to get to Kamloops. We usually drive straight through the Fraser Canyon, but it is a little risky to drive the canyon in the dark, so we'll get to Vancouver tomorrow."

Order to the cook. Coffee to the table. Food to the family. Money to the till.

Keep smiling and available to offer what people need. There is a kind of false face that I despise. There is a kind of genuine welcome and interest I try to convey. There is a contrast between the lifestyle I lead (no smoking, vegetarian, no coffee, clean language) and the clues I pick up from the people passing through (overweight, smoking, downing the coffee, shuffling back to their monster trucks). I cringe as I scrape the plates, wasting food, greasy food. I shudder as I make change for the cigarette machine, picturing the inner workings of this woman's body as her skin and yellow teeth show her age a decade early. I keep a rigid distance from how I feel and what

I say. I loathe falsity, but I am paid to do these tasks and keep a cheery expression on my face. Again and again.

More holiday travellers stop during mealtime. Some come this way annually and are familiar with this particular place. Others are passing through for the first time and ask about the highway conditions, the town, the local sights. I am new here but I try to answer or I relay the question to Gloria, the cook. She is almost as young as I am but she has lived here with her husband for three years and she knows her way around the local sights and can answer the kinds of questions people ask.

The morning waitress is kept on the run. Motel guests are freshly hopeful. Truckers who pulled over to sleep are unshaven and wrinkled. Loggers have been driving since 3:00am. Locals want to linger and laugh. Children are restless rascals. Older people pause to consider. Businessmen are in a hurry. Tourists ask curious questions.

The morning cook prepares so much, getting Today's Special ready, the baking, desserts, salads and plans for the day. Meanwhile, she has the short-order individual breakfast orders to cook on the grill. When the shift changes the grill must be stripped with the stone, scouring off the cooked-on food. The grease is scraped off with the metal paddle. The morning kitchen is left in order, but still active. Sometimes cooks change in the middle of cooking a guest's meal.

The evening shift is about restocking, cleanup, and returning everything to order. Everything must be ready for the quick start-up for tomorrow's early morning staff. Long haul truck drivers park here to sleep for a few hours. Regulars know that a hot breakfast will be ready in minutes first thing in the morning. If I omit any part of the preparations, I not only cause an inconvenience to my co-workers, and the neighbourhood clientele, but I could possibly also cause a delay for the truckers who deliver 'on-time goods' to the Vancouver port, their destination still eight hours away.

Now it is evening. Funny how some people come every morning and some people come every evening. The two local men who come regularly in the evening are quieter, cleaner. One bold, the other less dramatic, both are excellent storytellers. "I remember this one time..." Mike recalls an adventure. "When I was in the Yukon..." Jerry replies. "My Dad used to say..." These men like to be together and relive 'The Good Old Days.'

After the Moms, after the teens, after the supper hour slows down, it is time to get caught up with the dishwasher and start the final cleanup. And so I listen to their Tall Tales while I begin the evening cleanup. I find ways to stay close by where I can hear. I linger to check the supplies under the counter. I stall to rearrange something just to fill the time. I pause to water the plants. They are amazing stories. Who cares if they are accurate or stretching it a bit? And they are more interested in me giving them the attention of listening than of them giving me the attention of looking. I feel at ease. At least I can talk to a few people without blushing.

At about 8:30pm, I start to work my way down the list of routine cleaning duties. Fill the saltshakers. Wipe the ketchup bottles. Fill the napkin dispenser. Count out ten round, pleated, white paper filters and layer them with three measuring scoops of brown, ground coffee. Wash the ashtrays. Wipe out the cooler. Put the desserts and salads away in the walk-in refrigerator. Re-stock the shelves with bread. Open the case of canned goods. Turn the cans and jars on the shelves so the labels can be easily read by a cook in a hurry. Open crates of fresh fruits and vegetables and potatoes so they are readily available for the quick pace of the morning.

Stay alert. I'll hear about it and blush again if I make any mistakes. No one wants criticism from the following shift. There is great pride in a job no one can find fault with. There is a nasty little pleasure in discovering and announcing somebody else's flaw.

As 9:00pm approaches and there is less likelihood of a family stopping for a meal, it is time to mop.

First scrub down the washrooms, mirrors, light switch, sink, toilets, floor. Check the paper towels and toilet paper in the washrooms.

Put away the rubber gloves. Fill the mop bucket. Flip the chairs upside-down on the tables and get into the rhythm of swishing the heavy, wet, lemon-soap-smelling mop back and forth across the brown tile floor. The cook is scouring the grill. Moving through her own routine to leave things fresh and clean.

The place is empty. After all of these hours of carefully controlled behaviour, the small talk, the hot plates, the accuracy of the money, the dodging of criticism, the anticipation of what other people need, now I am alone and free to express myself. I start to sing. I let my mind wander through the songs I listened to in my room at home, the radio-alarm-clock bringing popular, cheerful, bright music to my imagination.

My 1960's and 70's repertoire comes from the Carpenters, Carole King, John Denver, Peter, Paul and Mary, Cat Stevens, Glen Campbell, Dionne Warwick, Joni Mitchell, Gordon Lightfoot, Anne Murray, Harry Belafonte and of course, the Beatles.

Anti-war songs. Nature songs. Love songs. The 1970's are a rich time for many voices. I feel a web of connection when I sing, yearning for familiarity in the darkness of this wilderness.

Blowin' in the Wind and *Where Have all the Flowers Gone?* were the first two songs I learned to play on my guitar. *Leaving on a Jet Plane* was the song I played to Kevin when he left to work out west. Sunday School and campfire songs. Songs of home and songs of adventure. Working men songs and lullabies. Folk songs and pop music. So many songs I copied out by hand to fill the pages of my notebook. So many songs illustrate and inform my dreams of married life, encouraging the effort we have for 'making the world a better place to be.'

Since it's Christmastime, I start into *The Twelve Days of Christmas*. Will my mopping speed match the rhythm? Will I finish both at the same time?

"*Twelve drummers drumming, eleven pipers piping, ten lords a leaping, nine ladies dancing, eight maids a-milking, seven swans a-swimming, six geese a-laying, five golden rings, four calling birds, three French hens, two turtle doves and a partridge in a pear tree.*" I finish with a flourish.

The clock tells me it is time for the last task. Garbage. In the kitchen, office, washrooms, near the exit and behind the serving counter, all the bags combine into three.

The garbage goes outside, down the stairs into a locked plywood bin under the stairway. It is frosty tonight and I pull on my boots and coat. I leave the door ajar so as not to be locked out. I kick my way down the snowy steps. It is dark and a little slippery. I really don't want to get hurt at the last moment of the day. I shudder to remember the autumn evenings when there were bears roaming through the town and this garbage bin, with the tempting smells of French fries, bread, meat, and fruit attracted them to tear open the door and wait nearby when it got dark. Was it a help or more danger that the menfolk, including Darlene's Dad, brother and fiancé were driving up and down the roads, looking for bears with their guns at the ready!

But now the bears are hibernating in their winter dens. There is only muffled silence and the nippy, clear air and I return safely to the warmth and light of the dining room with a sigh of relief.

Now to count the money. Darlene checked it before she left her shift. Now I must count every cent and reconcile it with the tape that has been recording the price, payment and change I have been handling for each customer all evening.

Pennies, nickels, dimes, quarters, bills, notes recording local IOUs, a cheque was cashed, a couple of credit card slips. Again, I hold my breath, not wanting criticism or fault finding. I count twice, three times. Not again! Once it was 11¢. Once it was 37¢. Today I am out by $1.41! How can this happen? I ask Gloria to re-count. It is not part of her job to do this and she sighs heavily. I feel myself blush. Yes, I am short by $1.41. The other waitress pays it back with her tips. But today there are none and I have no change with me. I leave a note, put the cash in the bag and shove the bag into the office drawer. The office door is locked up and Gloria sees to the final inspection before the lights are off, thermostat reset and the front door locked for the night.

Kevin is out in the van, engine humming, waiting in the warmth. He will tell me about the progress he made today. The dog will be glad to see me. The drive through the snow will be safe. The log bridge will cross the river. My bed will be warm.

It was a normal day filled with normal words, actions, feelings, thoughts and people, routines that do not vary, yet details that are always different.

Leaving the smell of the mop, the cigarette smoke and the coffee pot behind, stepping out into the brisk, clean rush of cold, and quickly into the VW van with it's smell of sawdust, dog and boots, I am glad to be back in my own world.

As we pull out onto the highway and get up to speed, we have these minutes to share our thoughts and feelings, our day and plans.

"I was out again," I sigh. "One dollar and forty one cents. It just doesn't make any sense. How could I be out by such an odd amount of money? It's not like I made a big mistake, nor that I miscounted one coin? I just don't get how it happens... and so often it's that same amount?" I sigh again, deeply, aware of my many mistakes throughout the day. "This obvious one I had to confess to the boss with a note in writing for the next morning. The whole staff will know."

"I wonder..."Kevin is musing quietly. "Add this up for me." And he lists off: "25 plus 10 plus 5 plus 1...How much is that?"

"41," I answer.

"Now add to that 100." He sends me a little grin sideways across the dark van.

"One hundred and forty one."

"Well?" He waits for me to see the obvious.

"I don't get it." I'm too tired to be clever. My eyebrows frown.

"I think maybe someone is playing a trick on you. Is it possible that someone took out one of each coin just as a prank to see what you would do?" Kevin's practical world view helps me make sense of so many things.

I sigh heavily. "No! Really? Well, let me think. Yes. Some of the teenagers who work there on weekends were at the till. There was silly whispering. They ring in each others hot chocolate and other drinks. But, would anyone really do that? I try so hard to be honest and careful and friendly and polite all day long, especially to the people who are our neighbours here."

"This is so embarrassing," I continue, now moaning. "When my till is out do people think I am stupid or sloppy or a thief? But, come to think of it, there are a lot of times when I leave the note and nobody says anything the next day."

Silent miles.

"Kevin! Do you think someone from the other shift could be part of the prank? Since they get there before the boss in the morning and one of them counts the money back into the till and the teens come early before the school bus, then they could put the amount they took out in the afternoon back into the till the next morning and the whole thing would be just for the fun of bugging me...Do you think that is possible?"

The world has become a tricky place.

More silent miles.

"Kevin?" There is something else on my mind. I want to confide in him and seek his opinion about an ethical question I am uncomfortable to ask my co-workers.

"Cecile takes home empty gallon glass jars. She uses them for storing flour and rice and beans. Jennie takes home a piece of day-old Matrimonial cake when her husband comes home from logging camp. Cheryl asks for the raw vegetable scraps and peelings to feed her chickens. Darlene's fiance is raising a pig and she saves the plate scrapings for him."

"So?"

"Well, when I clean the washrooms at night, they told me when I trained that I should throw away the last tiny bit of toilet paper and replace it with a new roll. I just can't see throwing it away. Do you think it is wrong if I bring that tiny roll end home?"

"Hmm, I'm not too sure," is his not too specific answer.

"The way I see it is this. If the other ladies aren't stealing, since they are only using things that were going to be thrown away... then, I'm not stealing either." I wait. "What do you think?"

Kevin has worked in a factory. It was a serious no-no to take anything home.

Silent miles.

"You know what else I was thinking about today?" I open a new conversation, my voice bright, my posture upright.

"What's that?" Kevin's voice is warm and soft and quietly curious and welcoming.

"I was thinking while I was mopping. I was making a dirty thing clean. You know, sometimes I am not so sure whether or not I am 'making the world a better place to be.' If I serve a hugely obese person a plate of greasy food, am I helping or harming? When parents buy gravy and French fries for their toddlers instead of a healthy meal, am I helping or harming? When I hand out change for the cigarette machine, am I helping of harming? But, when I mop the floor, yes, I am making something clean. And clean is good."

Eager to share my thoughts, I speak rapidly. "The ladies were talking about the Christmas Concert last night. You know I miss going to church so much. It got me thinking about Mary's part of the Bible story. Most of the tasks I do in the restaurant: food preparation, cleaning, serving others, are all tasks that Mary did, too. Daily, normal, nothing grand. She did them out of love. I decided to try to do that, too, change my attitude. Not 'Poor me, why am I stuck with this job?' but I have decided to try to adjust to a more cheerful motivation."

"Then, since I was working to make things clean, I thought of Jesus making people clean, whole, well, healed. It is kind of unusual when you think of it. He touched people who were unclean: lepers, the dead and the woman who had an issue of blood. In the Jewish law, if you touch an unclean person, then you become unclean, too. But Jesus touched the unclean and made them clean and He did not become unclean."

"So, how about Mary? She had Him within her! When He was a Baby and Child, she touched Him every day over and over again. She would have been made clean by Him, I would think."

"There are so many views of Mary," I continue. "Some say she was any ordinary peasant girl. Some say she was pure and totally without 'sin.' Some say she was raped by a Roman soldier! That would make her a liar if she said, 'an angel came and told me that the Power of the Most High would overshadow me. The Holy Child that I am carrying is the Son of God.'"

"The Church community I was raised in taught me something entirely different. They said that Jesus had a human mother so that He could inherit all of her 'heredity evil.' All of the troubles of the human race came to Him from her. She was somehow contagious and she polluted Him so He could have all the rotten human character qualities through her genealogy. During His lifetime, He would have to work through all of the battles of temptation because He already had a dose of all the evils passed on through all those generations through her."

"I rejected that view as soon as I heard it! I was about twelve years old, I think," I shudder.

"It's weird. It matters so much how you see this one tiny detail. Who was Mary? What happened when Jesus was conceived? Was He a normal baby who became God? Was He already God Himself? Was He some part of God? Or a sidekick? The angel Gabriel told Mary that He was the Son of God. Since she was His mother, it would be logical for everyone to call her 'The Mother of God.'" I wonder aloud. Pausing. Sighing. "That's what I was thinking about. What do you think?"

Kevin's familiar smile that is just for me shapes his face into a kind of warmth. "I think that you think a lot."

Returning to my earlier, basic thought, "Just think of it! Whatever Mary was doing, she was doing it for the Lord," I mumble. Now louder, "Kevin, your traditional Mennonite grandmother always wore that little white bonnet, didn't she? That was a symbol of always being at prayer, right? But those women wear it all day, every day. I wonder what it would be like to remain always in prayer, even while working at daily tasks." Scanning my activities and inner mind-set I wonder at the focus and intention. "I am going to try it: thankful, aware of the Gifts and the Giver, listening for Prompts, aware of service, desiring to be led. I think that would be a worthwhile challenge."

And we're home.

Well, it's not actually our home. It has been six months and five days since our wedding. Tonight we will spend Mid-Winter's Eve in a borrowed summer-style camper. Tonight is the last night of 'homelessness,' of wandering, borrowing, sleeping in other people's living rooms.

Tomorrow! Tomorrow we are going to move into our new home!

Chapter 2
December 22, 1978
Friday

My friend
shall forever be my friend
and reflect a ray of God to me.
— *Henry David Thoreau*

"Today is the day!"

It is wintery dark. In a flash from asleep to awake comes this bright realization: "Tonight I will sleep in my own house that my own husband built with his own hands!" Ideas and effort, dreams and determination, these intangibles have become reality.

I reach for the clock to see if it is morning. With mid-winter darkness lasting until dawn slowly arrives at 7:30, it is hard to wait.

Not yet. It is only 5:00 in the morning! I roll onto my tummy to peer out the window of the camper. Bright moonlight is glowing through misty fog reflecting on the snow.

Only two other people are sleeping on this side of the river for nearly 25 miles in either direction. Karl and Annika, from Holland, live in an old trapper's cabin nestled in the forest near the river. Great roots of driftwood show the high water mark on their silvery beach. Rounded rocks show the sand-scouring work of the river. Level benches show how the riverbed has been changing channels over time. Deep, black soil shows how centuries of fallen leaves have enriched the soil in the low land opening they use for their garden. The lowest logs of the 50 year old cabin are rotting into the ground it shows that the damp location for this building was not chosen for frequent sunshine. Their dream of 'Self-Sufficiency' is similar to ours. All together five couples share ownership of 160 acres of river-side, mountain slope, forest and rocks.

It was all Howard's idea. A retired accountant, he set up this company and we five are shareholders, owning the land as the company's asset. Karl and Annika were the only year-round residents, until we came. Howard and Opal come to stay in their camper during summer weekends. Glen hasn't started to build yet and Pete took one look, bought in and hasn't returned.

Kevin and I have been staying for seven nights in Howard and Opal's camper. Up on stilts, sheltered from the snow with a sloped tin roof, Howard also built an 8x8 foot insulated addition. It's their summer cottage. Such a compact space is toasty warm with a full-sized wood heater. Tucked into this tiny cube of warm shelter we are two isolated humans surrounded by complete wilderness while hibernating bears, yapping coyotes, silent moose and winter birds populate the unthinkably 'empty' winding river valley. Sedimentary slabs, folded humps, layers of lava, glacier scars, tumbled boulders, rounded river rock, nature's pressures and forces have shaped this valley. But few man-made marks can be seen. Pitch dark. Winter whiteness. Nasty cold. Cozy warmth. It is a place of contrasts.

If I let my mind realize just how alone we are, no phone, only these two neighbours, unmaintained road, condemned bridge...a wave of fear and dread will keep me from going forward.

So, I quickly, firmly, turn my mind to pleasant things.

I will snuggle down into my toasty warm covers, be still and enjoy an hour or two of memories. Oh, how delicious to have time to recall the years, months and days that lead to this day. Like stepping stones, I sense the way the Lord provided for each occurrence, governed each happening, prompted us at each turning point, guided each decision.

Deliberately, so as to fix it in a permanent place in my memory, I remember the sequence: meeting, romance, travel, letters, wedding, honeymoon, trip west, find land, build together. This is my life. This is my story. I know how I got here. I don't know what will come next. So far, so good. I know one thing for sure. I want to live and experience more...with my husband.

Six months ago we were on our honeymoon. Six months ago this was all a dream. Six months ago we didn't know where we were going or what we would do. All we had six months ago was one idea: 'West.'

"I remember the first time I saw you..."

Saturday, February 16, 1974. I remember specifically because it was Winter-Fest.

I had invited Hal (a boy I was flirting with who sat in front of me in Science class). He did not yet drive, so he invited Kevin (who had a VW van). So I invited my friend, Lisa, to make it two boys and two girls.

I first saw Hal. But I noticed Kevin. He was standing beside his green VW van, coat open to the sunny, snowy day, keeping a step away from the others, watching the winter fun without joining in.

Getting to know each other, "How old are you?" was one question passed around between us. Lisa was fifteen and not yet allowed to date (although her parents allowed her to go on group outings). Hal and I were sixteen. Kevin (in a way I learned to expect) answered the question without answering the question. "I got my driver's license the day I turned sixteen. In five days I will have had it for one year." OK, so that would mean he's turning seventeen.

Sledding, skating, snowmobile rides, snow sculpture and snowball fights were all part of the annual Winter-Fest event held at our church every year on a Saturday in mid-February.

The flat lawn behind the church was a gathering place for the adults to watch all the activities, cameras ready. The steep slope behind the church was perfect for tobogganing. Blue and purple crazy carpets, red saucers, wooden toboggans, brightly coloured snow suits and trendy scarves made for a colourful scene. Sledders in line watch those going ahead. Teams huddle and decide to attempt a mild, moderate or steep slope. At the top of the hill, choosing your crew, waiting your turn, decisions must be made together. Who sits in front? Shall we follow a known trail? Will we seek or avoid bumps and jumps? Daredevils open new trails. The snow on the tall dry goldenrod plants sprays off as the laughing sledders swoosh, breaking the bowing stalks.

Dads on snowmobiles slowly tow the children on sleds across the school playing field. Moms stir cocoa and serve sloppy-Joes passing the hot food and drinks out to eager hands through the kitchen window. Teens team up for a hockey match. Tots help build snow men. It is a day of cooperation, variety, happy voices and community spirit.

After the 'Dads vs. Lads' hockey match, there is time for free skating. The rink boards are set up every year on the flattest part of the playing field, near the Pastor's house, where the hoses will reach for night-time flooding. A coming of age duty of the boys in the Church community is to meet up with the young men who prepare the ice every winter. Winter-Fest is a time when over a hundred people will share the ice and enjoy the possibilities of a whole day of wintery fun together. However, neither Hal nor Kevin have brought skates. They stand on the snowbanks. Eager for our favourite part of the day, Lisa and I circle and pose. We have been practicing simple figure skating moves together since we were children. As we move through our routine, I wonder why I am noticing Kevin's eyes on me more than caring whether or not Hal is watching.

My mother invited Kevin and Lisa, Hal and I to our family's house afterwards for cocoa. My Dad, still snapping his camera, asked each of us to hold for a portrait. And so it happened that in this moment, on the first day I met him, the face of the man I would marry four years later is captured on film to treasure for years to come.

After we rested and dried off, listened to records and ate more food, we went to Lisa's house, riding in the VW van for a whole two blocks. Lisa's brother, Michael, was a master of improvisation on the piano. In a sunny room, furnished only with a piano and bench, we all sat on the floor while Michael entertained us with his flying fingers and ridiculous funny faces.

When Kevin recalls his impressions of that day, he likes to smile and tell his version about, "The rich Swedish people who sit on the floor!"

And so, the four of us ended up as a group for the winter. Driving around every weekend in Kevin's 1959 green and white VW van we climbed hills and went sledding, made bonfires for a cookout, threw rocks in the river to see the splash, went target shooting with a .22 Coey, explored back roads, and finished off the day with 'hot apple pie' from McDonald's. That was the only time in my life that I was part of a group. And we had a very good time. Although we were not really two couples, it was assumed that Hal and I were dating and Kevin and Lisa were a pair. But it was always a group and not really seriously sweethearts. Nothing seems to be so much fun as dropping snow down your boy friend's back. Unless it is wearing his sweater. Or waiting for his phone call. Hal was a flirt and a tease and a show-off, 'The Jester.' Kevin was always quiet, on time, the driver, 'Mr. Reliable.'

By Easter, while we confided in each other about how the romance was going, Lisa and I were startled to realize that Hal was two-timing us! A good night kiss given to two girls on the same evening? No way!

He got slapped for it and rejected by both of us.

Suddenly our fun Saturday drives were gone. No more hot dog roasts. No more invitations to church or Sunday dinner. No more afternoon hikes. No more flirting in Science class. No more rumbling of the VW engine. No more reason to see Kevin.

Unless I needed a ride?

"I remember the first time I actually talked with you..."

During the time we drove around every weekend as a group of young people, I never really paid that much attention to Kevin. He was a good driver, safe, dependable, focused on the task at hand, a good teacher, not a braggart or wanting to be the centre of attention. Still, I didn't know him to talk to or anything about his family, decisions, beliefs, plans.

Until the one day came which neither of us will ever forget.

At this time in my family, while we were teenagers, my Mother and Dad took in infants through the Ontario foster care program. Babies who were to be given up for adoption had to spend three months in foster care before the adoption went though. As my four siblings and I learned more about caring for babies, my Mother enjoyed every moment, cuddling, singing, providing for the baby's every need.

To preserve confidentiality, the social worker never told us much, but some of the babies had fifteen-year-old mothers or came from poverty or drug related situations. But one little boy had a mother and father who were nearly eighteen. The parents of these young people were very supportive and there was a strong possibility that the birth family would be able to work out the details and keep their son. The social worker came several times, taking the child to visit with his parents and grandparents. Everyone had their hopes up. Extensions postponing the adoption were granted again and again. The boy stayed with us until he was nearly a year old. And then, all of a sudden came a change of plans. The adoption was arranged. My Mother, I could see, was very upset. During the last few months, as the child was learning to talk, play and almost walk, Mother had been trying to convince Dad that we should adopt this little sunshine child into our own family.

But now it was not to be.

Mother explained to me how the sequence of events would happen on the day of the adoption. The social worker would come to our house, meet with my Mother, take the packed up belongings, including gifts my brothers and sisters and I had made for him. Then she would drive with the little boy to a nearby town, meet the adoptive parents at the office, sign the final papers and they would take him home. Mother invited me to stay home from school that day so I could say 'good-bye' to the little foster brother I had come to love. But I knew the real reason: she wanted to have me home with her when the baby left. She needed someone to share the silence and sadness. I knew her heart would be struggling with a mix of feelings. She would experience waves of gladness, knowing that she had done a good thing while waves of grief would also swirl as she admitted that this was an irreversible good-bye. Protected by law, the new family's privacy would close the door and we would never see this little lad again.

So, in order to help my Mother, I asked Kevin to help me. We made a plan to act in civil disobedience. I knew I was breaking the law. Yet, more seriously, it seemed to me, I was going to go someplace in a car with a boy and not tell my mother where I was going or when I would be back! I had never ever done such a thing in my entire life! I battled different layers of conscience as the clock moved slowly at school that afternoon. However, this risky action was a deliberate decision designed to comfort my Mother's heart. Not that she wanted to invade or interrupt the new family. But our plan would calm that anxious, ancient fear of a baby disappearing into the vast unknown. I could see that it was too painful for my Mother to experience. She had given this child so much of her heart, time and patience. She would have so many happy memories and hopes and imaginings suddenly tangled with feelings of anxiety as if the child was dropping into a chasm of the unknown with no information or place to finalize the end of the story. So, in order to put a period at the end of the sentence, Kevin and I took action.

Because I already had a plan with Kevin I turned down my Mother's invitation to stay home, as if I had no sympathy for her, I said, "No, I don't want to stay home from school to say good-bye. It's too sad. I'll just do it in the morning before I go." My heart was pounding as I looked into his blue eyes, memorizing his rosy cheeks and lock of curly blond hair. I knew I was hurting my Mother. I knew I was lying to my Mother. But, I knew I was still doing the right thing, even though I was breaking the law!

Three o'clock. As the school bell rang, Kevin and I dashed out the door, into the parking lot, we were first out of the driveway. I had the address and Kevin knew the roads. Meanwhile, at 3:00 the social worker would be just leaving our house, which was a little nearer the destination than we were. We would have to hurry to arrive at the meeting place. Kevin's steady driving and the VW's 55mph speed limit made for a slow hurry!

Parking across the street, we anxiously watched any cars entering or leaving and watched intently for a couple carrying a small child leaving the social worker's office.

It seemed like a long time, but at last I saw her, the social worker I recognized, the car, the baby's clothing. And soon another car pulled in. A man and woman stepped out with a helium balloon, a huge stuffed Donald Duck, a diaper bag, and a shiny new car seat.

It's them!

While we waited, anxious and alert, while the new parents got to know their new son, while the social worker arranged the papers to sign, the instructions, questions, interviews, laughter, and the moment of beginning a new family, while Mother dried her tears and tried to soothe her aching heart... Kevin and I were waiting and waiting in the van across the street. It was the first time I had actually talked and listened to him.

We were asking each other questions.

What do you want to do after high school?

Where do you want to live?

What do you imagine the perfect life to be?

How could it be that we had such similar dreams? I felt like he was reading my mind!

And for each thing I spoke aloud, my mind was racing with pictures of my future life.

I said, "I don't want to work for pay. I want to be a stay at home Mom."

I have been a babysitter, a live-in Nanny and worked at a day-care. Because there are so few career paths available for women at this time, mostly tellers, cashiers, service and hospitality jobs, as well as traditional teaching and nursing professions, many women have income significantly lower than what is available to men. While women shout loudly about this unequal pay, and laws begin to change, the newspaper still lists 'Help Wanted: Female.' When I work for families, I see how the mother's wages drain away to pay for child care, the gas for the second car as well as insurance and maintenance, the haircuts, clothing, shoes, make-up and purses she needs to be dressed properly in the workplace. It seems to me that she feels guilty about being away from home and tries to ease her strain by buying her kids gifts. They whine and want more. Her wages are used to replace the work she would have been doing at home: pay for a housekeeper, disposable diapers, she serves food out of a can or a package. I notice that the kids just watch

TV without a parent to stimulate their interests. I don't want my family to be like that.

Aloud I added, "I want to read aloud to my children. I want my children to play pretend."

My great-grandmother read aloud to my grandmother who read aloud to my Dad who read aloud to me. I love to play hide-and-seek and dress-up and build forts and stir mud and sketch with sidewalk chalk and invent new hop scotch patterns and scavenger hunts. I love exploratory bicycle riding and improvising skits and pretending to be ponies in the circus.

I mused, "I guess I'll have to learn how to bake bread so I can afford to not work for pay."

In a flash I realized that if I want to get married and have a whole bunch of kids, but not work outside the home, then, the thing is: what kind of 'cost of living' would it take? Our family would have to find ways to get things that were not expensive, like second hand clothing, bartering for furniture, expenses for only one car. We'd have to be deliberately thrifty at every decision. It would be necessary to have a garden, learn to prepare foods to store for the winter with canning, freezing, drying. And, it would save a lot of money to make our own crafty gifts. There must be a way to do this!

Besides the self-sacrificing decision to live with less money there would be valuable benefits, too. We will have more family time together, more play, more reading, more crafts, more clever inventions, more imagination and more learning how to do practical things. We wouldn't hire repairman or landscapers. We would learn to do many tasks ourselves. I could even give haircuts to my husband and children. Christmas and birthday decorations and gifts wouldn't come from a store. Family members will make things for each other.

For sure the family would have better nutrition with home-made soups and jams, pickles and bread, meat and vegetables without artificial colouring, artificial flavours and preservatives.

And self-reliance would be part of it, too. Some of the children I babysat couldn't get dressed by themselves, the Mom was in such a hurry she did it for them every day or expected the babysitter to do it after she left. The kids didn't learn how to do chores or even make a sandwich. Adults did everything for them.

I continued, "I want to teach my kids to take care of daily chores and try new things and keep learning."

I am not going to hand them every little thing because they are whining at me. We will have pets so the children will learn to be dependable.

I concluded, "And, woven throughout each day, I want to teach them about the Lord. He made us. He loves us. He sees us and hears us. He is near. He calls us. We can turn towards or away from Him. I want my children to know why holidays are Holy Days."

Then it was Kevin's turn to tell his life dream.

I turned to face him, focusing my eyes and ears to really listen to this very quiet person. I made an effort to link together the little bits of information he was willing to share. My heart and mind became open, sensing the foundation and character of this individual, the world view he was forming, the experiences and contrasts which had shaped him.

Kevin said he was interested in the RCMP, but didn't want to move so often. He was interested in the forest, but didn't want to be posted in the middle of nowhere watching for forest fires. He was interested in mechanics and machinery, but didn't want to work indoors every day with fumes and exhaust.

What would he do if he had a completely open door with no restrictions? No obstacles?

"I'd go out west, find a small piece of land that would grow food, put all my practical skill to work."

He had spent summers on the farms of his parents' friends, helping with sheep, turkeys, cattle and horses. He could fix things, build, drive tractor, hunt and make a fire. He could read repair manuals. He liked to maintain tools and machinery. He had radio experience.

Like a bright blue-white flash, my own dreams and his seemed welded into one. I looked at him again. From barely noticing him, I now wanted to know all about him. From wanting to express my own individuality, I now wanted to adjust my thinking to be influenced by his. From wanting to stand alone, I now wanted to seek his knowledge and ideas, ask his perspective on issues. From holding back, unwilling to confide in anyone, I now wanted to offer what I believed and valued to complement his views.

My turn again:

"In a perfect world, where there were no obstacles I would get married, go out west, build a log cabin, live off the land, have a bunch of kids, teach them about the Lord, volunteer in my community and then write a book about it." That was my dream, although I had never spoken it aloud, now it was crystal clear.

Movement across the street alerted us to the reason we were sitting in this particular VW van in this particular parking lot on this particular day. The new Mom and Dad, now carrying the baby I recognized as my foster brother, were leaving the building and preparing to buckle up in their car.

Kevin started the engine and we began the tricky part of our plan: following them without being discovered.

It was a little red hatchback car. The rear window allowed us to peer in. At every stop light the Mom and Dad would turn back to coo and smile and comfort and speak to their new son.

It was charming to watch and a detail I would convey to my Mother when I told her the story.

We followed them through the traffic lights of the city, up the slope to the old part of town, along a tree lined street of elegant residences. Suddenly they turned into the driveway. We were right at their house! They were so intrigued with their new arrival that they had no notice of the green van which kept so closely behind them. As Kevin realized we had reached our destination, he lurched forward while I jotted down the house number and street name. We made a u-turn and drove past again, slowly, to look more closely at the home: stone, Victorian, wide porch, nice up-keep, bigger than a cottage but smaller than a mansion. It looked like a doll house. Surely only good family times happen here and this precious child will grow up safe and secure, well provided for with music lessons and pets, cousins and family traditions.

I couldn't stop the flow of tears. Kevin turned for home.

It was such a relief to have some facts, to be able to envision a 'tomorrow' for this little lad.

I was not asked why I was late coming home from school, nor why I did not take the school bus. Mother was in her room with the door closed. Looking at the faces of my siblings, I realized that none of us knew what to do. Without our little foster brother in the house, it certainly seemed unusually quiet.

I had planned to wait to tell her what Kevin and I had discovered. Hearing her sobs, I gently tapped on her door. I told her everything that night. The change that came over her while I described our plot and success, each event and detail was worth the risk that we took that day. She was glad to know that the baby didn't disappear. He was actually safe and in a good place. The details I had observed demonstrated the parents' kindness to the boy.

My Mother called me 'Miriam' after that. It was like the day when Moses was hidden in the basket in the bulrushes along the Nile River to protect him from Pharaoh's command to destroy the baby boys. His sister, Miriam, stood at a distance to know what would be done to him. In the same way, I had followed to see that my baby brother was safe.

I phoned Kevin to relate to him the happy ending. From that time on, Mother had a very special respect for Kevin, trusting his judgment and appreciating his skills.

"I remember the gifts you gave me..."

Within weeks of this adventure, school was over for the summer. Kevin travelled by train to Alberta. He was hired to work on a ranch helping Lawrence, an old friend of the family, with his chores. Kevin tilled the fields with a big tractor, preparing acres and acres for crops, tinkered on machinery and finished the interior of his employer's self-designed house.

When he returned, I left to live and study at the Church boarding school in Pennsylvania.

The next summer and fall were the same. I came home for the summer. He left for Alberta. He came back. I left for school.

We were friends. We were sweethearts. But we were not in the same place for very much time.

We wrote letters, made phone calls, made gifts, sent cards.

Kevin gave me books of poetry. Every page filled with words of wisdom, hope, faith and love. Beautiful photography illustrated each quotation. I made him notebooks. With my own handwriting I copied words of songs, Bible verses, poetry and words of wisdom from many varied sources. I collected pretty nature pictures from calendars and magazines to illustrate the scrapbooks. Kevin learned to engrave words on little metal plaques and glued them onto wooden carvings he made.

A day came when he gave me a locket: a man and woman square dancing together. He engraved our initials on the back! My eyes eagerly sought his. Is this a casual trinket, or does this gift mean that you have chosen me? I wondered.

Very soon, the question was answered with his proposal and the gift of an engagement ring. Now wispy glimpses of the future began to take shape. Our story was shifting from dreamy possibilities to specific, structured steps towards a tangible goal. The engagement ring featured three diamonds. The central, larger, raised one representing the Lord guiding the husband and wife. While each draws closer to the Lord, they also draw closer to each other.

Then, the once in a lifetime gift given with witnesses: the wedding rings. Kevin made them. Unbroken bands repre-senting unending commitment, gold as a symbol of purity. Inside, where only we could see, Kevin engraved our wedding date, our initials and two birds flying together over a sunrise glowing between two mountain peaks. A pathway beckoned towards adventure.

"That's us," he explained the symbol he had created. "The sun is the Lord. The mountains represent the challenges and difficulties we will face together. But the path leads forward. We will Journey 'Twogether.'"

At last, now that we are married, I can give the gift to my husband which only a wife can give, the promise and commit-ment of loyalty as my physical love unites my mind, heart and spirit to my husband. At last, now that we are married, I can accept the gift which is only given by a husband to his wife, his own body giving sparks of life to grow within mine.

Until we have some security after all of this travelling and searching, we have agreed to postpone new life. We are unwilling to destroy, block, or tamper with this precious gift and sacred partnership with the Creator. Our 'Back-to-Nature' philosophy combined with 'Trust God' and the awareness that life begins at conception, guides our decisions. I do not want to chemically change my body's natural cycle. I do not want to make uninhabitable the welcoming nest within me. We have learned how to notice changes in my cycle, how to govern ourselves with responsibility and wait, trusting that our home and income will soon be secure, until the time when we are able to provide for the children we so hope will be given to us.

And so, the story of our gifts continues today, in my own house, itself a gift. Today I can unpack the special box marked 'Memories' and set out the books, cards, engravings and carvings he gave me. The entire world and every minute of my life feels like one big extended gift!

"I remember the first time we worked on the Christmas play together..."

During the four years from when we met until we were married, with so many months living so far away from each other, it would not be surprising that we might have drifted apart. In 1975, after only three months at college, I came home to find that no one had signed up to direct the annual Christmas play at church. So I stepped forward. "I'll do it!" This significant event is highly valued by young and old. Creative care must be taken to combine traditions and 'we always do it this way' with something unique and beautifully new. While quiet music sets the atmosphere, the Pastor narrates the story of Christ's birth from Luke and Matthew and actors pose in

Tableaux as living illustrations portraying each scene of the Nativity in Bethlehem.

I asked Kevin to be on my stage crew with ladders and wires and hammers. I asked Lisa to be Mary, wrapped in blue, singing the *Magnificat*. Her gestures conveyed both maternal gentleness and awe-filled reverence for the Baby Lord Jesus. I asked the young married couples to be the angel choir, wearing traditional white robes, but with the nontraditional addition of brightly coloured sashes. I cast members of the congregation as the shepherds and wise men, Joseph and Gabriel.

"Kevin?" I asked, "When the Narrator reads, 'And the Word was made flesh and dwelt among us,' do you think you could make a platform to support an open copy of the written Word and slowly lower it into the manger?"

Brightly lit, slowly lowering, curtains closing at just the right moment, hushed audience; it was a golden moment. Our eyes met and I knew that I wanted to overcome any obstacles that distance and time were attempting to keep us apart. I knew that this was the man I wanted to Journey with for all the adventures life would bring.

"I remember our wedding..."

The wedding ceremony was outdoors on the flat lawn behind the church. It was the same place we first met four years ago at Winter-Fest. The summertime setting had been transformed with generous bouquets gathered from the neighbours flower gardens and sparkling crystals hanging in the wide-spreading beech tree behind the log altar.

The wedding party went out early that morning wandering into the nearby fields picking wild daisies. "Will it rain?" A crew was setting up the tables for the breakfast reception inside and chairs for the wedding ceremony outside. One fellow took a towel to wipe away the sprinkle of rain. "Do we move inside?"

"Dear Lord, we hope to be outside to honour You in your beautiful Creation. Please, bring a pause in the rain so that we can share our Vows in Your sight."

And suddenly, sunshine!

The children I have been babysitting and reading to, volunteering with and teaching Sunday School lessons to were seated on picnic blankets in the front while their parents and grandparents were seated on folding chairs.

My sisters, Julie and Carole, and my friend, Lisa, were our bridesmaids, wearing softly flowing homemade gowns. Lori, a friend since summer youth Church camp when we were fourteen years old, had composed a song from Psalm 128 just for this day.

Blessed are they that feareth the Lord
and walketh in His ways.
And thou shalt eat the
labour and the fruit of thine own hands.
And ever more it shall be well with thee.
Thy wife shall be as fruitful as the vine beside thy home
With children like olive plants around.
And thou shalt see the good of Jerusalem for all thy days
And see thy children's children.
And happy shalt thou be and peace eternally.[3]

My brother, Andrew, was the photographer. My brother, James, wrote a piece of music for two flutes and guitar. Friends did the sewing and baking, decorated with a mural and arranged lodging for out-of-town relatives and guests.

The people were standing, hushed and reverent while the white robed Pastor opened the Word, signalling God's presence. Here. Now. Guitar strings pluck the rhythm, Lisa, my sisters and Lori were singing in harmony, *Morning has Broken*.

Kevin and I stepped out, hand-in-hand. We held the gold wedding rings he had made. We wore the clothing I had made. Hand-stitched, my flowing white cotton gauze wedding dress complemented his white linen tunic. We each wore a golden braided circlet in our hair as a symbol of virginity.

Our nontraditional setting made a memorable impact on our guests. Our vows came straight out of our Church's customs. "I promise to love, honour and comfort you and cleave unto you alone that we may dwell together in the holy state of marriage according to the ordinance of our God." But, unlike other Churches, the phrase 'til death do us part' is not included. Believing that the marriage of one man and one woman may continue in the life after death, the seriousness of our vows is really intended for all eternity.

In the reception line, the children brought us flowers! Classmates, relatives, neighbours wished us well. Long tables held a selection of muffins, banana bread, pumpkin bread, apple sauce cake, carrot cake and the three-tiered fruit cake my Mother and I prepared together. Decorated with fresh daisies, one helper discovered a daisy with a double centre for the very top. It seemed a fitting sign for our marriage. "Two shall be one."

Gifts included practical things like blankets and towels, finery such as serving dishes, and a sum of cash that would cover our travel expenses as we headed west. My parents gave us $1000 which we decided to use as a down payment on our land.

I remember our trip out west, finding land and the first tree you cut down...

Kevin had been working steadily to outfit our 1971 red and white Volkswagen van. He built a platform over the engine in the back to be our bed with a foam mattress on top and with storage built in underneath. Our inventory included: a Coleman two-burner stove and food box, how-to books and winter-ready sleeping-bags, work clothes and down parkas, cooking utensils and shiny new pots and pans from my parents (including a pressure cooker which will quickly make boiled beans for our vegetarian diet). In addition, I had packed up and itemized 21 boxes of belongings for my parents to mail out to us when we have an address.

Canada is a big place. Lines on the map became rivers, railroads, highways and topography as book learning transformed into living experiences as we rolled along the miles. Welcomed by strangers, we entered a new chapter of our lives in Avola.

Always there was this questioning hesitation before a decision was made. I looked into Kevin's eyes, we paused to sense the Lord's guidance, we think and weigh and wait and try to foresee the consequences. Then we agree and move forward another step.

This pattern repeated itself. Until, six months after our wedding day, we arrive at this day. Here. Now.

"Kevin?"

"hmmm?"

"I can hear your heart beat."

"That's a good thing."

"Kevin?"

"Yes?"

"Today is like a blank page. It's a new chapter. We get to write our own story."

"That's a good thing, too."

"I want you to be in my story."

"Me, too."

I look at the clock again. 7:00. It is morning. I stir in the sleeping-bag and locate the kitten. What fun it is to have the purring and snuggling of this tiny black and gold calico kitten. Kevin brought her back from Kamloops exactly a week ago. 'Amber' I call her for the gold specks in her black fur. Or maybe 'Ember' as she looks like the embers in the early morning fire after the logs have burned away.

Quietly I slide out of the warmth and poke the fire. New wood will catch in a moment with the heat from this deep bed of coals. I slide back beside my husband and bask in the happy feeling of success and satisfaction that today holds.

"I'm so glad I picked you," I murmur my often repeated early morning greeting to my still slumbering husband. "Today is the day, Kevin, today is the start of what we have been aiming towards for four years!"

I can't stop myself. The first music that pops into my head comes bubbling out of my mouth.

"*Country roads, take me home, to the place I belong!*" delivered in my best John Denver imitation!

Let's go!

I light the kerosene lamp and let the dog out. I boil the water and stir the oatmeal. I wash up the dishes and stuff the sleeping-bags. I gather the bedding and put all the clothes in boxes. Kevin is out loading the van. There's not much left to take over.

I count to be sure: We have moved five times since we arrived in Avola four months ago.

First we slept in the van while we were on the road. Water, food, tools, camping gear were all stowed. Stripped to the minimum, the van was our home for over two months as we looked and toured and explored.

Second, we slept in the van at Fran and Archie's in a meadow of their little farm.

Third, when it got a little frosty at night and our cabin was not done, they invited us inside to sleep on their fold-out couch in the living room of their house-trailer. Lacking privacy, we soon moved on.

Fourth, in November, Glen, another of the five co-owners of the land, invited us over. He was renting a place about five miles down the highway. It was an original homestead. The hand-hewn log house with a unique pyramid roof and generous four rooms, near-by creek, functioning out-house and 45-gallon drum wood stove, back porch and kerosene lamps would be a good midpoint for us to experience as we left town life and stepped ever closer towards our 'Back-to-Basics' pledge. He welcomed us to come and share his space since we were almost finished building our cabin.

Fifth, and I shudder to think of how we narrowly escaped disaster, it is only by a mini-miracle of Providence that we are living in this camper.

For no particular reason, except to save money on gas, last week, we decided to move as much of our stuff into the cabin now that the roof is on and it is waterproof. Without the additional minutes and miles back and forth to Glen's place, there would be more opportunity for me to help at the cabin every morning before I go to work in the afternoon. I am still chinking the cracks between the logs with moss. Kevin just has to finish the loft and ladder.

Our foam mattress and Polar-tec CannondaleTM mummy-style sleeping-bags, my guitar and music, our box of precious religious books, Kevin's double-bitted axe, bow saw, hammer, level, chalk-line, shovel and mechanic's tools, our kitchen utensils, pots and pans, the food box with our stock of supplies and our wedding presents were moved out of Glen's log house.

The day after we moved out of Glen's place, Kevin made a run to the city with my endorsed cheque on payday. Since the original $1000 wedding present we used as the down-payment on the property back in August, every penny has gone into building supplies. Now we can pay Howard and Opal another $100, thankful that they have been willing to trust us and wait four months for further payments.

As a Grande Finale to celebrate our achievement, Kevin bought a beautiful, brass 'Aladdin' kerosene lamp. The elegant shade, tall glass chimney and fragile silk mantle will shine a brighter light than the old fashioned cotton wick lamp we found in an old shed. He was also inspired to stop at the animal shelter to surprise me, bringing back my new kitten.

Headed home from the big city after a tiring day, in the early evening darkness, rounding the corner to the straight stretch of highway past Glen's place, Kevin was horrified to see the glow of 30 foot high orange flames. Shocked in disbelief he pulled in the driveway to see fire devouring the entire building. Glen pulled in behind Kevin, jaw dropped, eyes wide, but thankfully alive. Only an hour ago, he had returned home from his job cruising timber up on the mountain, cold and wet, he had come inside to light the fire in the stove, dashed out to fetch some groceries at the gas station fifteen miles away.

While he was gone, the metal elbow chimney pipe had shifted away from the concrete part of the chimney. Hot sparks shot out of the collapsed pipe, setting fire to the wooden walls, floor and furnishings. All of Glen's belongings were destroyed. His university text books, typewriter, skis, saddle, ten-speed bicycle and other outdoor sporting gear, boots and accessories, tools, chainsaw, kitchen and personal belongings. Even his winter supply of wood and food were incinerated. Gone.

He had his truck, his dog and what he was wearing. Fortunately, he had strong friendships and soon found lodging with co-workers in Clearwater. But the shock of the loss left a deep hurt. That unique 'joy of life' look in his eye was almost snuffed out.

After Kevin made sure that Glen was going to be OK, he continued to drive to Avola where I was waiting for him at Fran and Archie's place and told us the news. We made a long-distance telephone call to relay the news to Howard and Opal in the city. Their genuine concern to be of support to both Glen and us included the offer for him to move into the camper as soon as we moved out.

It has been a tight fit. But, without this tiny detail, this 'just-for-now' sleeping place we by chance decided to shift in to, all of our supplies would have still been in Glen's house and our worldly goods would have been nothing but ash.

Now, with urgency, we knew we needed to finish our home and be done with this moving about as homeless wanderers!

Yes! Today! Now! Our own place!

My excitement and the clock finally agree. Let's get moving.

"Bye, thanks for everything!" I blow kisses into the empty room. And we're off. It is such a short drive, less than half a mile. But, oh! The difference it makes. No more asking, waiting, being careful not to offend, not to take up too much space, not to make too much noise, not to use too much hot water, not to stay up too late, not to get up too early, not to need more of anything than has been offered. It is great to have so many people helping us, but what a difference now to be able to 'do it myself.'

We trudge up the path through eight inches of snow.

The world is monochromatic. The purple-grey overcast sky, not yet lit by the lazy late-to-rise sun makes the brilliantly white snow seem a tint of shaded grey. The bowing branches of snow-heavy evergreen trees seem black. Birch bark's white wrappings and bare branches of summer's shrubs have no distinguishing colour, but enter the eye as darker and lighter greys. The mountain walls shape the twisting valley with rock slides of granite grey. We round a curve in the snowy path to see our brand-new old-grey cabin. It is built of weather-aged logs, left standing, striped of bark and branches after a forest fire. This man-made structure is not an interruption to this colourless scene with each untreated log showing variations of soft grey. Even the solid black surface of the tar paper roof looks grey now covered by a fine dusting of new snow.

The only man-made structure as far as the eye can see, it is just as we left it, so familiar and also so new. It is not a building project any more. Home!

With every step I take, eyes feasting on the truth of this goal now within view, I want to shout our victory. This small, cube-like enclosed space is 'home' the symbol of protection and plenty. The sturdy cedar-fragrant logs thickly mark the boundary between 'out there' and 'in here.' Each piece is deliberately placed. Every effort is a gift from my husband.

It is hard to find words for the glory of it all. It is hard to reconcile the splendour inside my heart with the bare minimum definition of 'shelter' which is physically in front of me. Walls, floor, roof, door, three windows, wood stove. And boxes, sleeping-bags, tools. Our domain.

Perhaps other brides find their dream-come-true first home equipped with trendy features, fashionable furnishings, up-to-date appliances, magazine-photo-ready rooms. I am overjoyed with this rough-cut, axe-marked, from-the-land, rugged, raw, one room, compact, trimmed to the essentials dwelling place. No papers to sign. No mortgage. No building permit. It is the once-ever creation of my husband's mind and hands. It is a heart-to-heart expression, a piece of art, a symbol of dedication, of focus and endurance.

It is our first home!

I slide the wooden latch through the curved driftwood handle. "I have such a clever husband!" I push open the door with my foot, the box in my arms sliding to the floor. I see the changes Kevin made since I was last here. The tools are set aside, the sawdust swept away. The boxes and bags he has already stacked in the corner. The grey tin slop-water bucket on the floor behind the stove and the white enamel washbasin hanging on the nail on the wall behind the wood stove say, 'We live here now.'

The dog comes bounding in. He has been here every day since the golden leaves signalled mid-October. Kevin went to town for hinges for the door, read the bulletin board and came home with 'Sam,' a huge, black and tan male German Shepherd. He is well trained, but his owner is headed north and cannot take him along. Tame, obedient, strong, with a thick undercoat for the out-of-doors. He'll eat a lot, but he'll be a loyal companion and a trusty guard for our place.

Kevin has the kitten in a box until we are done opening and shutting the door. She mews and calls and scratches. "Sorry, Amber. It is not time yet!" I try to reassure her.

A few more loads and we can start to get set up. But we have to watch the clock. I have to be ready to start work at 2:00 this afternoon. Counting back from washing up when I get there, the drive two miles of dirt logging road back out to the highway, the miles up the highway, allowing time for warming up the van, we should leave at 12:30 after lunch.

So I have about another four hours to experience the entrance and then focus on the exit. The newly hung thermometer announces today's temperature. Kevin calls these days 'Mild' when it is a few degrees above or a few degrees below freezing. Since we're here for a while, I'll light the stove. I've had a little practice!

As soon as my hands are warm enough, I turn to finish my cabin-building task. The log-work was too heavy for me. I have no skill with tools. But I have been chinking the cracks between each log, between the logs and the floor, between the logs and the roof, between the logs and the door and window frames for several days. First I have to chip away at the frozen pile of moss heaped up in the middle of the room, loosening enough to put it in the oven in the old, dented roasting pan Fran gave us. Soon the steamy, tropical smell signals that it is thawed enough for me to continue my chinking project. I can scrape the last bits of summer's green off the floor boards with the shovel. Until spring melts the snow, that's all the moss I've gathered. I think it will be enough. Well, it has to be enough. That's all there is.

Kevin is getting things lined up to cut lumber to finish the loft. We have the use of Howard's gas generator. Kevin pulls the rope to start it. He plugs in the skilsaw he brought from Ontario. He has already measured the cuts he wants to make. One long piece of lumber will be cut lengthwise to prepare the upright sides of the ladder we will climb to the sleeping loft. A second piece of lumber will be cut in half length-wise, then shorter pieces cut to make enough rungs for the ladder.

I love the sounds of work: the low chugging rhythm of the generator, the high screaming whine of the saw, the ring of the hammer, the little ping of the chalk-line.

Resting, we open the box and Amber (or Ember) leaps out, hisses at the dog and climbs up onto my lap. I stroke her and talk to her and slowly show her where we are.

Kevin likes to plan ahead. While I stir soup for lunch, he gets things ready for three more fires. By the time he gets back from taking me to work, by the time he gets back from picking me up after work, and first thing tomorrow morning we will need more kindling, small wood, longer lasting big wood.

He'll be making saw dust inside all day while I'm at work. If the loft isn't quite finished, we will unroll the mattress and sleeping-bags when I come home after 10:00 tonight.

Oh, look, it is time to go already.

In the staff locker room I wash up and change into my uniform.

It is hard to describe the buoyant feeling of this day. Smiles for everyone. Quick step. Cheerful replies. I am gushing with stories and memories I want to tell the women I work with, much more than ever before.

I am dancing in my heart with gladness about the man I have picked for a husband. I think he is handsome. I think he is smart. I think he is strong. I think he has good ideas. I trust his judgment. I completely trust him with the money that I earn. I know he is safe. I know he does not drink or cuss or smoke or gamble. I know he does not whistle at girls. I admire his hands that invent and build and put together and take apart. I am amazed at the knowledge he has of the machinery we have used, the van, the generator, the chain saw, the skilsaw.

I depend on his knowledge of old-fashioned things: planning the design of the cabin, installing the chimney, lighting the fire, sharpening the axe, how to use the lamp, storing the food, obtaining clean water, preparing the outhouse, making a hinge for the door, fitting the windows. It is all so wonderful to be able to participate with someone who knows so much. I would not be able to survive out here without him! I would be blotted out. It is unthinkable. This lifestyle that I have wanted all my life would be impossible without the skills, strength and determination of this man. And not only that, he is kind, gentle, honest, on time, respects me and has an inner wisdom that is not wordy, but fundamental to how he makes decisions and consistent from deep inside to action.

While I am moving through my daily duties as a waitress, my mind is elsewhere.

I serve the food...Tomorrow I will cook for and serve my husband with food that I earned the money to buy.

I wipe the table...Tomorrow I will wipe my own table.

I stack the dishes in the dishwasher, steam seeping out of the cracks of the metal door...Tomorrow I will wash my own dishes in the water I have heated on the wood stove.

I sweep the kitchen…Tomorrow I will sweep my own kitchen with my own broom.

I restock the shelves…Tomorrow I will set up my own kitchen supplies.

Each task that yesterday seemed so dull and repetitive now has life and promise, interesting details and choices, achievement of purpose and domestic satisfaction.

I am linked to every young woman who reaches towards the moment she will survey her little kingdom and make every decision, arrange each item to her own satisfaction, choose how to spend each hour, plan meals, choose colours, budget income and name babies. The finished product is not what interests me. It is the process, the gradual, ever-changing development of the home-built furnishings, learning skills, building traditions, discussing options, choosing as a team, making memories, doing it all together. This is what is happening. Today. Now. With each breath. I am living in the moment. I am hyper-sensitive to the meaning behind each gesture, word and interaction. I am focused on remembering each detail to write letters home, to tell my children, to remember in my old age, to write in my memoirs.

To me it is all so grand and idealistic, and yet, it is really just a simple cabin in the snowy woods. Barely fit for humans, barely finished, barely closed in against the cold. But it is mine… ours…No one else did it. No one else knows. No one else can claim this victory, this accomplishment, this mountaintop. I get to tell the story because it happened to me. I made it happen. I entered the dream fully expecting to experience the reality, every single turn and change and shift.

After work I felt like I was pushing the van to get home faster! Out onto the highway, we turn left to join the westbound traffic headed for Vancouver. High beam lights dimmed, we greet the northbound truckers headed east for Edmonton. Around the tight curves and rock cuts, along the straight stretch past the swamps we come to the left turn, down the slope on the dirt road towards the river. Across the bridge, ignoring the 'condemned' sign, now into the dark, trees close to the road, we travel along deep ruts in the snow. The road narrows, passing the ridge. The lights are out where we slept last night in Howard and Opal's camper.

Now we are near. Right turn, up to the flat parking spot. The dog comes bounding out to greet us and we're home!

The pathway seems longer in my anxious hurry to step inside. Kevin lights the lamp. I poke the fire. There is a tiny collection of embers and I drop kindling in criss-cross, blow and watch the flames return.

Oh happy sigh! This is it.

Kevin has everything ready. It feels so romantic to see that my husband made our bed ready. Since the flooring of the upstairs tent-like loft is not quite finished, we will sleep on the downstairs floor tonight. There is a clean, new, blue tarp under the foam mattress to protect it from the bare floor and any remaining sawdust, shavings and mossy bits that have been frozen there these last few weeks. The sky-blue sheet is tucked in. Wedding gift pillows are in place. Kevin already zipped our sleeping- bags together. So rustic and so cozy. Complete. That's how I feel, like nothing is missing.

Tonight the temperature outside is still 'Mild,' so by morning, the indoor temperature will feel just the same as though we are camping. On top of the sleeping-bags, with a flourish, I ceremoniously spread over both of us the quilt I made for Kevin as an engagement present. The colours, the love and the wool layers will all keep us tucked in and cozy tonight.

While I was in boarding school for my last year of high school in Pennsylvania, I made the quilt from shirts I bought at the church rummage sale. I filled two huge bags with cotton blouses made in the 1950's. Back in my dormitory room I snipped off all of the buttons, cut away the collar and cuffs, opened each blouse flat and started to trace around a template of cardboard five inches square. I could get almost twenty squares from each shirt.

It was fun to lay the squares out, putting the pretty old-fashioned prints checker-board style making an overall pattern alternating dark and light. Here are green vine-y leaves. There a nose-gay of pink. Here is a shamrock. There is a snowflake. A curved green fern, a grey geometric pattern, a cluster of berries, autumn leaves, tiny people in a row, little ponies prance, birds fly, paisley and plaid and stripes and dots march and dance and invite and contrast. I build an unchanging sequence of light and dark with an entertaining variety of colours and designs. Inside the quilt is a wool blanket, also found at the rummage sale. The back is a thick, green striped, flannel sheet. I tied the corners with red yarn.

Two years ago, when we were newly engaged, we sat together in my parent's living room. I was hand sewing every seam while he told me interesting things about what he had read, learned on TV, where he had travelled, what work he knew how to do, his thoughts about the sermon, his opinions, interests, hobbies.

The quilt covered Kevin's bed while he was away for a year at the Church College keeping him safe and warm while he was so far away from me. I have been waiting for this day when we sleep together, married, in our first home.

The past hopes for the future have become this present peaceful moment.

It is late. There is nothing else to do. We get settled in and just grin in the darkness, our family of four, Kevin, Eleanor, Sam and Ember (or Amber). For the first time, we sleep in our own home, bought and paid for. Tomorrow is a clear blank page to write another chapter of our adventures.

As my eyes close, I can hear the comforting chorus from *Hansel and Gretel*.[4] There is nothing so wonderful in all my life.

When at night I go to sleep
Fourteen angels watch do keep
Two my head are guarding
Two my feet are guiding
Two are on my right hand
Two who near my left stand
Two who warmly cover
Two who over me hover
Two to whom 'tis given to guide my steps to heaven!

Chapter 3
December 23, 1978
Saturday

If a man does not keep pace with his companions,
perhaps it is because he hears a different drummer.
Let him step to the music that he hears,
however measured and far away.
—*Henry David Thoreau*

The night before last night we slept in our last stopover in the cozy camper. It was a real resting place. There was no work to do. No chores. The camper bed was clean and new. The little framed addition was so small that it was toasty warm from the large wood stove heater. The wood was plentiful. The location was convenient. It was less than a dozen steps from the van to the door. The invitation and welcome to stay in the camper was warm. But, it was not a place to live. You could barely move around to get dressed. It was a place to sleep and keep out of the chill.

Now, we have to walk up the snowy path, carrying every item from the road to our cabin. Moss and sawdust are frozen to the floor. Soot and snow track in. The firebox of the heater wood stove in the camper could hold four or five big round logs. The fire lasted all night. The little firebox of the kitchen cook stove in the cabin is so much smaller. Only two or three pieces of one log that has been split into quarters can fit in the firebox, like puzzle-pieces. The fire needs to be fed every hour or two. We won't be able to sleep through the night *and* stay warm. The camper was small and insulated. The uninsulated cabin is larger, colder.

But it is ours.

Yet, we feel not that we have less, but that we have more. Built with our wits and time. Built by our own dreams and muscles. Built of forest-found, store-bought, bartered and salvaged materials. It is our very own home, we paid cash for the building materials as we went along. With satisfaction we can say, "Built with our own bare hands."

Tonight, our first night in our cabin, as the wind softly stirs the tree-tops, as the ripples of the river rhythmically stroke the sand, as the moon glides across the star studded sky, as myriad sparkles dance on the crystal snow, as the animals burrow into their nests, as the dawn slowly opens the day, as all living things seek the sun's rays, so I gladly share this night with my husband, after yearning and striving, sacrifice and focus, struggle and reaching for this moment, at last we are together. Here. Now. We experience the closeness of husband and wife as part of the cycle, balance and beauty of nature's wholeness surrounding us.

This is what we wanted exactly. When he proposed, Kevin drew a picture which I have on the cover of my journal: a log cabin, garden, forest, mountain ridge, river winding, pathways. It is remarkable how alike they are: the drawing of his dream and the structure of this reality.

If this was a play or movie, the grand, heart-warming chords of music to demonstrate the satisfaction after endurance would be playing right now.

Kevin is rattling the stove. I know it is morning. He says, "Stay in bed until it gets warm in here."

It's my weekend. Actually, I'll be home for four whole days: Saturday, Sunday, then Christmas Day and Boxing Day. Hurrah! No watching the clock. No trip to town. No uniform. No waiting tables. No nosy co-workers. No teasing locals. No demanding customers. No embarrassing mistakes. We can savour being together, make plans, enjoy teamwork and settle in.

The night-time temperature dipped to -10°C.[5] Kevin announces after he returns from the wood pile. "It's 'Right Balmy!'" he grins.

I make a dash for the outhouse. The morning is just beginning to be blue. I will be glad to see clear blue sky! The more mild temperatures have kept the sky dreary grey and overcast for well over a month. The dawn begins, barely light, so it must be after 7:30. The sun will not climb above the walls of the mountain to shine on our little haven until after 10:00. Kevin has the fire crackling and I feel the warmth when I return from my chilly venture and enter our nest. "Balmy indeed!" I dive, shivering, back under the covers. "I'd say 'Brisk' is more like it." I am cheerfully eager to begin our first day.

Kevin installed a thermometer just outside the door. The red line will tell the scientific truth. I'm not sure I believe any of the tall tales the menfolk told me while I poured their coffee at the restaurant. Were they offering me advice? Or were they scaring me away? Or were they stretching things a bit and later laughing at my naivete? 30° below, 40° below, 50° below, wind chill factor...How many days and nights of deep freeze...How deep the snow gets...Are these true stories?

I've heard tales of water pipes freezing under the house-trailers. The man next door will help a women whose husband is in the bush. He might use a hairdryer or a fiery propane torch to thaw the pipes. When water freezes it expands, bursting the pipes, which means the home owner has to drive 45 miles to town to buy new replacement parts.

"We won't have broken water pipes since our water comes from melted snow," I offer a positive conversation opener. "Do you think it's true that the river could freeze solid?" I simply can't imagine it. How cold would it have to be for this vast, swiftly moving force to become locked in ice?

"Sure," Kevin replies. He has spent some time swapping stories with the older men when he comes to town to get the mail and pick me up after work. "Mr. Gibson told me that winter is the best time for logging because the river becomes a highway for the horse teams. You know that brown church building right behind the log school? It was originally the first schoolhouse built of lumber from the local sawmill when the early settlement was two miles downstream. Most people moved away after the forest fire in the early 1920's. In 1927 that school building was dragged up river to Avola by horse teams pulling it on the ice."

"What about equipment?" I continue, comparing fragments I have heard with what he has learned. "I don't get it when the men try to explain the way the cold affects their machinery."

"Extreme cold causes liquids in the engine to gel. Hydraulic fluid, lubricating oil, fuel oil and even the anti-freeze will change consistency in the deep cold. Cold shrinks some things but expands water. Seals leak. Lubricating oil is like mud. Fuel oil and propane won't flow through the lines. You have to have the right kind of engine oil or it will work against you. Without the proper antifreeze mixture, the fluid will freeze, expand and crack the engine block."

"Seriously? Cold can break iron?" I am aghast.

"Yes, deep cold causes metal to contract and become brittle. Tools will chip. Welding rods shatter. Rails on the railroad crack. You will have to be careful not to use the axe if it gets that cold."

"Well, what will the loggers do? What do all the people do if their engines won't start? They say it can stay that cold for a whole month?" I feel like I have been transported to live on one of the distant planets. The rules of 'normal' are distorted.

"At their homes in town, people will plug in an electric block heater to keep the coolant in their truck engine warm. In the bush, the men leave their equipment running all night and hire a guy to stay awake all night to keep watch. Or, if the engine does get too cold, they use a propane torch or toss a parachute or tarp over the equipment and keep a heater going all night." Kevin is speaking English, but it is hard for me to comprehend.

"Sounds awful. I don't like the cold. We'll be OK, won't we? I have cotton long johns, wool pants, a thick wool sweater, down parka and those special man-made ThinsuliteTM fibre mittens you gave me. I'm glad we found those felt-pack men's boots that fit me. They sure are warmer than any lady's fashionable boots." I try to convince myself with confidence. "So far my normal jeans seem to be OK."

"I want you to have silk or wool or man-made fibre long johns. Cotton isn't good enough. It holds the moisture.

Man-made fibres wick the moisture away from your body. It is so important to stay dry." Kevin seems to know so much and wants to protect me. "Frostbite is a very real danger. And you will have to be careful when you work outside not to breathe in too deeply. If you feel your thumb getting cold, pull it into your mitten with the other fingers until it warms up. And take your boot-liners out to dry every evening or the moisture will freeze inside your boots." I'm starting to feel anxious about all of these precautions. "If it gets windy, which doesn't seem to happen very often here in this deep valley, be aware that the wind chill factor will make it more dangerously cold, but it will not register on the thermometer."

Well! Who knew that the silent, silvery, winter wonderland was so hazardous?

Meanwhile, Kevin has added wood to the kindling and poked the fuel so the heat will flare up into the space under one of the round lids on the cook stove. Removing it with the lid-lifter, he set our small cast-iron frying pan over the gap. The orange flames tickle the bottom of the pan.

"I didn't know you could do that!" I exclaim.

"A single layer of cast iron will get hotter faster than two layers. That is a big advantage of this wood cook stove design. The food will reach the boiling point faster if you remove the lid and put the pot directly over the flames." So, from that moment on, all of our nice new wedding gift pots and pans are initiated into the back-woods life with their black, smoky bottoms.

"Why are you putting the egg shells into the fire?" I'm curious.

"We will burn all of our food scraps, empty cans and other things that smell," he explains, "We don't want to attract bears and other..."

"Varmits!" I finish his sentence using a 'Hill-Billy' word to show I know a thing or two about country living!

"How come you know so much?" I ask in appreciation of this man who seems to be right at home in this place which is so foreign to me.

He has many experiences both at the farm house which his family rented as a summer cottage and while working for Mennonite farmers in Ontario and visiting relatives in Alberta who not-so-long-ago lived this lifestyle. His frequent camping experiences have also given him the knowledge, practice and confidence to know he can rely on himself to carve a human habitation in these rugged mountains.

Eggs sizzle. Toast laid on the stove top browns nicely. My husband is making me breakfast in bed! He steps outside to scoop up snow to melt for water. Eventually I will also have mint tea.

Somehow I just can't stay in bed while he has all the fun. Reaching into one of my boxes of treasures, I pull out a Granny Square afghan my Mother crocheted for me which I love to use as a shawl. I come closer to watch and ask more questions... and soak up some of the heat from the stove.

Kevin brought me the stove for a birthday present. Abandoned in one of the rotting homestead cabins, he retrieved it and set it up for me.

At first I could see only a confusion of black lids and shiny chrome knobs. The massive cube of the cast iron body and the tall, cylindrical chimney seemed ominous. Each feature had mysterious powers I did not know how to control. How would I ever be able to govern a blazing fire inside of my own house?

One by one I began to see the purpose and cleverness of the four main parts: stove top, oven, warming oven and water tank.

The door to the firebox was on the upper left side. As the fire burns the ashes fall through a grate into the metal ash box below. When the lower door was opened and the metal ash box pulled out, the corners could be scraped bare with a little hoe-like tool.

The stove top seemed easy to understand. But why are there six lids? Pots and pans must be moved to find the ideal temperature to sizzle, simmer, boil or melt. A lid can be removed and a cast iron frying pan placed in the empty hole with the fire directly contacting the bottom of the pan to provide direct heat.

The oven was harder for me to comprehend. Hot air rises. How will a fire over on the left heat the oven over on the right? When I open the chrome decorated oven door, I can't figure it out. All I see is an empty metal box.

By lifting lids and opening doors I could uncover the mysterious inner workings.

But first I needed to understand one basic fact.

Fire needs air. Open air vents allow the wood to burn hotter and more quickly. Closing them slows the fire's heat. There are three sliding or turning doors which I can open and close to control the air.

First and most obvious, the sliding knob on the left wall of the stove, just beside the firebox, opens several windows. Best to start a fire with these wide open, allowing the hungry fire to feed on the fuel. Soon the slots can be reduced to a sliver so the fire will maintain a steady heat. Later these draft openings can be shut all the way to reduce the oxygen, slowing combustion, to make the fire last longer.

The second air control is the chimney damper. This chrome spiral-wire knob is above the stove, just within reach. When the fire is starting, this is open to allow the hot air and smoke to rise unobstructed. When turned, a flat, round disc inside the chimney closes. This slows the smoke, chokes the fire, pressing the flames down to glowing coals, making the fire last longer.

The third control is for the oven. It is harder for me to understand this one at first. On the back of the stove, under the cooking surface, where the stove top meets the chimney, there is a long, rectangular sliding door. I can see what it does when I lift the lid away and watch the opening to the chimney slide open and closed. But what is it for?

I had to think of the fire as something flexible. When the chimney control is open, the fire's heat and smoke go directly from the firebox straight up the chimney. But when the stove is hot and the smoke is eagerly drawing upwards, the slider can be closed. This forces the heat and smoke to wrap around the oven, seeking the available passageway across the top, down to the right, wrapping underneath and then behind the oven and at last, up the chimney. This amazingly clever design heats the oven to the perfect baking temperature.

At about shoulder height, the chimney passes through the warming oven. It is so civilized. Imagine this: after a winter's night with the kitchen fire gone out, warm porridge, scrambled eggs, toast or pancakes will lose their heat immediately if served on chilly bowls or plates. To combat the cold, while the meal is being prepared, the cook places the plates, bowls and mugs into the warming oven. It is a huge advantage to serve the food directly onto warm dishes. The meal can be enjoyed with an added bonus. Early morning hands find comfort holding each warm bowl or mug.

The final feature of the wood stove is the copper water reservoir with a hinged lid along the right side of the stove. By the time the meal is ready, there is also hot water ready for dishes. Before bedtime, warm bath water is ready.

In this 'Back-to-Basics' lifestyle, one last detail is a luxury. Above the firebox there is a little shelf for my teapot! Ready at the ideal temperature, I will be able to pause mid-morning and enjoy a second cup.

After a little trial and error I will learn to prepare granola and muffins, cookies and pies, bread and biscuits, baked beans and corn bread, casseroles and gingerbread all toasted and fragrant coming from that Moffat wood cook stove oven.

"This is just like our Honeymoon!" I exclaim. "Remember? You got up to light the wood stove and bring me breakfast. That was such a darling little cabin beside the lake. We had the leftovers from our Wedding Day breakfast. I'm so glad my Mother thought of packing up a box of goodies for us. Fruit cake, pumpkin muffins, fruit salad, grape juice, banana bread. Yummy!"

"And peach pie!" Kevin remembers finding that treat when we spent our first afternoon as 'Mr. and Mrs.' exploring the local shops and Farmer's Market.

"Yes, I remember," I rapidly recall details. "After we left the wedding reception at the church, my house and our families, we drove to the Toronto airport taking the guitarist, Lori, to her flight. I cried so hard when we said good-bye. When we were at the airport, I thought I was going to collapse. Your strong arms supported me so I could walk. I was just so sad to be leaving everyone and everything I knew behind. Saying good-bye to her was a symbol of leaving behind everything familiar. No more church. No more music. No more friendships. No more childhood. No more old familiar places."

"As we left the city and passed through villages and towns we passed by six weddings!" I continue my reminiscing. "Gowned guests going into their churches. Festive flowers held by clusters of families posing for photos. Dreamy couples getting into their decorated cars! Then we wandered all over the countryside until we got to a place where we could see cabins beside a lake and you signed us in for the night. We were officially Mr. and Mrs. Kevin Deckert!"

Shaking my head and slightly blushing I remembered, "In the morning I was so embarrassed to realize that we were in a fishing camp. All these old geezers were grinning at us, a young couple so obviously in love. I could tell they were thinking 'wink-wink!' I wanted to be invisible. I wanted to evaporate. Oh well, maybe they smiled and remembered their own youth with the gladness of sweet love!"

Kevin cast me a sideways glance as I gesture, exaggerating my flirtations, tossing my hair and batting my eyelashes.

He reaches into the warming oven where the two autumn coloured plates my siblings gave us for our wedding have been waiting, warming. I re-wrap my shawl and come to sit on my upright log, like a high stool. Kevin made the table from the piece of plywood that had been our bed in the van. It is supported on two sides and three corners with lumber Kevin nailed level to the south and west walls of the cabin. The fourth corner is held up by an upright log of the same height.

The kerosene Aladdin lamp looks so fine, all shiny brass and glittering glass on the bare plywood table. This brand-new old-fashioned purchase is so much brighter than the old wick lamp. But, we won't need to light it for breakfast, daylight is reclaiming the sky.

"Wow! Look at this! The eggs are from Fran's chickens. The bread is a loaf Cheryl gave us for a housewarming gift. I saved one of the jars of jam we made together from the wild blueberries we picked back in August when we first arrived. And the tea is from Fran's dried herbs! This is a foreshadowing of things to come. Oh, Kevin! Someday these things will all be from our own garden! I wish we could start right now!"

"There'll be plenty of work to do today," he smiles at my eagerness. "I haven't been able to finish the cabin and get firewood in as well. There are only scraps and bits outside ready to burn. We will have to start cutting right away."

But first I want to feast my eyes on what we have accomplished...We? Kevin! I have been at work full-time and he has built this cabin as a one-man project.

Sam, our sturdy German Shepherd, is stretched out across the doorway on the east wall of the cabin. The cold draft is kept out by the black tar paper stapled in place to line the lumber door. Beside him, nails for our coats and a box for our boots and a stack of firewood and kindling, birch bark and paper are ready to add to the stove. The southeast corner is now a stack of my 21 boxes from home. My parents have been sending them in the mail. Soon, we will build shelves in this corner for books and an altar for our Bible, candles and other symbols for worship.

The south wall has two windows. Kevin surveyed this orientation with his compass so as to best enjoy the benefits of light and heat from the sunshine. The southwest corner is where we are now, the plywood table is two feet wide and four feet long. It is just the right size for two people. When we get unpacked, I will find a table cloth and use straight pins from my sewing supplies to hang up the colourful Christmas cards we have received from family and friends. These textiles and pictures will be the only decorative artwork to break the grey logs, grey plywood table, grey lumber floor, grey underside of the roof boards.

Along the western wall, between the table and the kitchen area there is space for the foot of the ladder. Yesterday, Kevin built the ladder. Today he will nail the last of the lumber to the log beams to be the floor of the sleeping loft. Underneath the ladder, in the low slanting space, we will place the blue food storage box from the van and the tightly lidded white plastic water buckets.

The northwest corner is the kitchen area. Now, empty space. Soon it will be shelved and a work counter with just enough room for either the dish pan or a cutting board or to stir a mixing bowl. The northern wall is all about the wood stove. It is necessary to leave empty space behind and beside it for safety sake. Nothing can be near the heat of the flames. I block my mind from thinking how readily the cedar kindling caches fire from only the coaching of crumbled paper. Our entire dwelling place is made of this combustible material! I must never allow a towel, or a coat hung up to dry, or a fallen page of newspaper, or any other flammable item to be left for even a moment against the stove. The slop-water bucket, my chamber pot and the kitten's litter box are all on the floor behind the stove.

The northeast corner will soon be Kevin's shelves for tools, books, hardware, ammunition, gloves, hardhat, outdoor gear.

The one room cabin is a comfortably tight fit for the two of us, measuring only 14x14 feet square. We have and need no furniture. Only the table and two stumps to sit on. There will be room for storage of my boxes under the eaves at the foot of the bed in the sleeping loft. Above the wood stove is open space so the hot air can rise and so nothing touches the chimney. The loft is just big enough for our mattress. There is not enough height to stand. But, I have learned while camping how to get dressed in my sleeping-bag.

And now, my visual tour complete, my eyes return to Sam, trusting us to take care of him in this new place.

Amber (or Ember) jumps off of my lap and sniffs cautiously at Sam. It looks like they'll get along just fine.

"Do you know what I'm doing right now, Darling?" my voice quiet as I turn my head surveying the scene.

"What would that be?" Kevin turns his head to study my expression.

"I am memorizing this moment: this place, the pathway we took to get here, the sequence of your work to build this cabin. This moment, this exact moment will be in the book I write someday. I hope I will be able to find words to describe this blissful satisfaction."

The fire crackles and snaps. The dog lays his head on his outstretched paws and sighs. The cat has returned, curled up on my lap. My husband flips the toast.

"And you know what else?" I come out of my musings for a moment to try to find words. "In a way we didn't do anything! In a way this whole thing is a free gift!"

Turning in surprise, his muscles remembering every stroke of the axe, every lift of every part of the dwelling place we are now so comfy in, the pounding of every nail. Kevin's eyebrows show at once his question, but also his interest in the sometimes puzzling, often unusual form of logic this new wife will share as soon as she can formulate the sentence to convey her thoughts. "How's that?"

"Well, we asked the Lord to lead us and He did! We asked Him for just about exactly this. You even drew a picture that I have on the cover of my journal. Kevin, all we did was follow instructions, follow the trail He blazed. Our muscles did the physical work, but He *did* it all, got it all set up...We just stepped in and agreed to do what He got ready for us. Do you see what I mean?"

"How could our advertisement seeking land have been printed in the same magazine as Fran and Archie's invitational letter? How could we have even walked into that exact health food store to buy that exact magazine on that exact day? We never saw that magazine any other place on this whole trip! How else could we have known how to find this place? Remember? It was the only copy left on the magazine rack! We are here only because He knew what we were looking for and He kept sending us hints and we kept listening! Even the forest fire that came through here, way back before our parents were born, has provided us with these logs. And conversely, our belongings were spared from Glen's fire. If our sleeping-bags had been destroyed, we wouldn't have been able to pay for new ones. Who knew there would be a job for me? And one more thing. Whoever heard of building a house with cash as you go along when you are only earning $2.57 an hour! Seriously! Whoever heard of building a house for $300? How is that even possible? Only if Someone was helping us, showing us, leading us, providing for us."

Stroking the kitten I add, "I am bursting with gratitude right this moment. How can I ever show how thankful I am? I wish we could have a huge Thanksgiving banquet for God right now. I wish everyone could know how happy I am right now. I wish other people could experience this security and sense of Him leading. Trust. I really like trust! Trust is..." my hands gesture in a wide arc...I run out of words for this foundation, this central, essential quality. There is no peace of mind, no hope, no security, no bonding, no freedom of expression, no belonging, no sense of fairness or purpose or satisfaction or calm without Trust.

Now the plate of warm food is handed to me. *"Praise God from Whom all blessings flow."* The words and melody fill this tiny cabin, this shelter from extremes, a sanctuary, now blessed and dedicated to the Giver of all that is good.

Content, we have our first Thanksgiving feast...for breakfast! Two people, a small kitten and a big dog, in the middle of nowhere. Showered with gifts. Warm. Safe. Dry. Twogether.

Back in August it only took two days to choose this spot. Here at last was what we had been searching for as we drove all the way across Canada, up and down the highways and valleys of BC, and after touring several local properties.

On August 17th, when we first pulled into their driveway, Fran and Archie took us in immediately. That afternoon they showed us their property which they called 'Brooksong.' We also explored the Rody homestead which had a flat open field where townsfolk used to come to play baseball. Another cabin up the slope had a rotten roof, but could be restored. They described to us that there were many small homesteads up and down the valley, started in the 1920's-1940's, linked to the outside world by the passenger and local freight trains. Most of the early families had a double economy. The rain, soil and sunshine made it possible to support a sustainable family garden, while a cash income could be had from cutting poles, railroad ties, fence posts, shingles or logs for the sawmill. Many of these pioneer homes were abandoned fairly recently when the 1969 completion of the paved highway made travel easier and the younger generation left for the city life.

On the second day, August 18th, Fran and Archie introduced us to the Gibson's. We were welcomed with tea and cookies as they told us stories of local history. Now about 80 years old, Mr. Gibson told how his parents had come from the prairies in the 1920's to take part in the early days of logging. As the country opened up, Canada needed quantities of telegraph poles, farmers needed fence posts and the railway needed miles and miles of railroad ties. The forests here were the kinds of trees that were needed. It was very attractive to people feeling the call to move west.

Mrs. Gibson brought a civilizing influence to the tiny village of Avola, isolated by the dirt roads which were often impassable from deep winter snow or slides, flooding and mud in the spring or ruts dried and hard in the summertime. Mrs. Gibson had a piano. She ran the store and post office. She taught Sunday School and led the local Canadian Girls in Training. She wrote a weekly column for the valley newspaper.

They had raised four children on their land beside the river. The rich, black soil of their large garden fed the family. Mr. Gibson worked four to six months a year, felling trees for the cash they needed and ran a small sawmill for the lumber they used to add buildings to their homestead.

When we left them, I quietly whispered to my husband, "I want to tell these same stories 50 years from now. I want us to be just like them."

And I wanted to be like Fran, too. Her knowledge of the plants, birds and animals astonished me. Her garden in August was overflowing with herbs for tea and medicine, root vegetables and greens, flowers and fruit trees, berry bushes and corn. Jars of home canning lined the shelves of her back room. The root cellar below the house was stocked with even more baskets, bags, bins, boxes and jars of food. The freezer was full of wild game, poultry and meat they raised. Goat's milk and eggs came from the barn daily.

As if pictures in the books I had collected before our marriage had come to life, these people knew the things I wanted to learn. Their generosity and instruction was the ingredient we needed even more than we needed a specific piece of land.

After our visit with the Gibson's that day, Fran took us down the highway to meet a young couple, Karl and Annika, who were living the homestead-style life. A retired accountant, Howard, and his wife, Opal, had purchased 160 steeply sloped acres three years ago, intending to fix up the old trapper's cabin as a country home.

But, after several weekends when they came up from their home in the city to make improvements, they saw the vandalism and theft as someone saw both an opportunity for themselves and a disregard for the owner, stripped a generator, broke windows and rummaged through cupboards. Howard and Opal posted an advertisement in the newspaper asking for live-in helpers. Karl and Annika, itinerant farm workers recently emigrated from Holland, were attracted by the idea of a free place to live out the winter.

Ever inventing creative solutions to problems, Howard set in motion the paperwork to create a jointly owned company with five shareholders. And all of this came into fruition just at the time of our arrival.

As we walked through the land, learning from Karl and Annika about how the property was set up, we discovered this one particular spot.

"Kevin, isn't this what we have been looking for?" I asked, my eyes meeting his hopefully.

The forest was young jack pine. Open to the sunshine, knee-high blueberry bushes were hanging heavy with fruit. Tall dead cedar trees were left from the forest fire five decades ago, their grey, bare skeletons would provide building material for our log cabin. No effort would be needed to strip the bark or branches. No time would be lost waiting for the sap to dry up and shrink the logs.

Kevin sized up the situation. "Here is wood to build with and to burn, clean water in abundance, south facing slope to later build an earth sheltered house and a root cellar, good soil in a flat sunny space for a garden to grow and plenty of wild edible plants to harvest. Others have done it here. We can, too."

"I'll be able to work at the restaurant while you work on the cabin," I added hopefully, "and we can even get in before winter if we stay focused! September, October, November and part of December," I counted four months on my fingers.

So, on August 19th, on the third day after our arrival, we became the third couple on the land. We were off to Kamloops to meet with the original owners, Howard and Opal. And we signed up! The $1000 wedding present from my parents became our down payment on the $4800 for our share.

That is how it happened. After a two month search, with only $40 cash left from our travels, in only three days we had a quick realization of our goal. After a brief interview, I was hired at the Avola restaurant. In a few days the students who were working there would be back to school. In a few days I would start work and earn the money we would need to build.

Until I was needed at the restaurant, Kevin and I returned to the site. A line of young pine trees to the north looked like they had been deliberately planted in a row behind our proposed cabin. To the south, a small hollow seemed like a perfect play place for our future children to explore and pretend, yet stay in sight.

Unlike me, Kevin doesn't talk very much while he works. I like to observe him and try to follow his thought process. Sketching with a pencil in the evening before a project begins, he organizes his ideas into a plan. Bright and early, clip board in hand, pencil behind his ear, focused on inner questions and non-verbally solving anticipated problems, he begins. I sit at a distance, silently watching. He places a stone as a starting point, uses his orienteering compass to align himself with 'south' to his left shoulder. Then he paces off, using his size 11 boots, toe to heel. He planned the cabin to be 14 feet wide with two windows on this south side to allow maximum sunlight in. A diagram in a do-it-yourself book demonstrated the summer and winter angles of the sun at our latitude. With this information he planned the distance the roof would overhang, shading in summer, unobstructed in winter. Marking with another stone, turning at a right angle, pacing the same way along the western side, he measured another 14 feet. In the same way, the north and east walls were planned.

The stones now marked the corners of the 14x14 foot square. I walked about, imagining the size and placement of the kitchen, stove, shelving, table, places to sit. "There is not enough room for our bed," I mentioned.

"It will be in the loft," he replied. I gladly agreed, thinking of Heidi up in her straw-filled loft with the shutter open and the spectacular mountain views from her Grandfather's chalet.

"Hot air will rise from the wood stove below. Yet, we can keep an eye on the stove from above." He had thought it all through.

The next day, at each of the four corners, he dug holes about three feet deep. In each hole he planted a broad, upright log, tamped in firmly. That was the foundation.

As I watched in amazement at the reality of it all, using his double-bitted axe, he felled the first huge cedar tree. The earth shook when it fell.

"It's a widow-maker," Kevin pointed out.

"What does that mean?" I asked, alarmed that the term 'widow' might have at the moment referred to me.

"See how hollow it is? Although I notched it on this side because I wanted it to fall in this direction, there is no way to be sure. Since the timber is weakened and the weight of the tree is altered by the uneven hollowed core, it could have split apart or fallen in an unexpected direction."

Gravity doesn't care if the workman is standing in the wrong place. Unforeseen danger could have blotted out my husband's life and a very young widow I would be. "Dear Lord in Heaven, Please, protect my Husband," became my silent prayer from that moment, every day, every breath.

That particular stump was so near the cabin site we would be able to show future visitors, children and grand-children: "See this stump? This is where Kevin felled the first tree."

I cut brush to clear a pathway and define our 'yard' dragging it into a high burning pile to be lit when the autumn rains started. I imagined our children running here and there, the garden crops stored in the root cellar, the crafts in the winter, the hikes in the summer, the snowshoeing, bicycling, canoeing and discoveries the years ahead would bring.

From this point on, I was at the restaurant every day, wondering at his progress, decisions, energy, dedication, anxious about his safety. Kevin worked alone.

Over a year ago, one of the first things Kevin did to prepare for our western adventure was to order his 'Mother's Finest' axe from the 'Mother Earth News' magazine which was so popular in the 1970's 'Back-to-the-Land' movement. In addition, Archie loaned Kevin a five-foot long bucksaw asking only, "Do you know how to sharpen this?" The flat file for the axe would also sharpen the two-inch long saw teeth.

Archie also supplied tie-tongs used for moving railroad ties which would be excellent for moving logs. Kevin opened the tongs with a firm grip on the handles. He could stand with his back towards the cabin site, straddling each log, closing the pointed tongs near the lead end of the log. The sharp points dug into the wood, allowing him to lift the log and slide it between his feet. Progress was made one lift at a time. Keeping a secure grip on the log with the tongs, he stepped backwards again and again. Each tree he felled was a little farther from the building site. Each log was a little further to drag to the site.

The floor joists had to be in place before the second row of logs. One long, thin, strong joist was notched in across one way, then shorter cross pieces spanned the distance from the centre floor joist to the sides. It looked just like the 'Lincoln Logs' my brothers played with when we were small.

My pay cheque started coming in to buy things we needed as we went along. Fran and Archie charged neither rent nor room and board, so we could get moving forward as quickly as possible.

The sawmill 25 miles away had 2x8 inch hemlock boards priced at $100 for 1000 board feet. One sling of lumber was enough for the floor. A second pay cheque for a second sling would be needed for the roof. Kevin took 8-foot lengths so he could haul them in the van. I could help hammer down the floor boards on my weekend. Kevin framed in a trap door so that a future root cellar could be finished later.

In late September, Kevin arranged for my birthday present. The cooler weather had recently begun and Fran and Archie insisted that we move into their living room, to sleep on their fold-out couch. After everyone was asleep, Kevin slid out from under the covers whispering, "I'll be awhile." I heard the van start up, no headlights, he crawled slowly, quietly down the driveway. Parking so that his headlights shone into the abandoned homestead cabin across the road, I could faintly hear the clatter of metal and the grunts of his effort lifting. Again the motor rumbled, now fading away as he drove the curved dirt road to the highway. I dozed. I watched the clock. I waited. He arrived back to me after delivering the elegant, but long unused Moffat wood cook stove to our property. If anyone ever recognized it, they never said anything. Salvaging what has been abandoned is a legitimate claim to ownership in this rugged, rural life.

That weekend, when I could spend two days at the building site, I could see that Kevin's axe had made good progress. The logs were three rows high now. It was splendid to walk on the floor. Our floor. To get the feel of the space. To imagine the finished project.

"Kevin? Can you estimate how much more time you will need to finish?"

"Well, each row takes a little longer to build. I've already felled the twelve trees that are closest to the cabin. Now I have to search for more good wood. Since some trees have hollow, rotten centres from standing dead for so long, I sometimes have to cut away the lower part and only use the upper part. Plus, each log takes longer for me to drag the extra distance and then rest up before I can go back again. Also, for safety sake, I have to take more precautions. Each time the walls get higher it is harder to lift, roll and fit the next log into place."

"I wish I could help. But I don't see how I could? I'm just not strong enough and it might cause an accident if you were relying on me and I couldn't hold up my end."

Time was important, these golden autumn days would not last forever. We asked old-timers how soon to expect snow. Kevin confided in me that he felt like he was constantly looking over his shoulder, watching the calendar pages turn and the days becoming shorter, cooler, like a threatening force he knew was coming. Preparations were essential. Pressure was constant.

Then, rain.

Day and night, more and more unceasing rain. In the evening, while we enjoyed Fran's wholesome meals, Archie explained how this area was moderated by coastal weather. The mild temperatures brought heavy precipitation inland. Just like the diagram in a Grade 4 geography text book, warm moist air rises off of the ocean, moves inland, gains elevation crossing over the mountains, cools, condenses and pours down rain.

Not the billowing purple cumulonimbus storm clouds in Colorado drifting in from the prairie. Not the frightening, violent storm lashing hurricane-force winds I had experienced in Florida. Not the cheerful spring rains of Ontario nor sudden summer thunder showers. This is long days of dreary dark overcast skies. I-can't-tell-where-the-sun-is dimly lit days. Drizzling all day and all night. Penetrating. Saturating everything.

Unless, of course, the temperature drops below freezing and the precipitation falls as ever deeper layers of snow.

Waitressing continued, but the heavy curtains of rain made for neither safe nor effective work conditions. After work I asked Kevin, "What progress today on the cabin?"

Although he had nylon rain gear, Kevin had to stop and think about his options. "I took the day to drive. Explore. I'm curious about the logging roads."

He described several homesteads he had found along the low road, following the curves of the river. Along the high roads he watched the logging operations through his binoculars. Views of ice-capped mountains, crystal clear lakes, roaring waterfalls and golden autumn aspen groves lifted his spirits and confirmed his commitment to the decision to settle here permanently. He noticed signs of deer, moose, bear, eagles and beaver in the varying habitat. Man-made evidence left signs of trappers, gold panners, railroad, mining, homesteads.

But, while these discoveries encouraged him, Kevin was also experiencing an unseen struggle, leaving him staring at the unfinished cabin for hours at a time, virtually paralyzed day after day.

Only three months married, it was hard for me to decode his down-turned face, his smaller gestures, his dull tone of voice, his heavier posture. But, I could see that something was weighing him down. Of course, he was physically tired by the end of the day. Of course he was thinking, solving problems, addressing challenges. After two months of accepting the help of this fine couple, it was also a strain to be a guest at the table every day, make up the fold-out bed, share conversations with others. Lack of privacy wears on anyone.

The first weekend in October when I returned to the cabin, I was shocked to notice that there had been no progress at all. "Kevin? What's happening?" I tried to keep my voice soft and coaxing. Sometimes in a movie the passage of time is shown when the calendar pages blow, turning faster and skittering leaves and whirling music build up the tension.

Kevin leaned his head down on his hands. Pent-up emotions filled his chest heaving, his breath gasping, his words blunt, his voice a shouting whisper.

"It is as if I can still hear the mocking jeers of the fellows at the factory!"

"You'll be back."

"You'll never make it."

"What a dream."

"Your wife will leave you."

The physical work, the difficult obstacles, solving the challenges of how to safely work alone, the endurance test of the wits, these were one kind of effort. But this erosion of courage was such a personal strain.

My hand gently, firmly on his shoulder, I teetered between disbelief and empathy. I had seen Kevin upset a few times over our four-year courtship. He had shared with me the emotions he experienced at the time of his father's death. He had described unpleasant scenes, times he had stood up to unjust teachers, ways he coped with disappointments. But, these were all retelling events from the past. I had come to appreciate his character qualities and the ways he had overcome hardship, his morals, his self-discipline. This was the first time he was immobilized right in front of me. And so much depended on his on-going progress on the cabin.

"It is strange how much it hurts," I began calmly, almost murmuring. "How can people who don't even know you, who are thousands of miles away, who will never see your accomplishments, who don't care one speck how this turns out...how can what they say matter enough to hurt you so deeply?"

Kevin shuddered, sighed and listened.

"I am the one you are working for. I am your wife. I am your friend. You are my friend. I am not going to hurt you. I am the one cheering for you. I am the one hoping for your safety and strength and endurance and creative problem solving." The tone of my voice became rich and deep. The pledges we made, clothed in white, flowers and music and friends all around, were being tested. "This is our story. Twogether. No one else can damage or erode or rob us of this day."

My mind searched for some comparison, some example to draw strength from.

Suddenly a bright, clear realization: "The laughter and taunting you hear is part of the Journey! Jesus heard it, too. Over and over again people said, 'If you are really God then show me a miracle' and 'Why don't you save yourself?' Kevin! Right now it feels like an insurmountable barricade. But maybe it is a necessary part of the Path."

More words tumbled out of my friend's heart. Unlike anything he had ever shared with me before, and yet part of the whole person I was committed to Journey with. Gradually,

I was able to decipher his tangled memories by asking questions, prompting and gentle listening.

"Doesn't it seem like the book we read?" I reminded him of one of the first things we shared while we were in high school. 'Jonathan Livingston Seagull' crashing through the breakfast flock! Those factory workers back in Ontario had already given up. They've settled for the daily routines, the bills to pay, the lawn to mow. Having a dream? Reaching for a goal? They can only laugh. Otherwise it would hurt inside themselves too much."

And so, after sorting through and verbalizing pent-up emotions, Kevin stood and gripped his axe. He could begin again.

I walked back to the van to make lunch on the camp stove. I found myself humming as I stirred the soup. I recognized the tune which arrived in my mind. It was a yearning, hopeful, idealistic song.

"There *is* a place for us. It's right here! There is a time for us. It's right now! Peace and quiet and open air. Yes!" I felt buoyant and confident while my voice carried the song through the forest.

Like Maria and Tony in 'West Side Story',[6] the love that binds us is so strong and new and sweet. Forces in society will try to pry us apart, cast doubts, tear our hearts, assume we would fail. But, we keep striving, hoping, believing.

When I returned, he was sitting again. Like a statue. Focused intently. It seemed to me the hour glass was spilling time away.

Then in a flash Kevin had an idea!

"I knew I saw it somewhere! If the rest of the walls are built of shorter upright logs, like palisades of a log fort, they would be easier for one person to move, go up quickly and make use of the sometimes less-than-ideal trees."

After that historic day, Kevin's cheery energy returned and every day was full of positive progress.

And that was a good thing, too. Silently, I was ever mindful of the days lost and the shortened time to finish before winter snows blocked the road, slowed progress and made construction work icy and dangerous.

Echoes of mocking laughter and the erosion of self-doubt had made it hard for Kevin to keep going. Added to that was the local gossip I had to contend with. So much energy is lost when people sneer. When 'they' say it is impossible it feels impossible. During these times, our meals with Fran and Archie were a balm. A word of encouragement is like a fountain of energy renewing the muscles and mind, bringing clarity of thought and courage to the heart.

Now that he had a vision, I helped Kevin prepare the level surface along the top of the three-log-high wall with a snap of the blue chalk-line. He had a clever little level, only about four inches long, that had two hooks to hang on the chalk-line. With the markings on all four knee-high walls, he used the hand saw to score the log down to the chalk-line. It looked like a bread knife slicing partially into the top of a loaf of bread. Then, with the double-bitted axe, he could accurately chip off the wood to prepare a level surface. Next, spiking down an eight-inch wide board, he created a consistent surface for the five-foot tall upright logs to be toe-nailed in place.

Ants were already resident in some logs. Later I had to sweep up little pyramid shaped piles of their sawdust as the ant colony bored more channels in their home which was now also our home.

Kevin started this new method in early October. When Fran and Archie brought their camera on the golden autumn

Thanksgiving weekend[7] Fran took a picture of Kevin placing the upright logs along the second wall.

When the final upright was in place, Kevin planned to add one course of horizontal logs spiked securely into the uprights to tie the structure firmly together. Making a ramp with poles, hammering in spikes at intervals, Kevin was able to lift these four large top-plate logs one end at a time, held in place with pegs, lifting first the left then the right, climbing up and up until they were in place. What a celebration when those four corner notches were done!

With the successful experience of designing the first set of floor joints, the floor joists for the loft were quicker to install.

By chance, Rod, Gloria's husband, showed up one day, curious and offering to lend a hand. And just in time for a two-man lift. Earlier, Kevin had spotted a specific tree which was straight and solid which he wanted to use as the ridge pole. The only problem: it was 300 yards away up a steep slope. Kevin felled and bucked to the correct length, but knew he could not move it alone. So it was perfect timing for Rod to offer to lend a hand. Together they wrapped rope on the lead end to lift and to guide it as gravity helped move it down the hill. They agreed on the route and together, hooting and hollering, breaking branches and brambles, the men skidded the log down the slope to the site.

By the end of the day, they had wrestled the ridge pole up on the wall.

Now, Kevin had to estimate how high to make the ridge pole supports, knowing he would be lifting the ridge pole log into place alone, one end at a time. "This is as high as I can safely lift this weight," he demonstrated to me as he held the end just over waist high, "so this is as high as our ridge pole will be," he told me. More notching. More spiking. High off the ground, he was concentrating on his own safety during every move. I sighed a huge sigh when this hazardous phase was complete.

Roof rafters were next, made of slender, but sturdy poles. When payday came, the lumber for the roof took several trips to haul. More money was needed to buy the tar paper and rolled roofing and the chimney. Every pay cheque was stretched and tugged to feed two people and the van, a dog and the house.

Unexpectedly, here was another obstacle which Nature put in our path. Tar paper is light weight and inexpensive. The more costly rolled roofing will crack in the cold. And every day the temperature was teasing us. Frosty at night. Chilly in the morning and afternoon. Warm enough at midday if the sun shone. But would it rain? If the optimum temperature was mid-afternoon and I needed to get to work, would the interruption to bring me to work at 2:00 cause a delay of an entire day? Perhaps that one perfect day would be the only one for an entire cloudy week? Without a telephone, without a weather forecast, with me not able to drive myself, was there nothing to do except accept the fact that there would be valuable time lost?

It was beginning to be stressful. Tension between us caused a lot of silence. There is nothing we could do to change the weather. Attempting to move forward when it was too cold would damage and waste the costly materials. This would cause an even longer wait until the next payday.

Could we heat up the roll of roofing near the stove? Maybe, but it will cool off by the time it is delivered up the ladder, rolled out to measure and fastened down.

Limitations seemed to be pressing in. I wanted answers. But Kevin could not see the future. My silence was anxious. Kevin's silence was patient.

The wood stove was set up just in time. The chill on bare hands was relieved. And my hands were getting rough and red from the task I was doing.

To chink the gaps between the logs, I gathered moss that grew on the steep north slope down to the river. I pulled thick carpets of wet moss off the rotting fallen logs, huge boulders, the forest floor. I filled up plastic garbage bags and carried the heavy load. To occupy my mind I was always estimating: time to harvest, weight to carry, wait to rest, time to chink. To estimate the total amount needed I counted how many gaps I could fill with one bag of the spongy, fern-like moss. Then I counted how many cracks there were all together. Then I multiplied that to estimate how many times I would need to return with the soggy, heavy load. I realized I should harvest, carry and save up enough for the whole project first and then do the chinking. Otherwise, the entire project might be doomed if deep snow prevented me from safely lowering myself down the slippery slope.

Kevin made me a wooden wedge and mallet to hammer the moss firmly into the cracks. Little-by-little I worked my way around the inside walls. My hands got chapped from the wet, cold work.

November brought frost, rain, snow crystals and crusts of ice to my bare hands or soaked my work gloves. I hurriedly brought eight more bags full of moss, heaping them up in the middle of the cabin floor.

During the night it froze rock solid. The next day I had to use the chisel and mallet to pry chunks and slabs off of the pile. Lighting the fire to keep ourselves warm while we worked, racing the sky, I used an old roasting pan to heap up frozen moss to thaw in the wood stove oven, soggy and steaming. "Mmm, what's for supper?" my husband would tease. But, there was one advantage. Now my fingers were warm. I realized that

I would not have time to chink the cracks along the outside, too. Winter was really coming now.

And then, working long and hard one sunny afternoon, the roof was covered.

Kevin asked a small sawmill owner if he could have enough slabs to close in the two triangle ends under the roof. Borrowing Howard's generator and using a skilsaw, he sliced and fitted these free boards, lined the inside with tar paper and won the race with winter at last! December 21! We made it!

As Kevin and I look back this morning, talking over the sequences and accomplishments, we realize deeply that there is so much to be proud of and thankful for as we share this 'Homecoming Breakfast.'

The snow has melted by now and heated up for dish water. We have been camping for two months during the summer as we travelled and searched, so I have my dish washing routine figured out.

The shallow, white enamel dishpan hangs on a nail behind the stove. I pour steaming hot water and squirt the dish soap in and set the pan on the table. I lay out a towel for the clean dishes and begin to wash the least dirty dishes. I also have a pitcher of hot, clean water handy to pour over the newly washed dishes while I hold them over the basin. This rinses off the soap. I save the sticky pots for last. Often I can only partially clean them, washing off the oil and sticky food in the first wash. I have to wait for more water until more snow melts and heats up so I can finish the job.

"Here's one advantage of a wood stove," Kevin offers a suggestion. "When the wash water cools you can put the metal basin back on the stove to keep the water hot." Kevin brings in more and more snow to fill up the water reservoir, but it shrinks away so fast. It seems to be about ten parts of snow to obtain one part of water.

"Do you know one of the things I like best about our house?" I ask my heroic husband.

"I couldn't begin to guess," he replies, eyes meeting and curious, hoping for a compliment.

"The windows," I answer.

Kevin looks a little surprised, after all his physical achievements, clever problem solving and courageous heavy lifting.

"Remember when you borrowed the chainsaw and brought it into the house and asked, 'Where do you want your windows?' I showed you where I would stand to wash the dishes, hoping a window there would provide both natural light for my workplace and a scenic view for my enjoyment. Then you pulled the cord and started up the chainsaw right inside the house and cut the space out of the log wall to my exact recommendations. At that precise moment I felt like the wealthiest woman in the world!"

The windows had been salvaged from some old building and Kevin found them leaning up beside the goat barn at Fran and Archie's place. "What are they worth to you?" Archie asked with a twinkle in his eye.

"I have eleven dollars in my wallet," Kevin replied, looking.

"Eleven dollars and all three are yours." Archie was pretty easy to get along with.

They don't match, but two let in the sunshine to the south and the other one faces to the west in my tiny kitchen area.

During these four months of construction, Kevin used two chainsaws for short and specific times. One he borrowed from a neighbour for a very short time. The other chainsaw was borrowed from Jim, Archie's son-in-law. But, Kevin found that maintaining a machine cost money, was frustrating to repair and slower overall than doing the work by hand. Howard let us use his old, somewhat stubborn gas powered generator. "I think this thing is older than I am," Kevin muttered as he struggled to keep it running. The generator barely had enough power to run the skilsaw Kevin had brought with us from Ontario as he cut the lumber for the floor and ripped the slabs lengthwise. So, except for a few days of using power tools, the entire cabin was built with an axe and a saw.

Construction was finished, but every day working on the cabin was a day gone by with no firewood gathered. Now it would all have to be cut with the two-man cross-cut saw.

Breakfast cleanup is done now. It must be 10:00. The sun has just hit the house, brilliantly lighting our interior which has been gloomy grey all morning. I've rolled up the bedding and covered it with the blue tarp. There is no use sweeping because Kevin is lifting boards up, measuring, cutting. The sawdust smells so good. The ring of the hammer is music. I am so glad to be here and watch and help him work.

Kevin has finished the ladder and loft. And so, as a Grande Finale, I get to test it out.

"I feel like a squirrel in my nest when I look out of the little window and see the nearby birch tree." Kevin cleverly hinged a shutter near the head of the bed so we can look out, let fresh air in and see the sunrise to the east. The loft is plenty big enough for our mattress and storage, but like living in a tent, we can't stand up.

We wrestle the mattress up, Kevin hands me the bedding. I can do the rest.

"Yoo-Hoo!" Voices are coming up the trail. Our only neigh-bours, Karl and Annika, are pulling a sled loaded with some big object. What could it be?

As they approach and the dog stops barking, greetings are exchanged, smiles and welcome and cheer. Annika explains that they have brought us a housewarming gift. It is a large shelved hutch they had which Karl was using in his wood-shop. Since he has built a better shelf for his tools, this one is for us to get our furnishings started.

We share our excitement at moving in and a big "Thank-you" and a cup of tea enjoyed with some muffins that Annika brought.

After our guests leave, Kevin really wants to get going outside on the firewood supply.

I really want to start opening my 21 boxes that have been mailed from home.

He gears up and heads out.

I am alone and ready to satisfy my desire to unpack and claim my territory.

I have a list of the belongings inside each box, so I can quickly prioritize. The boxes of clothing I take up the ladder. Most of it is city clothes, summer clothes, things I do not need at this time of year, so they are stored in the lowest eve where the roof meets the loft floor.

The books can be unpacked later as there are no shelves yet and very little lumber left to build any.

I open two of the boxes to enjoy my childhood treasures. Like a movie flashback, scenes of memories blur my vision and slow my movements. Here are my report cards from Colorado,

Florida, Ontario and Pennsylvania. Here are my art projects, first grade workbooks, articles torn from magazines I thought were of interest, programs and ticket stubs from concerts. I kept a memento from each of the ballets and plays I was in. I kept brochures from trips our family took to Pikes Peak, Mesa Verde, the Grand Canyon, the Statue of Liberty, the Empire State Building, Washington DC, Ottawa.

All of this is behind me. Yet, in the collection there are also items I kept in hopes for the future. My baby clothes and blanket: will I someday wrap my own child in this soft warmth? I saved samples of my school work: planning to find a remote location to raise our children, will I need these things to provide for their education? My Brownie and Girl Scout uniforms and badges: as I raise our children I want to remember to include emphasis on good citizenship and loyalty, volunteering and a wide variety of skill development.

My most precious possession: a photograph taken in 1897 of a little two-year old girl sitting on her mother's lap. It is my great-grandmother who is reading a book to my little-girl grandmother! And she read to my Daddy who read aloud to me. And, Oh how I will enjoy the moment when my husband can take a matching photograph of me reading to our children!

In an extra large box: colour. Before I left home, I raided Mother's fabric closet. Here are pieces of leftover cloth from Christmas dresses, nightgowns, table cloths, gifts, school clothes. I want to make a quilt for our bed which will, like a scrapbook or photo album, bring memories of these times, places and people that I love.

Curious, I open another. Ah, yes, here it is. The jewelry box my brothers gave me and the rings, necklaces, beads, tiny treasures it contains. I check to see. Yes, my engagement ring is safe. Yes, we have made a good start to live the meaning of the three diamonds. The husband and the wife continually seeking the Voice of His guidance.

Here is the pottery bowl my sister, Julie, made and gave me last Christmas. My sister, Carole, carefully wrote out a beautiful poem as a wedding gift. My heart tugs to touch these things and not see the face nor hear the voice of my family members. My siblings pitched in their money to buy a set of autumn coloured dishes for our wedding: two plates, two bowls, two mugs and a teapot. I ceremoniously set them on the new shelf.

Now I am finding other wedding gifts, many of which I do not unpack. They are from dearly loved aunts and cousins, however, the fancy dishes are not essential for this time of life: a crystal three-legged serving bowl, a glass salad bowl with six matching individual bowls, our wedding clothes, photo album. Reluctantly I close this box of fine things. I move on looking for practical items we need which quickly find a home on the newly delivered hutch shelves.

I find two pieces of four foot long lumber and rest one end on the hutch shelf that is counter-top height. I hammer a leg to brace up the other end to make my work counter. Below this I build another two shelves, using scraps of 2x8 wood left from the roof and floor. I hammer nails into the logs behind the stove to hang up pots and their lids, the cast iron frying pan, the dish pan, the towels and hot pot holders. The slop-water pail, the chamber pot and the cat's litter box are on the floor behind the stove, too, out of the way and out of sight.

Now larger items will go below the counter-top: mixing bowls, casserole dish, pressure cooker, as well as the box of potatoes and onions. We have a plastic bucket with a snap-on lid for storage of rice, beans, split peas, oatmeal and other dry goods. I do not want any mice to find and spoil our food!

The higher shelves are for dishes, including six pottery mugs sent as a wedding gift. Each delicious for the eyes, holding fragrant tea, they also warm the heart like a hug from my favourite aunt. I ceremoniously set in place the hand-made blue and golden glazed casserole dish and lid which we bought on our honeymoon. Purchased on that day, anticipating this day, we will enjoy baked yumminess from our wood stove for dinner tonight.

Then I unpack one more box marked 'kitchen' and tears burst out to my surprise. Here is the set of silverware my parents gave us last Christmas. One year ago we had hopes and dreams. When I opened this gift last year, I stopped to marvel at the spoons my babies would one day eat from, the knifes that would butter bread I would bake, the forks that would lift tasty vegetables from our garden. Now, here they are, arrived like a message in a bottle, like travellers in time. They are in this place and time and the future has become the present while yesterday's present has become the past.

This is really happening.

Kevin's boots tromp off snow, the squeak of the door opening, the crash of wood landing on the pile. His face shows alarm when he sees my tears. When I meet his eyes I see the whole four years since we met pass by and also glimpse the years ahead. This silverware will be in every story we live together. Every child, every guest, every celebration, every 'here we are at the table' photo will have these simple, otherwise insignificant, common items.

Kevin admires my efforts and I admire his. There is enough wood for the day and enough space cleared and prepared for me to stop and consider the evening meal and closing down for today.

After camping and cooking on the two-burner Coleman stove since we left Ontario, I am eager to try the wood stove oven. I have beans I prepared in the pressure cooker yesterday. In the honeymoon casserole dish I mix the kidney beans with a can of tomatoes, chopped onions, minced garlic, a dab of molasses and a dollop of ketchup. With the lid on, I pop them into the oven and mix up a batch of corn bread. The smells are a wonder in this untamed wilderness and this cube-like space of civilization.

And then a surprise. As Kevin lights the kerosene lamp, he brings out a parcel he picked up from the mail yesterday. It is a Christmas gift from his brother. I scold him for opening it two days early, but what can I do?

A radio! And batteries!

It is a little shocking to hear modern rock music in this hand-hewn cabin. It is a little out of context to hear news of far away places. It is a little invasive to have the DJ rattling on. Even a little disturbing. I go outside for a moment to collect my feelings.

When I return, Kevin has found a station with a quieter tone and Christmas carols. My heart surges with emotion and I ask Kevin to turn it off again. I can't take the delicious "At last, we are here, now" feelings and the bitter "We are so far away from everyone we love" feelings in contrast at the same time.

After supper, I very soon climb up into the loft. I feel like a teenager at summer camp when I peek down over the edge and wave at my husband below. Cozy and content, I stretch out for the first time in the sleeping loft. It is indeed warm up here, since the heat rises from the wood stove directly below. I relax after the many decisions of the day. I hear him rattle the stove, fitting the maximum amount of fuel, sliding the controls to slow the flame.

I peek over the edge when I hear him in the kitchen area. "What are you doing?" I quiz him.

"Last night I noticed rustling and gnawing sounds. So I thought I'd better set the mouse traps where I saw their 'calling cards' this morning. Now that we've moved in, it's time for them to be made unwelcome." He dippers out water to wash his hands, then pours it into the slop-water bucket.

I hear Kevin turning the dial and exploring the possibilities with the radio. He begins to climb the ladder. "Are you still awake?" he whispers. "I think I found treasure!"

We can hear an advertisement for 'Sears Radio Theatre' on the station from Seattle, KIRO.[8] They host radio plays every weekday evening! Drama, westerns, comedy, romance, and murder mystery. It is like we're back in the 1930's with the family pressed around the radio stimulating the imagination each evening with sound effects, audience laughter and creativity. It is exciting to hear familiar voices. Lorne Green hosts the westerns. Andy Griffith hosts comedy night.

But today is Saturday. We have to wait a few nights to find out what it will be like.

Tonight is a talk show, followed by a murder mystery. I realize that Kevin has fallen asleep! I am alone in the night with my heart pounding from the thrill and fear! Next the radio programming offers a preacher and I rinse out the scary criminals with the sounds of familiar hymns, texts and uplifting message.

Three hours have passed. It is time to creep down the ladder and feed the fire.

As I return to snuggle into bed, I can hear a little tapping sound. What is it? Clink-clink-clink. It sounds like a spoon tapping on a dish? I lie on my tummy, slide part way up, out of my sleeping-bag to shine the flashlight down over the edge of the loft onto the kitchen counter. Ugh! A mouse scampers away, off the plate and down under the counter. Yuck!

Soon the trap snaps! My every muscle grips, hating the sound. I thought death was instant! But it's not over! Horrible clattering continues as the death struggle flaps the trap, dragging it this way and that. Slowing...quieter...less...until at last the little beast is dead.

In the morning I will have to search for the nasty rodent. Where did the little creature pull the trap? I will have to move the cardboard boxes of pasta, paper bag of flour, plastic bag of apples, box of potatoes, until I find the trap. I realize that these wrappings will not stop the gnawing pests. In the morning, sure enough, tiny black mousy 'calling cards' can be found littered near the food.

Kevin will take the corpse out to the slop-water pit or out house. I will tie a string from the trap to a nail in the wall so I won't have to play 'Hide and Seek' with such an unpleasant goal. I think we have three traps. 'Eleanor's Trap Line.' Kevin will chuckle while I cringe.

I calm myself, realizing that they were indeed here first. We are the intruders. Mice survive the way they always have. I just have to outsmart them and establish that my home, in this part of the Great Canadian Wilderness, is not also their home. Soon the kitten will be old enough to lead the hunting party.

In the morning I will rewash every pot, bowl, cup and plate. I will store them upside-down on their shelves. I will put the silverware in a metal box with a lid. The 2x2x2 foot cube-like food box from our camping gear is secure. That is where all of the paper and plastic-wrapped food items should be stored.

Sigh. Reality check. They don't talk about this part in books and movies about roughing it in the woods! And yet, there are plenty of picturesque, romantic scenes happening simultaneously.

Today was our first day in our new cabin. Beginning a new chapter. A moment to remember. Mount a flag on the top of a mountain. Cheering crowds. International news. Trophy, announcements, fireworks, trumpet blasts, handshakes, portraits!

So many decisions. So many new habits. So many emotions.

As we sleep, this day, which we have so long worked towards, slides from the present into the past.

Chapter 4
December 24, 1978
Sunday

Stand still and look
until you really see.
—*unknown*

My nose knows, poking out of my sleeping-bag.

The fire is out. Brrrrr!

It is way too early to get up. Besides, there's no alarm clock today and it is ever-so cozy to snuggle up wrapped in the arms of my warm husband and snooze some more.

Today is Christmas Eve!

Some wonderful librarian in my mind swiftly supplies my inner senses with the crisp precise notes of the 'Nutcracker Suite Ballet.'

In the darkness, I let the music fill me with colours, movement, costumes, the shadowed wings of the stage, blinding beams of light. Outside of me is isolation and silence. Inside my mind is crowded with a world of rich textures, choreography, tradition and every note is sharply clear. I follow the conductor, hear the orchestra, anticipate the solos, enjoy the instruments, imagine the printed sheets of music. I drift away from this log cabin in the forest in the mountains. I allow time and space to shift into imagining, remembering, focusing on details, trying to re-enact the entire production.

First: the Overture.

I am aged 10. My ballet class Christmas recital is in Colorado Springs. During the overture three of us portray the toys in the work-shop where Uncle Drosselmeir is putting the finishing touches on us. A dab of paint here, testing the wind-up mechanics there, now he is satisfied with his work. I am a toy soldier, a drummer boy. I am a gift Uncle Drosselmeir is preparing to take to the Christmas Eve party for the children. Dressed in my uniform, a tightly fitting red jacket, brass buttons gleaming, royal blue pants with a long white band down the leg, I hold drum sticks poised to rat-a-tat the marching beat. I stand stiff and straight in front of the thick, red velvet curtain. Bright lights. The orchestra pit is so close beneath us. We invite the audience to enter the world we are creating.

When the applause dies, the curtain opens to the ballroom scene. The wealthy Victorian family and their guests are gathered for a feast, dancing, decorating the Christmas tree. Uncle Drosselmeir has brought a huge bag. He has gifts to present to the children.

Downstairs, I wait with the other soldiers in the dressing room. We sit up straight and tall, careful not to smear the thick, greasy make-up on our white faces, round red cheeks and boldly outlined eyes. We dare not touch our perfectly pulled-back hair. We play Jacks on the floor, pretending not to be nervous or excited, casually waiting for the signal to return to the stage. The Jacks are scattered. The red ball bounces. Honour-bound to remember how many Jacks we picked up last turn, we each add variations and difficulty as we progress without a mistake.

Meanwhile, on the stage, the girls dance with their baby dolls, rocking them gently. The boys interrupt with their swords, chasing the girls in a frenzy. Fritz grabs Klara's Nutcracker, smashing it on the floor.

Comforting Klara, bidding good night to her guests, Mama restores peace to the family, gently tucking her children into bed.

Curious Klara returns to the parlour to find the magic of Christmas Eve beginning. The Christmas Tree grows to gigantic proportions. The mice come out to do battle. The Nutcracker leads the soldiers.

I am in the line of soldiers, standing at attention, holding very still in the darkness of the wings off stage. Then, I hear my cue. I am hurrying in the bright lights onto the battle ground. There is a chaotic struggle for the triumph of good over evil. No one has told me to take off my glasses, but my vanity is stronger than my common sense. Starting and stopping, marching and turning, drumming and saluting, I avoid collision with the regiment of soldiers, the scampering mice and the handsome Nutcracker. Klara throws her shoe at the King of the Mice and saves the day.

Back off stage I can hear the music slow and become regal as the Snow Queen comes to invite Klara and the Prince on a tour of her magical kingdom.

Not until we moved to Ontario was I able to see the rest of the ballet on stage. The Toronto production took my breath away. The snowflakes formed ever-new patterns. In a barrage of colours and contrasts, the pastel tulle of the Flowers, the Chinese dancers' huge round hats, the silky swirling veils of the Turks, the rhythmic Spanish tempo and astonishing leaps of the Russians each displayed their own movements, energy, traditions and surprises.

As fabulous and grand as this world-class presentation was, there was one other amateur experience I remember which makes me smile in the dark.

During a small school Christmas concert, when I was about 12, I danced the part of the Sugar Plum Fairy! The audience stood along the wall of the gymnasium, leaving the entire floor space for me to point, step, reach, pirouette and travel in a slow, precise, elegant circle. My custom-made tutu of pastel green was decorated with clusters of real candies stitched to encircle the waist and form a sash across my shoulder. I had to concentrate and steady my face as I passed close by my friends, teachers, the old folks, my little brothers and the other schoolboys. Blushing and uncomfortable with so many eyes and smiles both encouraging and mocking, I circled the room, ever closer to the centre where a basket of wrapped colourful candies was waiting. When the music changed, fast and spinning, I looped and leapt and tossed the candies for the children to gather. Squealing, their hands clutching their treasures, they turned glowing faces to their parents. And suddenly, the Sugar Plum Fairy was gone!

For a moment time travel is so real. I can enjoy this collage of experiences, recalling this wealth of music, stage sets, traditions, scenes.

Strange for me to realize that at the same time that this music was first composed during this Era of elegance, culture and abundance, the inhospitable part of the world I am in now was uninhabited. Even the aboriginal people who came here in the warm seasons, spent the winter further south. Early explorers, trappers, gold panners and surveyors for the railroad had just begun to penetrate this vast mountain-walled wilderness.

Shuddering at the contrast, I return from my fantasy.

Now I am once again in my bed, in the loft, in my cabin, in the snow, in the mountains, in Canada.

Now it is morning. I feel energized for my first Christmas away from home. I want to add another page in my own life, a story to tell, a new experience, a day to live out and someday tell my children: My first Christmas celebration with my husband.

Barefoot down the ladder, I brave the empty stove and begin a new fire.

I am still very new at this and cold fingers slow my movements. Open the firebox door. Crunch paper. Weave in birch bark. Lay kindling criss-cross. Layer small split pieces. Strike a match. Open all the air vents and the draft up the chimney. Stay close by. Watch and listen for the snapping of the wood. Shall I poke it? Shall I wait? Is it OK to step away? Shall I add more wood? Will it all fall in on itself and smother the hope of a first try success? Blow. Poke. Wait. Blow.

While I wait, I hang up my jeans, long johns and sweater near the stove to warm up.

Checking the fire as it begins to catch and grow strong, I make three mistakes which I will doubtless repeat until I master this skill. Poking the fire with a piece of kindling, I touch the hot metal with my wrist. A red burn mark shows the place. Blowing to encourage the flame to spread, I inhale smoke, coughing. Leaning forward, I tuck my hair back behind my ear, brushing my fingertips across my cheek and forehead leaving a trail of soot across my face.

As the fire grows strong and the hot air lifts the smoke up the chimney, I slide the air vents, scraping metal on metal, to wrap the heat and smoke through tunnel-like chambers around the oven and up the back of the stove. There is smoke coming out of our chimney! From one spark, there is now warmth. In this wilderness place, there is now a spark of civilization.

Now I can move about the room as it starts to get warm. Using the lid-lifter I can take out one of the round stove top lids and put the pot of water directly over the flame. I can poke the wood to arrange the orange, dancing flames to lick the bottom of the pot. I can control the heat to boil the water to make Christmas Eve porridge for the start of our happy day.

3 cups of boiling water. 1 ½ cups of oats. Stir. Wait. Warm the bowls. Call the husband.

I am sitting on my upright log, holding the warm bowl of porridge between my chilly hands. I am watching the butter and brown sugar melt. The smell of the cinnamon warms me, too. The raisins offer sunshine from California.

This is my home. This is my moment. This is my life. I am so happy and eager to unwrap the day like a long anticipated gift. I want to soak in every experience, remember each decision, observe myself think and feel and learn and explore. Although I am entering this 'Old Fashioned' lifestyle, for me everything is new. Although we are doing things that people did 'then,' for us everything is 'now.' Although these routines will become second nature, today everything is significant. Although the repetition will become dull, today everything is sharply focused. Although the long winter months may become boring, today I am keenly interested. Although we share universal morning preparations, today everything is mine.

Inside, I quickly wash up and sweep and dress.

Outside, Kevin prepares to go wood cutting.

When I join him, I ask Kevin about Christmastime in his family.

"Somebody handed me a $20 bill," is his short reply. "There's nothing much to remember. Too many people. Too much drinking."

The subject is closed.

I wish I could hook up a wire from my memory banks to his and give him some of my happy memories. So I chatter on, describing details while we push-pull the bucksaw, carry and stack the wood.

I don't know how much he is listening, but it is entertaining for me to continue my monologue. It distracts me from my muscles, helps pass the time and makes a bridge from 'then' to 'now.' I suppose that all newlyweds spend a part of their first Christmas Present telling each other stories of Christmas Past while they begin to construct traditions for Christmas Future in their own home with their future family.

While we work, I have just enough breath to ramble on.

"My earliest Christmas memory is this. Every year in our family, we were given a book from the Church and allowed to open it on Christmas Eve. When I was three years old and my twin brothers nearly two, I opened a beautifully illustrated book of the Christ Child which quotes the Bible texts from

Matthew and Luke. I remember teaching my brothers the story of Jesus. It was my first experience as a Sunday School teacher. Imagine! I still love to do what I did when I was three!"

The birch log thumps to the ground and Kevin starts the next cut. Slow, straight, drawing the saw repeatedly along the same line, the cut begins. Then I grip my end, and the rhythm returns.

"That was when we lived in Pennsylvania. Daddy took a picture of us, sitting, legs straight out, on the floor, shoulder-to-shoulder under the Christmas tree. I was wearing a green paisley dress my mother made for me. The boys had white shirts and bow-ties. Our little hard leather shoes and fresh haircuts make me appreciate how much Mother did for us to be ready for Christmas Eve church."

Kevin marks each length of wood to fit in the stove. As we move down the log, we adjust the end to lay across a fallen tree, holding it up so the saw can move without digging into the ground. After a few cuts, I bend to stack the pieces. Kevin rolls another birch log into place.

"In Colorado, Daddy took us kids out to search our 50 acre property to find a Christmas tree. Our new house had a two-story living room and we could choose a giant tree. I began to watch Mother's preparations and think, 'I will have children. I will need to know how to do this'...like making the turkey and pies and decorating and reading the Bible and singing Christmas hymns and choosing gifts." I pause to hold the memory carefully. "Once we all had 'Winnie the Pooh' toys poking out of the top of our stockings."

My breath puffs out in the cold. But our muscles warm us while we work. Kevin takes off his green down parka and continues with the wool long johns and work shirt. I open my dark blue parka and loosen my scarf.

"In Florida, we were all so sad. This scrawny, dried up Christmas tree was given to us by the little old ladies at church. It was pretty bare by the time we brought it home on the top of our van! Julie and I shared our big present: a bicycle. The twins had a bicycle to share, too. Carole was three years old. Her curious eagerness was my only happiness that year. Who wants a bicycle for Christmas? We wanted to go sledding and skating! We went swimming on December 27 in the Gulf of Mexico. But we were sad."

Giving our arms a rest, we carry the wood back to the cabin. Walking towards our own home is the happiest feeling on earth. Every armload of wood is a significant addition to our resources.

"We were so happy to move to Canada! Because it was a Church school, there was emphasis on the beauty of the story of Christ's birth. Mother practiced special pieces on our piano at home so she would be ready to play for the church service. The voices of the congregation filled the church with age-old meaningful hymns, while guest musicians added to the celebration with trumpet, clarinet, violin, flute. I was so happy to live in a place where everyone came to honour the Baby who came to be our King."

I wait while Kevin finds, rolls and settles another log onto the fallen tree. It is just the right height for us to work. The snow is not too deep. We can keep finding dead wood, the small ends of the cedar logs he built with, birch trees he cut down while he was borrowing the chain saw.

"All the time, like anyone else in their teens, I was gathering ideas, storing up experiences, learning music, collecting skills, shaping my beliefs about the Christ, looking inwards at my own skills, talents and interests, looking outwards reaching towards my own life choices and career path." And now I have to stop working for a moment. Emotions are strong. My muscles have gone weak.

Kevin has been working steadily. His method, rhythm, sequence and determination carry him through many repetitions. It's a little daunting to admit that we have an entire winter supply of wood to cut by hand with a saw and carry in our arms back to the cabin. Slow and steady is an excellent stride.

But, he has been listening to me. He senses the change in my voice and looks up to ask, "What is it? Are you OK?"

It is more than the spilling of sweet memories. More than a nostalgic tour. More than sharing glimpses in a scrapbook. More than a longing for the past and my idyllic childhood. More than grieving for times gone by.

Kevin already knows the story I am about to tell, but somehow, as I have so quickly spoken my autobiography under the theme of 'Christmas Celebrations,' one turning point stands out with a new jolt of pain.

"I can never be sure, Kevin. Was I crazy? Was I wrong? Did I misunderstand? Or is it really possible that the Lord 'calls' a person to do a specific thing? When I was about thirteen, I went to my Pastor to tell him, 'I want to be a minister.' I thought he would welcome this news and encourage me. It was so obvious that my interest and focus was all about the Lord. My questions and comments, my listening and writing were all so intensely focused on continual deeper understanding. The joy of teaching Sunday School when I was fifteen, the eagerness to participate in every event at church…How could he not see that? But his answer was immediate and clear. 'A woman cannot be a minister.' It was not 'may not' like it was about permission, nor 'is not capable' like I was lacking education or training, nor 'should not' like it was somehow risky, but 'cannot' like it goes against the structure of the universe.

According to the teachings of our Church, only a man can read the Word in public. Only a man can speak the words, give instruction, lead the gestures and rituals of worship."

"Kevin, I felt like I was going to die. I was dizzy and I felt faint. My heart was pounding and I could hardly see. I knew I had been given many gifts by my Maker. I could study and sing. I could teach and lead. I could organize and plan. I wanted to give every one of my gifts back to the Giver. I wanted to give everything I had been given to lead others to the Lord."

It's a good time to go inside for lunch. We walk slowly back, stomp off our boots. I slump onto my stump. Kevin pokes and feeds the fire. There are leftovers from the casserole to re-heat.

"I guess I should not have been so surprised," I continue, frowning, puzzling and slowly forming words. "My Mother was teaching kindergarten at the Church school. She was told that she was not allowed to read the Word aloud to the children! Only a minister!"

"I enrolled to attend the Church College and saw for myself how shut out the women were, not even allowed to enter the door of the theological school! I felt my heart turn to a dry weight. I just had to leave that school after only one term. I just couldn't take the inner on-going conflict."

"What could I do? Over and over again I put myself to the test. 'What do you want to be when you grow up?' I listened to other people tell how they decided on a career path, or selected educational studies, or began training for a trade. I went as far down each path as I could. In the secular world, I could study and achieve almost anything. But it felt like eating sand and pretending it was pie. I felt limp when I thought of those careers. But, within the Church, I felt like I was one of those trees clipped and geometrically pinned to the wall, or those hedges trimmed to an unnatural shape. Sure, I could be a Minister's wife, smiling, standing beside him. I'd have a respected role in the Church community. Maybe play the piano for church. Maybe teach Sunday School. As long as I did not read aloud or try to lead worship. I could get my Education Degree and become a teacher. As long as I never taught religion. Or I could quit this Church and go to another denomination. But that makes me feel like a Traitor!"

Silence.

Kevin added his observations. "When I went to the Church College, we had evening worship in the men's dormitory. Once I was invited to go to the women's dorm to read one evening. OK. That's nice. I asked if we could invite them to come read for us. The answer was a definite 'No.' Only the men are allowed to read the Word aloud. I thought it was kind of strange."

Finishing my meal but not finished my story I kept on, "I asked again, as an adult, thinking perhaps I had not spoken clearly while I was so young," with elbows on the table, head in hands, feeling heavy. "This time the Minister gave me the reason. He said that it was a teaching of the Church that a woman would go insane, although appear outwardly to be normal, if she attempted to preach like a man."

"Kevin! I was stuck between a rock and a hard place! How could I live if I turned away from what the Lord called me to do? How could I stay in a place that forbade me by Divine Authority from reaching, seeking, striving towards what I felt compelled to do? By obedience to them I threw away my potential? How could the Pastor I respected be wrong? How could I stay in the Church that I loved so much if they see me as insane because I want to serve?"

Dizzy with conflicting pressures I nearly shrieked, "How could I trust my own judgment if everyone around me agreed that this Church teaching was true and could not be changed?"

Unaware of the time and need to go back to work I kept following the train of thought.

"In an equally balanced tug-of-war I felt: 'I can't - I have to.' When I enrolled in the university, where my Dad was teaching, I took five courses, looking to see if there was anything that brought me light and excitement like I felt when I was preparing to teach about the Lord."

"I took: philosophy, psychology, world religions, social work and drama. Nope. None of these were the right path. I wandered through the university library looking for what would draw me in, like a thirsty person, seeking a fountain. I realized, 'If I take an academic approach to religion, I will spend my life learning Hebrew, Greek and Latin. I will read scrolls and go to lectures. I will write books and fill my life with words, debates and logic. But I will miss the whole point. How would any of this help an individual find the Lord and live for Him?' It is all so simple when Jesus speaks, 'Seek ye first the Kingdom of God and all these things shall be added unto you.'"[9]

"How could the thing I found most sacred and wanted to dedicate myself to be so impossible to reach? How could the beauty and harmony I sensed when I read the Word, let it nourish me, turned the Scriptures this way and that allowing the facets of colour to shimmer and dance be reduced to an academic study? How could the sweetness of following the Lord's Prompting lead me to a dead-end brick wall? It felt like the universe was set up to contradict itself?"

In a flash of clarity I thumped my fist on the table. Eyes flashing, strong and certain I asked, "Did Jesus say, 'Go ye therefore and teach all nations baptizing them'[10] ...and then in parentheses add, ('but not the women')? No. He didn't."

"I can't. I have to." I let out a long sigh. "Kevin. It was agony."

The daylight will begin to fade in another hour. We should be returning to our task. But my eyes seek my husband's face. I need to finish sharing my heart with him.

"So, then I met you, Kevin. When we spoke of this 'Back-to-the-Land' lifestyle. I wondered. I felt that same jolt of recognition, of being led, of His Guidance. I realized, 'When we live in a remote village, I could teach the children we find there who might not otherwise have any instruction about the Lord.' And when you and I worked together on Tableaux, I felt it again. 'This is the one I will marry.' We can work together every Christmas to bring the story of Christ's birth to others who would otherwise have nothing of the beauty, truth, love and gifts pouring out through the Bible story."

"So, here we are. The pain and agony of leaving all of the family-church-Christmas experiences behind is less than the pain of staying there and not being able to read aloud, speak or lead others to the Lord."

"Somehow this 'I can't - I have to' tension will be lived out and we will find what the Lord has led us here to do."

Pull on boots. Zip up coat. Tuck in scarf. The bright sunshine and brisk air gives me a sense of reassurance. Nature leads to the Lord, too. There seems to be plenty of evidence all around us which Robert Browning captured when he said, 'God's in His heaven. All's right with the world.'

Back to the pattern of work now. The sound of the saw. The smell of the wood. The crunch of the snow. The teamwork and effort and satisfaction of watching the stack of wood grow.

"Here's a cheery thought, Kevin!" I exclaim. "I just remembered the little family of teddies we made together last year. Remember? I asked Mother if you and I could be 'Santa' and prepare the stockings because I would need to know how someday. My Daddy teddy had a brief case and tie, my Mommy teddy wore an apron, you and I wore matching denim vests, James and Andrew held artist's brushes and paints. Julie wore fashionable earrings and Carole held a little bride's maid bouquet. It was my way of saying good-bye to our family. They have them still to keep now that we have gone."

The evening comes so early. The sun lowers behind the ridge at 2:00 and the darkness will be complete before 4:30.

So, dinner decisions must be made, the kerosene lamp filled, kindling prepared and the water supply renewed.

It is Christmas Eve. Tomorrow is Christmas Day. We will be leaving early. We have been invited for the day to Fran and Archie's place. Kevin and I have handmade gifts to bring them, small, but we want to show our appreciation for all they have done for us.

Although I do not want to, it seems practical to open the gifts from our family now. The cabin will be cold in the morning and there will be no reason to prolong our departure.

Kevin doesn't have a strong sense of tradition, but my nerves are stressed to break the 'no-no' and even peek at my gifts before Christmas morning.

Kevin has already opened the portable radio his brother sent. Being a practical older brother, Richard included batteries as we will not be going to town until payday.

Two parcels from Kevin's Mother arrived last week. She ordered from the Sears catalogue and they were delivered by mail. The cube-like one is revealed to be a dark, rich fruitcake, wrapped in red cellophane and temptingly traditional. The second one is a round, flat basket with dried fruit attractively arranged. Golden pears, dark plums, crystallized pineapple, fragrant apple slices. I resist, however, knowing that tomorrow we will feast with Fran and Archie's extended family.

Anticipating the guests we have invited for December 26, 'Boxing Day' in Canada, I know these treats will be a larger benefit if we save them for later.

I put the fruit tray in the lidded bucket and cover the fruit cake with an inverted metal mixing bowl.

Now I will unpack the gift from Mother. I found it while opening my boxes of childhood belongings from home. Last Christmas, when we took the decorations down, she handed me this shoe box saying, "These are all of your Christmas ornaments: the things you made in elementary school, the treasures your aunts and siblings have given you, the favourite ones from our tree. I want you to take them to be ready for your new home next Christmas." Our eyes met. She knew better than I did the significance of the gift. Now I know. This little box holds a lot of love from her hands. She protected these things for decades so she could hand something tangible and familiar to me as I stepped away from her into the unknown.

And here they are: the silver-glittered stocking I made in Grade 5, the doily-angel I made in Grade 2, the antique glass bells from our family tree dating back to when I was a baby. I touch them each as if they had value beyond measure.

There is also an envelope. It is from my Dad. I already know what is inside. He told me he was sending it. The card is a picture of an old-fashioned scene, hoop-skirts, a chandelier, a turkey on a platter and a table loaded with cakes and steaming bowls of food. It looks much like the family festivities re-enacted in the 'Nutcracker Suite.' Inside the card is a cheque for $100. I've never been given money for Christmas. Strangely it feels anticlimactic. I have already decided to buy something practical that I need, as well as something fun, hoping to give myself a sense of security from my Daddy's gift. I ordered snow pants and ice skates from the Sears catalogue, to be paid for and picked up next time we go to town.

Oh! There's one more thing. Also inside the card is an announcement. Daddy has given Kevin a subscription to a magazine for a year. It will be nice to keep getting something in the mail.

That's it. The gift giving is over.

Kevin clicks the radio on and turns the dials. Every channel is overflowing with Christmas music both secular and sacred.

Together with the darkening sky, the flood of memories, the meagre tree-less decorations which seem lifeless laying on the table, the lack of family faces, the contrast between what was and what is...I feel tears prickling my eyelids. I can't stop the pressure and give in.

I turn my face down, climb up the ladder to the loft, slide into my sleeping-bag. I don't want Kevin to see my face. An avalanche of memories is cascading into my mind. I miss the poinsettia, the red dresses, Tableaux, the singing, playing my clarinet, the choir, the band, the children, the wrapping paper, the food and family and snuggly feeling of waiting for Christmas morning. I don't have one scrap of this to look forward to tomorrow. I don't know anyone here who enjoys singing or actually believes that Jesus was real. I don't know what to do and the feelings overflow into tears. The cheerful radio parades a chain of songs. Each brings new memories and longing and images to my mind.

I want churches and candles and trees and decorations. I want lineups and malls and fancy dresses and Christmas jewelry and people smiling at me. I want to plan and prepare and search for gifts to give. I want to count my money and whisper secrets. I want to go into my room and close the door and snip with the scissors and tape. I want to help my Mother in the kitchen. I want to wash the dishes while I am wearing my best dress.

I want to sit in the crowded church and see all of the familiar people in their finery. I want to join them to kneel and stand and sing and watch and listen and have everything just the same as last year while everything is new and different, too.

I want to smell the turkey and pie. I want to taste the sweet potatoes and feel my full tummy. I want to tell the story of Bethlehem to children and watch the old folks smile.

I want to laugh and talk and hear stories and poems. I want to go to rehearsal and try on costumes and get props ready and wait back stage.

Each piece of music makes its own picture and causes more tears.

O come all ye faithful, joyful and triumphant: the bold brass, the thick warm chords, the many voices roundly certain. But I am alone, with no place to go and no one to sing with. Here, there are no 'faithful.' God's Name is spoken as a cuss word. Joy? Only merriment is found at the bottom of a bottle. I want my Daddy, his sincere voice and the security of holding the hymn book between us, his suit and tie, his polished shoes, his knowing these songs by heart, passed to him by generations of the faithful.

Now a choir of children so sweetly sing: *Come they told me pa-rum-pa-pum-pum.* It is the performance of a school choir. I hold my breath, soaking in every sound. I remember a specific day when I was in Grade 5 in Colorado. A team of technicians from the radio station came to our school to record our choir singing this same song. It would be played on Christmas Day. Pressing my focus to the speaker at precisely 9 o'clock on Christmas Morning, 1967, I could hear my own voice announcing *Drummer Boy* and *Do you hear what I hear?*

The urgency and the strain of longing is so painful, I stifle a moan. I want a stereo and speakers and all of the records my family is listening to today: the mighty Mormon Tabernacle

Choir booming out Handel's Messiah, the sweetly clear chimes of a bell choir. I want to attend or perform with ballet and theatre productions, school children learning traditional Christmas songs from around the world. Oh! how very much I want the repetition of my Mother playing the piano, practicing the hymns for church.

I'm all alone while gatherings around the world celebrate midnight Christmas Eve Mass. Santas ring bells on the street corners. Volunteers at soup kitchens and food banks hustle and serve. So many people collectively participate in this festive celebration of the new born King.

A quartet now brings the German *Silent Night*...Now I am yearning for my Oma. I wish I could go to Germany to explore places she once lived. I would walk through the tiny village where this song was written. I want time travel, too, so I could enter the story of the church with the broken organ on Christmas Eve long ago, prompting the musician to compose this simple song for guitar accompaniment.

I want my little sister, Carole. I want to brush her hair and zip up the beautiful Christmas dress that Mother made for her. I want to hold her hand while we walk in the dark snow to church on Christmas Eve. I want to hang up her coat and find our place in the crowded pews. I want to whisper and point and be sure she understands the story of Mary and Joseph, Bethlehem and the Baby Lord.

Like them, I have limitations. Like the Holy Family, I must find something beautiful in my loneliness to give to the King.

O Christmas tree, another German carol. And here I am surrounded for mountainous miles by nothing but evergreen trees, but with not one branch holding decorations and no room to bring flammable greenery into our compact cottage. The risk of a spark is just too high, so even this simple nature-based custom I have to give up.

I want the jewel-like fruit-filled traditional German Stolen, fresh from the oven and drizzled white icing my Mother makes for Christmas morning.

Tears stream down my cheeks. I silently scream. "I want an orange in the toe of my stocking." A chill passes over me as I recall the images in Hans Christian Andersen's story 'The Little Match Girl.' I am not so very far away from her poverty and want.

City sidewalks, busy sidewalks. Nothing could be further from my reality. I close my eyes to enjoy the memory of the bustle and jostling, the hurry and the impatient waiting, the swirl of colourful lights of the city while I isolate myself in my grey-dark lamp-lit, solitary, secluded home. I want to go wandering through the mall with James and Andrew. I want to 'go halfies' with Julie on a special gift for Dad or share with Carole a secret project for Mother.

Upbeat now and peppy, I recognize the intro to a piano piece Mother used to play as an incentive for us kids to step lively while doing our chores: *Santa Clause is coming to town.* Now her fingers tinkling the high keys sound like the brightly painted mechanical wind-up tin toys *curly head dolls that oggle and coo, elephants, boats and kiddie cars, too.* There's a little tug of my heart while I remember my childhood trust in 'The Man in Red.' *He sees you when you're sleeping. He knows when you're awake. He knows if you've been bad or good so be good for goodness sake!* I want to be with Julie, to dance together, to spin. To wait, to wonder with Carole.

The kaleidoscope of my imagination shifts, bringing geometric patterns of royal colours. The droning rhythm of the orchestra surrounds me as a trio of *Three Kings* trudge wearily on *following yonder star.*

I cannot sing along or even hum, my throat is choking as the sopranos and angels radiate *Gloria in excelis deo.* The distance between the heavenly bright message of peace, love and joy and my miserable self-pity is too much to endure.

Shall I ask Kevin to turn the radio off? Change the channel? I control my throat and call down into his lamp-lit circle, "Could you please change the channel? I think I've had enough Christmas music for now."

But, no, every notch on the dial brings another wave of familiar tunes, cheery secular songs and meaningful hymns. There is no escape. It is Christmas Eve and 'happy,' 'home,' 'love,' 'peace,' 'joy,' 'tradition'...is the re-occurring, bombarding message.

"Maybe we can have it off for a while," I say, deliberately steadying my voice.

Click of the button. Silence.

Oh, now a new pain envelopes me. Imagination can close the gap of 3000 miles. The heart can stretch to remember family comforts when the bridge of shared melodies and the wealth of harmonies supply a starting place. But silence? It is heavy and presses the heart, mind and spirit low.

"I think I changed my mind. Please turn it back on."

Scarcely whispering the words, my voiceless lips move as I sing along. Bethlehem seems so close. *Away in a manger, no crib for a bed, the little Lord Jesus lay down His sweet head.* Perhaps I am glimpsing now what I have never seen clearly. For a moment the luxurious red velvet and shining coloured lights, the tall candles and extravagant gifts, the glamorous golden glass balls and fresh smelling tree, the harmonious flutes and harps and French horns, the cathedral halls and village churches are not what I am so painfully longing for. For a moment I am in the reality of the cold, lonely stable. Rejected. Every door shut. Every face turned away. Shouting and carousing flood the streets as the noisy over-crowded Bethlehem villagers struggle under the pressures of Roman rule.

And what of the road-weary Joseph? How can he endure the poverty of the moment? Hospitality denied. Why this smelly barn when he saw the glory of an angel and believes this Baby is of Divine origin? Mary? Exhausted by the miles and the pressures of her enlarged belly is more alone than I am.

For a moment I can see the universal, the primal hunger is: 'Home.'

I have a home. However small, cold and distant from my family. I have a bed, food and my husband is with me. For four Christmases Kevin has been my friend. That has to count for something. We have threads woven to begin a new pattern of our own. Our journey of miles is over but the Journey of our lives together on our own land has just begun. We are in good health, provided for and safe.

The Holy Family had to run for their lives. Behind them an army on horseback thundered fear into the villagers' hearts and homes. We are not threatened by Herod, an illness-mad tyrant who commanded his men to draw swords and bathe the streets with infant blood.

I barely noticed their hardship before amongst the glittery stores and showy wealth, midst the velvet and lace and ribbons and wrappings, alongside the baubles and centrepieces and wreaths and gifts below the sparkling Christmas tree.

With less bombarding distractions, I can see tiny details. Without city sounds, I sense significance.

And so, the earth rotates. The season is upon us. The stars shine. The calendar dictates the actions of the masses. And, in confused ever-shifting emotions, I struggle through my first Christmas Eve away from home, yet in my own home.

I quietly slide to the edge and look down the ladder. What is my husband doing? His head is down on his hands, shoulders rounded, breathing slowly. I have no idea what he is experiencing. How he feels. What he remembers. What he was expecting. Whether he is aware of my sobbing.

I simply do not have the energy reserves, the mental clarity, or enough empathy to extend. I cannot take care of him. I can barely take care of myself.

The First Noel. Yes, this is our first Noel. Sigh. Be brave. You can do it. Let it pass. Try to rest. Breathe. Steady.

Kevin comes part way up the ladder to ask me gently if I want any supper. I feel so foggy and have no sensations to prompt me to eat. I fight back a wave of guilt. It is our first Christmas Eve and my red eyes and pale face are not what I would have anticipated. Why have I not planned a meal, a custom, a resting place, a positive expression for this meaningful day?

Kevin opens a can of mushroom soup and calls me when it is ready.

We speak quietly about how we dreamed of our family in the woods. I want those children now. I don't know how to be without children with me at Christmastime.

I sleep early. Kevin stays up late. The radio is on again, volume low.

Joy to the world! Only last year I played my clarinet for the Christmas Eve church service. It was a descant, soaring above the congregation, dancing with the melody of the trumpet. The last and most satisfying hymn for the service, *Let heaven and nature sing!* And here I am, a mere speck in the midst of unending nature with this man-made technology bringing me an entire orchestra.

I must somehow calm myself, still my heart, seek sleep, bring my mind to a new focus. The past, so rich in tradition is not available to me here and now. The future, also out of reach, filled with hugs and hopes and dreams, my own children and the satisfaction of developing our own customs. What can I do with what I have: here, now, this? What does this Christmas bring me? What do I have to give? How can all of this be a part of Christmas?

Sleep comes. Fragile, but welcome. Kevin blows out the lamp and the creaking ladder brings him sliding into the sleeping-bag beside me. The kitten is warm. The dog paces, settles, is still. The fire snaps. My own breath is deliberately slow and steady.

Time passes and the fire needs to be fed. Ever so slowly I slip out of the sleeping-bag and creep down the ladder. The fire is barely coals. I must have slept awhile. The flashlight seeks birch bark, kindling, split wood. I blow and poke and wait. I move my log stool near the stove. I wrap up in my Mother-made afghan-shawl. I reach for my journal and a pen.

While the coals catch the tinder, my mind is moving in a similar way. A tiny spark of truth lights up my dark, sad heart.

So. Here I am. This is me. Now. In this place. My grandmothers gave some sort of invisible wealth to my Mother and my Father, and they to me. The value of all of this effort, creativity, expression, belief, is central to every day and decision. What is the point of celebrating Christmas again and again? Emmanuel: God with us. This is my core. No amount of glitter will improve or embellish it more than the wonder that it already is. I stand starkly bare and alone adrift in memories yet with no tangible resources. Stripped to the bare essentials, I can see for the first time, that props are unnecessary, the message of the story is real. More real than any amount of pretend fairy-tale magic. The power of the Baby I cannot see is greater than the existence of the vast gulf of isolation ready to swallow me. The responsibility is passed to me now. For 'all generations'[11] this promise was spoken, carried, hidden, treasured and is now made manifest.

Yes, my aching heart is resolved with courage. My trembling voice grows firm. My curled up spine pulls up straight. I will carry the flame. I will bring the Good News. I will share and speak and sing and draw and write and re-deliver the message. I want to be one of the ones who says, 'Come. We have found the Messiah.'[12]

Suddenly, I feel the stance and courage, the against-all-odds strength that is born of suffering and loss. Realizing the small share I have had today in the great sea of human pain, I no longer feel intense longing for the things I do not and cannot have. I realize that I am a thread in this tapestry of Christmas. 'One' participating in an individual way with the 'All' around the world and through the centuries is enough. It is really all there ever is.

My needs are met. There is no threat or danger. I overflow with thanksgiving that my 'want' is so small. My resolve has shifted today from a school girl skipping through the daisies of dreamland to a foundation of strong certainty that the goal I am striving for is worthwhile, achievable and I will be provided for one moment at a time. Just as Mary's vision unfolded in ways she did not have foreknowledge of, just as Joseph's steady reliable one-foot-in-front-of-the-other assurance that now and now and now God was with him, just as the Infant Jesus was protected and information, resources and opportunities came to Him at the time He needed them and He recognized and took action as required. Just as it was for them, my future will be. Unknown to me ahead of time, yet provided for by the Author.

Opening the Journal that Kevin prepared for me before our wedding, I write.

Journal entry: December 24, 1978.

It is midnight on Christmas Eve.

The fire that was going strong at 9:00 is now just a few coals. Now, as I wait for it to catch and warm our little house, my thoughts turn to Christmas and I wish to record some of the things we've talked about, about Christmas.

Of course we miss the influence of the Church - both the traditional services and just the influence of people who know why we really celebrate. Tonight, many years ago, the Lord Jesus Christ, the Saviour of mankind, the Son of God was born to earth. This is an awesome thought. It brings me mentally to my knees. It is like brilliant lights blinding me that take several minutes to become accustomed to.

It seems that everyone around us, in town, on the radio and television, talk from the neighbours, is so caught up in the Santa Claus, party, presents, fancy decorations, booze, food, that few seem to remember what's really being celebrated. The Christmas cards that I see hung in friend's homes show winter scenes, Santa, cute puppies or pictures of a Christmas tree. In some homes, none of the cards at all are of the Baby Jesus, stable, shepherds, angels, star, wise men or any part of the story of His birth!

There are parts of the Christmas Story that have really touched me this year. He was born in a stable, with no special attendants, no perfect environment, not so much as a proper bed for an infant. And yet, things were probably timed perfectly. Mary and Joseph were travellers with no place to call home. But they still had a place prepared by the Lord, a place with privacy, warmth. It was just the place to show in our own life story that even if we just give Jesus a small, humble, dirty corner of our life, He will be born within us. He does not need silver trumpets to announce His coming. No splendid, elaborate parts of our minds to find a way into our lives. He will come in through whatever small opening we leave for Him and dwell there and bless us and grow a little stronger and bear fruit.

Sometimes the most humble place can be the best place even for important things, and, Providence guides during the blackest, most hopeless times right down to the minute.

This is what I've learned and I want to always remember.

Neither Yesterday Nor Tomorrow

Drained by the drama, I realize that I simply cannot get up all night over and over again to keep the fire going. I would rather sleep now and wake up to a cold house later. Deeply, deeply, I am sleeping.

2:00am

Why am I awake? After my mellow moments making the fire, pondering and recording the meaning of life in my journal, I am disgusted to hear again the scurries and rustling of tiny feet.

Maybe I can make this unpleasant reality go away with my imagination? Or reshape it with creativity?

Into my mind pops Beatrix Potter's charming little animal tales. Edwardian homes are inhabited by well-to-do mouse-y residents. With floral wallpaper, beautiful furnishings and lush carpets, her illustrations depict a little mouse-y cleaning maid or cook or nanny. Domestic, clean, well-educated and full of family fun, perhaps I am being too harsh with my trap-line method of destroying the little forest-folk.

After all, it is Christmas Eve. Tradition holds that the animals speak, kneel in worship and proclaim the Good News because they were the first to see the New King in the barn.

Surely there were mice in the barn of Bethlehem? What clever paws, tiny ears and soft smooth fur. What an amazing thing that so small a creature can survive in this inhospitable winter climate, raise young and find a way to thrive. With determination I will have to claim my territory within this place where nature is so beautiful, balanced and worth preserving. But, reality returns. I cannot let them eat my hard-won food, or worse, contaminate it with their disgusting every-where-present droppings.

Suddenly: SNAP.

The trap is sprung. As Kevin snores on, I hear the wrestling battle of life versus death. Eyes wide in the dark, what terrors play out below? Eyes shut tight in the dark, what torturous events are unfolding? Is the mouse caught by the tail or leg? Shall I go down to help the little fellow? Set it free? Why is it taking so long to die? Do all mice flip and writhe with such fierce effort? Less...slower...quiet. Ugh, now it is dead.

Now I have to remember first thing on Christmas Day to say, "Kevin, could you please put on these gloves and remove this beast from our house? Oh, and be sure to wash your hands."

But wait, if I let the fire go out, maybe the water will be frozen. It will take an hour to melt snow. But we are leaving right away to go to town. Ugh, I hope germs die when you rub your hands in snow and give them a shake.

How can I sleep...on Christmas Eve as we greet the Lord of Life...when I have just deliberately killed?

Chapter 5
December 25, 1978
Monday

Until you do
what you believe in,
You don't know
whether you believe it.
    —*Leo Tolstoy*

Well, I'm feeling a little fragile this morning. The emotions
yesterday came so swiftly and so deeply. I feel drained and
cautious, like the day after the flu. My head is tired from interrupted sleep. Am I OK? Will a storm of emotions overtake
me again?

We have been invited to Fran and Archie's place for Christmas Day. Yes, come for breakfast. Yes, stay all day.

So, we do.

We plan to arrive at 8:30. Kevin got up to feed the fire once more after my two turns, so now there are a few embers to bring the blaze back to life. The thermometer outside tells me that the temperature has dropped from a month or so of 'Mild' -5°C to a slightly more 'Bracing' -10°C which Kevin calls, 'A Little Chilly.' We stay in bed until daylight pushes the darkness back and until the fire shares a little warmth.

I pull the clothing I am going to wear into my sleeping-bag. Kevin taught me this trick. "Warm up your clothes with your body heat before you put them on. Get dressed in your sleeping-bag." Down the ladder, I add my parka and boots and move about the cabin to make preparations for the day.

We have made small gifts for our friends. For Fran, I have embroidered cross-stitched patterns on a blue gingham apron. For Archie, I made a puffy, red felt pillow filled with fragrant cedar for his sweater drawer. One rainy day in late November, Kevin made a gift for Jim and Cheryl's children. He cut scraps of our lumber on Jim's table saw. We sanded them smooth so the children would have a set of building blocks. The gifts must be packed up, the dog and cat fed and more kindling has to be cut to be ready to start the fire when we return. And we may as well scoop snow now. It will be pitch dark by the time we get home.

Empty this. Fill that. Put this away. Bring this in. Take that out. The house is tidy.

We have a standing invitation to take a bath whenever we visit Fran and Archie, so I pack up a special Christmas dress to wear after I am shiny- clean. We will return home with the layers of warmth we are wearing now: cotton long johns under wool pants, thick cotton top, then an acrylic turtle neck, then a favourite golden-brown alpaca sweater.

We also bring a bag of laundry: light, dark, sheets and towels. It is Christmas Day. Asking to do laundry is a little embarrassing. But the generosity of this couple is something we have come to rely on. Hopefully we will be able to repay these good people over time when we get settled.

We are quiet as we prepare to leave. I feel like I need to hold onto the banister, like I am a little light headed from standing up too fast, like I am on a boat that might tip, like I am uncertain of my own body's strength and balance.

Kitten stays home. Sam can come.

I glance at the clock as we close the door. It is 8:00. I count the time zones: 9:00, 10:00, 11:00. Right now the church service is starting at home. The white-robed priest enters the chancel while everyone is singing a hymn. The candle-lit service for Christmas Eve was last night. The church was packed and warm. Wide-eyed children were given hand-made gifts. This morning, with mostly adults present, the sermon will be more doctrinal. The Incarnation. The Virgin Birth. The Alpha and the Omega. Emmanuel: God is with us.

But it is all so far away.

Like a blow, this realization makes my heart feel bruised inside. Why did I leave all of the traditions of this Church when it matters to me so much?

But I did. And now I walk this path.

We walk single file down the snowy trail, between young, straight, tall jack pine trees. The tableland where we built our cabin in this narrow part of the valley has soil that was once river bottom, not the fertile silt we were hoping for, but the gravel and rounded stones of an ancient sand bar. A forest fire passed through in 1920's leaving standing dead trees, mostly cedar. These dry, light, abundant logs provided the free building materials for our cabin. The new, young growth is so easy to explore and clear that we have chosen this place as our part of the land.

The knee-deep snow covers summer's grasses, mosses, lichen and blueberry bushes. But the Saskatoon berry, pin cherry, wild rose and other unnamed shrubs cluster here and there, recovering the stark fire-bare slopes. Some provide twigs which the moose, rabbits and beaver like to nibble on through the winter. Like a forest of Christmas trees, the softer Douglas fir adds variety to the forest. Where it is wet the cedar trees have grown back. White birch trees are also part of the mix. Their golden leaves signal autumn on the mountainsides.

We load up the van. With no new snow during the night it is easy enough to back out of the flat parking space and head out.

It is just over two miles from our cabin to the highway as we follow the dirt logging road. Two miles is not so far when you drive and when the snow is not deep. But we do not know what the total snowfall will be nor how the van will fare in the cold. If and when the van is no longer able to make it, we will have to walk out. The road is no longer being maintained since the 'condemned' sign was posted on the wooden bridge spanning the 100 yard wide river. I shudder every time we cross, but Kevin assures me that the 'condemned' warning means that a loaded logging truck is too much weight. Our light van is in no danger of collapsing this structure.

We pass our tableland on the left, a swampy low place on the right. Sharply rising on the left, a very steep hill divides the land like a barrier and as the slope lowers, we enter the cozy nook where Karl and Annika's old trapper's cabin is tucked into the hillside. Their garden is deep, black dirt. The rich swampy soil has been layering fallen plant life there for centuries. The water supply flows in a tiny creek to the river only steps from their door. A sandy beach welcomes summer guests.

Cedar, pine and fir tree branches, drooping with the weight of the snow, crowd close to the road all the rest of the way. The world is black and white and grey. Black trees, white snow, grey sky.

The source of the North Thompson River is a glacier over 100 miles to the north. The glacier-blue water is tainted downstream by out-flowing waters from the aptly named Mud Lake. Generally wide, calm and shallow, this river was used by the Secwmpec First Nations people as a highway between summer and winter homes. For centuries, summertime families canoed upriver, gathering berries and plants, fishing for returning salmon in the late summer, waiting until the autumn hunt for elk, moose and deer. Smoked and dried, these supplies were transported down river. They wintered in villages about 100 miles south of our location at Kamloops, the Anglicized word for "Meeting of the Waters."

To avoid the harsh temperatures and deep snows, the people developed Keekwillies.[13] The design of these half-underground earth-sheltered lodges allowed these cold-climate people to survive. Housing as many as forty people, with a central fire, this round dwelling was ideal for the long, harsh winter. Earth was dug away to form the sunken, circular main room. Space for sleeping was along the outer rim of the circle. A strong log structure above ground with pole beams supported the branch-layered earthen roof. Thickly insulated, lit and warmed by the fire, food stored nearby, this form of communal living made sense in this place where snow covers the higher elevations for seven months of the year.

Our cabin is built to the northern end of this Native territory and at a higher elevation than the traditional wintertime area. The idea of two people living alone, above ground, all winter, was unknown to these people. Whatever our situation, it would not have been experienced in the same way by the more prepared, communal dwelling Native people.

The first European settlers, called 'The Overlanders,' arrived in 1862. Travelling across the prairies by cart, drifting down the river on log rafts, portaging to avoid the places where rapids could tear their rafts apart, the settlers, including the first white woman with her children, arrived in Kamloops just as winter hit. In 1914-15, the railroad bed was laid in the valley. Italian, Scandinavian, British and emigrants from other European cultures found land and set up homesteads. Needing cash, the menfolk worked away from home or cut timber while the women raised the children, garden, goats, pigs, chickens and sheep.

Rough dirt roads along the valley floor were impassable during the months of snow, high water in springtime and muddy spring runoff. The local train brought food and supplies the settlers ordered as well as shipments of coal and grain. The train also took produce to markets such as strawberries and livestock. Fur trappers shipped out their winter-gathered goods. School children received their books. Women sent for the doctor or packed up and went to the city to deliver their babies. Even the Catholic priest rode the reliable train to visit families along the 250 mile valley.

And the forest brought an income, too. Imagine the number of cedar telegraph poles, pine and fir railroad ties, farmer's fence posts and split cedar fence rails that were needed during these decades when Canada was first opening up. Men swinging axes and push-pulling two-man saws cut huge old growth timber. Horse teams skidded logs to float downriver to the steam driven sawmills and railroad loading decks. Trains loaded with logs, shingles, poles and lumber carried the forest away.

The single lane bridge we have to cross was built of logs so that truck-loads of logs could be taken to the sawmill. Since the 1940's, dirt roads have penetrated the mountains' secrets. Huge, heavy trucks gear down the slopes and risk the twisting gravel grades. The first time I saw the bridge I gasped with fear. I could glimpse the rushing water in between the two parallel deck planks which were only wide enough for the truck tires.

This morning, Kevin steers skillfully to find footing. If the slippery, snow covered deck causes the van to swerve we will have to dig and push to remount the narrow passageway. Guardrail logs on both sides are two feet high, protecting us from a plunge into the icy river below.

We have noticed that the ice is different at different temperatures and in different places. Thin at first it looks pale aqua-blue and only covers the places where the river scarcely moves. Later, colder, will it really become frozen all the way across? We have been told that the icy river becomes a highway when the temperature drops to more than 20°C below. Heaving up, cracked and broken, the river will sound with snaps as loud as gun shots if and when the temperature drops to 40° below, a thought that makes me shudder.

Not so long ago, horses pulled sleds up and down the frozen river-highway as people went visiting. Teams would skid logs to stack on the river ice awaiting spring thaw to float them to the sawmill. Trappers were glad to gain access to areas in swamp lands they were not able to travel through at other times of year. A hazard, yet an economy, the river is a primary link to commerce.

Thanks to Kevin's steady driving we cross the bridge with no event, look both ways and then bump over the railroad crossing and climb up the switchback curve to enter the highway.

There's nothing to see as we pass places with names which were once important railway sidings with crews living in bunk houses. Angus Horn, Wolfenden, Messiter, Cottonwood Flats, Wire Cache, McMurphy, Wabron, Irvine are some of the names of empty places that are no longer inhabited by workers, but are still marked on maps. Back in the day before heavy equipment and specialized machinery, manual labour was done by section crews who lived in company housing every eight miles to maintain railroad track. Every 25 miles trains had to stop for coal, water and to up-date their train orders through communication sent by telegraph using Morse Code. Once steam locomotives were replaced by diesel engines, machinery replaced human muscles and track phones relayed information, fewer men were needed at such close intervals.

Now that we are up on the highway, I can see across the river. Shadow-black man-made shapes of log buildings stand out in the snowy fields. Some homesteaders chose sites on the other side of the river which had more level land. They believed that the railroad would pass through their property and pay well for the right of way. However, the swampy low land was a worse obstacle to the roadbed than the effort to blast many rock cuts on the steeper side of the valley. The buildings of many homesteads up and down the valley now stand dilapidated.

As opportunities became evident and were abandoned, as resources were discovered and depleted, as adventurous young men moved in and moved on seeking new horizons, each settlement had a temporary, ever-shifting population. A permanent school, church, post office or store was not always established.

Avola, partly because of on-going homesteaders, partly because of the favourable geography, partly because of the railroad water tower and 15-man section crew, partly because of the abundant timber, somehow managed to remain a permanent town.

Up to speed, we can now see the full view of the valley. Rounded mountains on either side are robed with thick forests reaching north to the permafrost arctic, south to the dry Okanagan, east to the grassland prairies and west to the Pacific Ocean. We are a tiny red and white dot moving on this ribbon of highway, two humans in this endless wilderness, so still on Christmas Day. The swamp is frozen. Beaver lodges shelter families feasting on food stored for this season of ice. Tracks of moose stitch patterns across the frozen, flat swamp, empty of trees. A coyote darts across the highway, looking back at us, the intruders.

The highway climbs slightly, cuts a rock bank, curves up until we can see the town below to the right. Beside the river are man-made threads. The railway (1915), oil pipeline (1952), highway (1969), electric transmission line (1973) pass through this valley. To the right are the restaurant and gas station. Down the hill are the church, log school house, pub, post office and Community Hall.

We turn left onto the old gravel highway and pass the motel and two small homesteads which were once cleared and cultivated, now abandoned and overgrown. We reach 'Brooksong,' the newly resettled homestead that will welcome us for today's Christmas celebration. It looks like a postcard.

There are already five vehicles in the driveway lined up along the right side. Avola must have had a snowfall during the night. Only ten miles away from our place, the weather can be quite different. The air currents bring warm, moist air in from the ocean. The saturated air rises and cools in the narrowing of the valley and precipitation can be very sudden and local. The mountains twist as though wringing the clouds out like a wet dish rag.

Jim is hunched forward, pushing behind the snow blower. Fountains of fluffy white glitter sprays four feet in the air as the hum of the motor breaks the forest's silence. Grant strolls down to our van. Kevin rolls down the window.

"Hey, Kev! Hi, Missus!" he grins.

"What's the plan?" Kevin replies.

"Merry Christmas, Grant!" I greet the first person I've seen on Christmas Day.

"Jim's about done. If you want to leave your keys, I'll park your wheels," he offers.

"Wow! Valet service! I'll recommend this place to my friends," I tease as I move my hand to open the door, eyeing how deep the snow is beside the road.

"No thanks, I'll wait." Kevin doesn't like anyone to use his equipment.

I am anxious to enter this scene and participate in this day with these people, but I wait and watch and remember.

It has been four months since we first entered this quaint picture. It was as though God had read my mind. The three-generation family, the sense of belonging, the way they reach out to welcome newcomers with their hospitality feels like it was custom-made for our benefit. Kevin and I entered their story and they became a part of ours. The slope of the garden and grassy wildflower field, now blanketed in white, forms a broad entrance with the gravel driveway leading to the back porch and kitchen door. The picture window overlooking the garden allows the residents to view incoming guests and have the kettle on by the time they knock on the door.

The dark brown house was built of huge, local, untreated, hand-hewn fire-killed cedar logs. We have been told that the cedar trees which were surrounded by the forest fire have an especially high value as building material. When the sap in the living tree was heated it caused the wood to be better preserved and less susceptible to rot. The Community Hall, log school house and this homestead were all built at about the same time from the fire-killed cedar forest. Our cabin is made of the trees that were still standing from the same fire fifty years later and several miles away.

Behind the house is a barn full of two milking goats and their kids as well as about forty laying hens. A wood-working shop is beside. With six men living there, projects are always on to go.

Under the house is a dirt root cellar. The shelves are heavy laden with jars and boxes of food the garden has produced.

To the far left, down a short path, near a babbling brook that empties into Fran's lily pond, is the small house-trailer. Thrifty and resourceful, Fran and Archie have a cozy home here, stocked with garden foods, heated by wood, water supplied by gravity feed from the mountain stream. Some of the furnishings are homemade. Charming collections and family mementos fill the book shelves.

A smile tugs at my mouth as I look across the broad, snowy garden space and remember how I first got to know Cheryl. Although she is only four years older than I am, her life experience is so different from mine. It is as though I am a child when I follow her as she works her way through the day. I am continually asking questions and learning practical things.

"Do you always feed the animals at this time of day? Why do you milk this goat first? Where will you store the apples? Will you teach me how you bake bread? Who taught you how to make jam? Where did you get all of these canning jars? What is this strange looking kitchen thing-y for?"

And then there are the two questions I asked which we both will laugh about for years to come. One sunny September afternoon, I walked up to 'Brooksong' after work. Kevin would come when his log cabin building day was done. As I approached, I could see Cheryl with her children sitting in the green grass picking dandelions! Pleased to join them, I started to show the children how to braid crowns, put them in their button holes, decorate their shoes and wrap and twist them into bracelets and other flower fairy finery.

Thinking that Cheryl was having a quality, crafty Mom-time with her children, I was surprised and asked why she was plucking only the heads off the flowers and discarding the stems. "Why are you filling up that glass jar with dandelion flowers?" I asked.

"I am making dandelion wine," was her reply. She was thinking, "Isn't it obvious?"

Oh, how differently we see the world. I, with children frolicking in the meadow. She, with friends over for a party.

The second question really showed my ignorance. Cheryl grew up on a farm in Saskatchewan. Her days were filled with chores and gardens, younger children to keep safe, and many relatives to feed. She was used to on-going hard work as a young child. Her mother became ever weaker, fading until, by the time Cheryl was twelve years old, her mother was gone.

My life was music lessons and picnics. I have a very stylized view of lovely storybook farming. I have seen recipe books with glossy pictures of heaped up cookies and shiny jars of pickles.

But I have never actually gotten my hands dirty, or worked up a sweat, or eaten food that I dug up from the earth.

So, while picking mint leaves to dry and admiring the flower bed, I had asked Cheryl last summer, thinking I was asking a totally legitimate question, "How do you tell when the carrots are ripe?"

Instantly, I saw in her eyes a flash of disbelief. Silently she gasped and realized, "Was Eleanor, the fancy vocabulary professor's daughter, so unprepared for the lifestyle she says she wants?"

Instantly, I saw in her eyes that I had stumbled badly, showing my foolishness plainly. Of course! Carrots are roots, not fruit. They don't get 'ripe!' I fumbled and moved away, turning my head so she would not see me blush.

But, somehow, Cheryl had taken me under her wing. Her skills she willingly shared while I learned new things from her each time we were together.

Awakened from my reminiscing, I can see Cheryl's younger brother they call 'Red' shoveling a path to the A-frame wood shed, tossing puffs of snow that send sparkles into the air. His brother, Marshall, swings an axe, splitting cedar into kindling, spruce into quarters and birch into halves. By the time Red clears the path to the wood shed, Marshall will have the wheelbarrow loaded. The wood box on Jim and Cheryl's porch will take about six loads to fill, Fran and Archie's place will take about two additional wheelbarrow loads. Since these boys grew up on the prairies, these morning chores are as second nature to them as pushing up the thermostat is to a city kid.

While we wait, Grant begins to pull the trucks into place. Jim and Cheryl have a family SUV, Red and Marshall each have serviceable older pickup trucks, used for hunting, firewood and exploring up the mountain roads. Grant has a new black 4x4 parked beside Fran and Archie's light blue station wagon. Now Kevin pulls our red and white VW van into place and we join this three-generation family. The children wave to me through the window. I gather my bags.

As I round the corner towards the trailer, expecting to come across a bounding pooch or whining cat, I am startled for a moment to see Darcy, leaning against the porch railing.

"Merry Christmas, Darcy," I call out. He signals "shh" with his finger to his lips, and quietly lets me in on his plan. "Ma sent me out to help the guys with the firewood, but if I stand right in this spot she can't see me and neither can they!"

"Does Santa know?" I prod his conscience just a little and with a grin pass up the porch stairs to the kitchen door. Darcy is an adopted cousin, fourteen years old and a...hmmm, what word to describe him? A bit of a 'challenge' and one to keep your eye on.

It took me awhile to understand who was who in the family portrait.

After World War II, Fran married her pen-pal, a handsome First Nations man in uniform who had returned with the Canadian troops from overseas. They had four children. He died in a car accident when the children were very small. Bravely and with creativity and humorous cheer, she raised them alone in southern BC where her gardening knowledge benefited the budget.

Archie met his wife in England while stationed there in World War II. They had five children, raised on the wide Canadian prairies. His skills as a bee-keeper and Jack-of-all-trades kept the family fed. His wife died from cancer just as the children entered their teens.

Fran and Archie met through writing letters to the editor to the same newspaper. They wed and the combined family lived in the Fraser Valley in southern BC. They recently added Darcy, adopted from a relative's family. What a houseful of teenager energy and pranks. Their family portrait is proudly displayed in a prominent place in the entry way. Recently, Archie's eyesight has been fading. Sadly, he cannot enjoy the spectacular mountain views, yet still functions well with daily routines. Gradually he has come to rely more heavily on Fran for anything out of the ordinary.

Three years ago, now that all of the children in this combined family were able to be out on their own, Fran and Archie moved away from the coast to this tiny village and this picture perfect small farm. Just then, Jim lost his job, Cheryl discovered she was pregnant with their second child and her two brothers and friend, Grant, tagged along finding work 25 miles away in the sawmill.

So, instead of their plans to live in the sturdy log farm house, enjoying quiet days at home alone after Darcy caught the school bus, Fran and Archie moved into the little house-trailer, sacrificing the spacious house to the seven others. With our arrival there will be twelve for Christmas Dinner!

"Good Morning, Fran. Merry Christmas!" Hugs are exchanged. She is setting everything on the table for breakfast. Familiar with her habits, I glance at her arrangement, estimating that I have time to dodge over to Cheryl's place to start the first load of laundry.

"Good Morning, Cheryl. Merry Christmas!"

Breakfast was over long ago.

The children are sitting up on the counter, licking spoons and pinching dough. "I am embarrassed, Cheryl, to interrupt on this special day, but may I start some laundry?" Of course she has to nod, "Yes. And you can move my load around, too."

Any house built before indoor plumbing has to solve a lot of logistics problems when bathrooms and laundry rooms are installed. Jim has been the home handyman for the three years they have lived here, tinkering with the roof and electricity, plumbing and additional sleeping space by insulating the attic. It's a win-win situation, though. They pay no rent and Fran and Archie are getting the renovations done for free. The three extra guys help out. Cheryl feeds the hungry working men. The children have lots of interesting experiences and there is always an available lap for a snuggle.

When I lug my heavy bag into the kitchen there are four ways I could turn: straight ahead to the round, oak dining table and wood heated living room, or through a door downstairs to the root cellar, or to the right into a tiny bathroom, or to the left through the kitchen into the master bedroom which houses the washing machine.

"Excuse me," I greet the kitchen crew as I return from the laundry-bedroom, passing through the kitchen, the dining area and the living room to put Cheryl's wet load into the dryer in the far porch. Wires and plumbing are a bit of a mystery to me, but this is the arrangement and I will have to repeat this dance four more times to get my laundry done. At the moment, all of the menfolk are still out doing chores. But I can see already that I will be blushing when I carry my personal items through a room full of bachelors!

Torn wrapping paper and stray ribbons and the empty space beneath the Christmas tree tell me that the gifts have already been opened. "I'll be back every hour," I call over my shoulder as I make a hasty retreat. "And I'll come and help with the dinner preparations as soon as I can get away," I offer as I return the few steps to Fran and Archie's trailer.

It is a breakfast like many others we have shared at this table. The blue and white china, brown teapot wrapped with the homemade tea cozy, the sugar bowl and cream pitcher are all just where they belong. First we have porridge. Fran makes a special mixture of Red River cereal, oats and granola with raisins cooked in, too. The goat's milk in the cream pitcher has a hay-like taste which I have grown used to. When we have finished, Fran brings a plate of fried eggs which have stayed warm and covered in the oven, a stack of toasted homemade bread which we spread with her wonderful jam. Today the options are: apple butter from their own trees, raspberry and also strawberry-rhubarb from the garden and Saskatoon from the wild bushes which grow abundantly along the road sides.

This is a normal breakfast! "This is exactly how I hope my Christmas table looks someday," I smile as I pass the jam to Archie. "Of course, first we have to clear the land, plant and harvest the garden, learn to make jam and how to bake bread in a wood stove oven, raise a flock of chickens and build a goat barn," I eagerly forecast the future. "But, soon. Oh, I hope it will be soon."

Fran spontaneously chuckles at my enthusiasm and Archie gives a fatherly nod.

"I think I'll go move my laundry load," I excuse myself. "I'll be back right away."

My glasses fog up when I return to Fran's warm kitchen. We women catch up on family news and stories while we wash the dishes. Kevin and Archie swap stories in the living room beside the little Christmas tree. Up on the coffee table, it is wrapped and wrapped in silvery garland. I have never seen so much garland on such a tiny tree. The coloured electric lights barely shine out. The ornaments are hidden. My German traditions result in a very different looking tree: single strands of tinsel delicately hanging from the tip of each twig, the ornaments plainly seen. This garland, I am told, is a more English way to be-deck the tree.

Now we exchange gifts. Archie, who has already given Kevin much advice and loaned him tools through the building process, now goes out to the porch and returns with a grin. Holding out the five-foot long bucksaw he generously gives it to Kevin. Much prized and showing years of use in Archie's hands, sadly, his failing sight will keep him from using it in the future.

"This is the saw I loaned you when you first started to build your cabin. You took care of it. You sharpened it. You returned it. Now I want you to keep it. No one here has a need for nor the skill to use it," Archie explains.

The bond of trust and respect between this older man and this younger one grows even stronger as their eyes meet and the saw, a symbol of our newly adopted 'Do-It-Yourself' lifestyle changes hands and begins a new chapter.

Fran places a flat, hard, rectangular parcel in my hands. I know by the shape and feel what it is and my heart thumps loudly within me as another Christmas memory surfaces.

"Oh, Fran! It's a book! The best Christmas present of all. Every year for my whole life my Grammie has given me a book. Oh, I hardly want to open it! I just want the sensation of it in my hands." But I do. And the pretty red and green paper reveals 'The Trapp Family Singers'. It is Fran's own copy, published in 1949. Written by Maria herself, it includes the family's adventures once they arrive in America. I am eager to read it, wondering how her real life experiences compare to the hugely popular 1965 movie featuring Julie Andrews and Christopher Plummer.

"Oh, Thank-you so much! The year this movie was showing in theatres, every girl invited her friends to see it for her birthday party. Some girls were invited to so many birthday parties that they saw it six or eight times! The line ups went all the way around the block. I have such an interest in this woman's story. Thank-you again and again."

Fran admires the apron I made, ties it on and wears it for the rest of the day. Archie enjoys the sachet. These are such small tokens but given with so much appreciation for their on-going support during our newlywed months.

"I made something for you, too," Fran quietly presses another flat wrapped gift in my hands. In her tidy, careful handwriting, using an ordinary pen, she has written a favourite quotation on a sturdy piece of white fabric and glued it to a wooden dowel. It is intended to be a wall hanging. The words are new to me, but the opportunity to share personal values is especially meaningful to me today.

> Great is the power of might and mind,
> but only love can make us kind
> and all we are and hope to be
> is empty pride and vanity.
> If love is not a part of all,
> the greatest man is very small.
> —Helen Steiner Rice[14]

I read it aloud. "That's nice." I lift my eyes to meet hers. "I like quotations. I collect them in my notebook." I can see Fran's heart through these words. Hers is not a 'religion' with 'doctrine,' texts, translations, debate, scholars. Her practicality and good will is a plain, straightforward, way to live all day every day. Perhaps her teaching me is more significant than anything I can teach her?

"I brought my guitar." I tune up, open my notebook and bring music to these dear friends.

What Child is this who laid to rest on Mary's lap is sleeping?
Whom angels greet with anthems sweet
While shepherd's flocks are keeping?
This, this is Christ the King whom shepherds guard and angels sing.
Hail, hail, the Word made Flesh, the Babe, the Son of Mary.[15]

'Silent Night' and 'Away in a Manger' I can sing with a confident, clear voice now that there are others who share today's reverent sense of wonder. Grateful to have been led to this haven, the confused jumble of emotions I experienced yesterday have faded away. Being with these generous older people who have overcome many difficulties themselves brings a sense of comfort and perspective.

11:00...I count the time zones 12:00, 1:00, 2:00...my family will have opened stockings and gifts, gone to church, and by now they will be finishing Christmas dinner. "May I use the telephone?"

Carefully dialing one number after another on the rotary phone, I wait to speak with the operator to place a collect call. My voice travels through wires across half of the continent. One by one, each family member is called to the kitchen wall phone. I imagine each face, each person holding the telephone, surrounded by Christmas decor, discarded wrappings, yummy dinnertime smells. I didn't know it would be so difficult to think of things to talk about. I didn't know the distance of both miles and months would muffle communication, blur images. My questions interrupt their familiar reality and it is too much effort for them to stretch to comprehend mine. I hold tightly to my 'Christmas Cheer,' cautious not to allow myself to open the door to disturbing feelings.

It is easier to speak with Kevin's family. Light. Predictable. Polite formulas. Less yearning.

Now I slip out to move my laundry again while Kevin has his shower.

I hear Cheryl's voice before I open the door. "Red! Fill up the wood stove. Marshall! Bring me a jar of pickles. Jim! Get these kids out of my hair."

Red pushes past me to the firewood box on the porch. Marshall's head pokes up through the trap door to the root cellar. Jim hoists the squealing kids over his shoulder and heads for the far porch where their snow suits are hanging on hooks.

"I can take them," I offer to Cheryl. Jim has them dressed by the time my laundry loads are changed around. Cheryl is now five months pregnant and could use a few minutes for a nap.

Outdoors, the snow is way too deep for these small children to play in. The banks of snow are too soft to climb. The pathways are clear now, but don't offer much for the imagination. With so many limitations, we head for the barn. Bonnie is five years old and started kindergarten this fall. Jack is three years old and is always seeking attention. Bonnie is shy. Jack is rambunctious. It takes all of my child care skills to bring them both a fun experience.

I ask them about their gifts and what Santa brought. I listen to them tell me about the goats and how they help with the chickens. I prompt them with hints, but they don't seem to know much about what we are celebrating on Christmas Day. "Who's birthday is it today? Was His mother's name Mary? Did Joseph take care of the new Baby? Who told the visitors where to find the Baby? Was the Baby born in a barn, like this one? Did other visitors ride camels and bring gifts?"

With blank faces, I realize that this family has such a fast-paced lifestyle that somehow the story of the Christ Child has not been told, at least not in a way that they can remember.

So, content and cozy in the barn, I fluff up a mound of clean straw and nestle in, wrap my arms around them and begin to retell the age-old story including direct quotes from the Bible that I know by heart, quiet hymns at just the right place in the story, plenty of description of shepherds and angels and travelling kings. I use drama in my voice to emphasize the wonder and hope, the danger and decisions, the mystery and the beauty of it all.

Rosy cheeks and eyes wide, we return to the house where I promise to bring over the Christmas book I have had since I was Jack's age. "It has beautiful pictures," I coax them.

"It must be *very* old!" little Bonnie says with emphasis.

Stomping off the snow, we step back into the bustling kitchen.

"Did you get a nap?" I ask. Cheryl answers with a withering look. Hardly possible with the clock zooming and such a big dinner to prepare for a midday meal.

I return the soggy mittens, boots, coats and snow pants to their hooks and release the children. They run to pester their uncles who, beer in hand, lift, toss and dangle them up-side down and otherwise tease and pester them. Screeching and scolding, playful and annoyed, voices drown out the sounds of simmering pots and crackling fire. The TV blares and "Hush Up!" is repeated by every uncle to the scampering tots.

Rotating the laundry again, I realize that I have not added my two hands to the many kitchen tasks.

Cheryl has a huge pot of potatoes coming to a boil. The turkey smells great. There are golden pies already out of the oven. With both a propane and a wood stove to cook on, she has two ovens and plenty of burners. Pots of vegetables are just heating through: peas and carrots, squash, greens, beets. The quart jar of pickles is poured into a cut crystal pickle dish. The butter dish is refilled.

I see the need for the table to be set and the preparation dishes to be washed, so I roll up my sleeves and jump right in. Many times since our arrival in August, I have participated in this kitchen. I stay in one place while Cheryl flits, always moving, to stir and chop, season and taste, heat and pour, mash and blend. Twelve people will eat what she has made today. Her activities are well choreographed.

Look at the time! I have not bathed yet! I excuse myself and hurry back to Fran's.

The steamy warmth is so very pleasant. The citrus smell of the shampoo reminds me of home. The soapy scrub feels like the epitome of security. I wish I could stay and stay. But the clock is ticking and there are more parts of this day to enjoy. Squeaky clean, rosy and warm I emerge from the bathroom, wearing the red wool dress I made for our betrothal so far away in space and time, yet those pledges so central to this day and purpose.

Kevin carries Fran's sweet potato casserole dish and Archie carries a basket of hot biscuits. Fran has a bag of gifts for the children. And I bring up the rear with my guitar and a centrepiece for the table. I have a very small present for Cheryl's household: paper napkins decorated with poinsettia. She admires them, sets them in the middle of the crowded table. I notice that I am the only one who reaches to use one and place it on my lap.

Leaves have been added to the table making it a long oval. Cheryl's brothers have been fetching and carrying to bring enough chairs and benches and place the heavy serving dishes and platter of turkey in the middle where everyone can reach.

"Dinner's ready!"

And the twelve are seated. I wait for the silent pause, the bowing of heads and the calm thanksgiving before we begin. But people are already reaching across the table, hoisting loaded spoons, stabbing forks into meat, knives scooping up butter to bring back to the still warm biscuits, passing the dripping gravy boat.

My eyes must have signalled alarm because Cheryl's ringing authoritative voice cuts through the commotion. "Eleanor, would you like to say Grace?"

All eyes turn to me. Some curious. Some annoyed. Hands are frozen in space and then return to a posture of prayer. Eleven pairs of eyes dart around for a clue as to how to behave. The children are taken by surprise.

"Shall we hold hands?" I suggest.

Heads bowed now, my heart is pounding while eleven pairs of ears wonder what I will say.

"Dear Lord, we thank You for this feast and the hands that prepared it. We thank you for this abundant earth which grew so much of what we share today. We thank You for each family member here and those we love who are far away. But, most of all, we thank You for coming, for stepping from eternity and infinity into time and space, to live with us, teach us, help us and love us. Help us to hear You calling us to learn to love and follow You, making Christmas Day every day. Amen."

"Amen," eleven voices respond. And the feast is shared.

While many hands clear and wash, I draw the children near again and bring out the treasure I have to share. The children enjoy their new building blocks and Kevin spends some time with them stacking up a high tower. We sit together and I open the book of the Christ Child which I have re-read annually since I was three years old. I turn the pages, pausing to admire Mary's calm beauty, Joseph's reverent loyalty, wonder at the angels' message, whisper so as not to startle the sleeping Baby Lord, admire the shepherd's little lambs, announce the arrival of the wise men and sing the lullabies I taught them earlier today.

No time or place or pause for more guitar music and singing together in this house. The TV reigns.

Soon it will be dark. Reluctantly, we have to pack up and make an exit.

We return to Fran and Archie's place, reminding them of the invitation to come and see our new home tomorrow, weather permitting. They would love to see how things have turned out for us. It is hard to say "Good night," but I cheer up because I can also say my favourite words, so rare now that we live farther away. "See you tomorrow!"

Laundry folded, pretty dress off, practical layers on, gifts gathered, and away we go, into the softly darkening night.

Kevin is quiet. I feel distant. It was fun and noisy and full of people. My tummy is full. I saw the colourful tree and ate fancy cookies, but somehow it does not seem like a real Christmas.

What *is* a 'real' Christmas?

What was missing?

What does it all mean?

What do I believe?

What do I want for our family?

How is one family different from another?

How are they similar?

What customs will I keep and discard and create until I have fashioned a design for our children to best express what Christmas means in our family?

And what will they do when it is their turn to pass on traditions to the next generation?

When we arrive back at our little grey cabin, empty of decorations, silent and cold, I am not much help with necessary evening chores. The guitar and folded laundry are hoisted up the ladder. I worry that the cold might damage the guitar so I loosen the strings. I sort the laundry into 'his' and 'hers.' Meanwhile, my flashlight pierces the dark of the loft as I struggle, kneeling on the spongy mattress under low roof rafters of the eves to put away our clean clothes in their orderly cardboard boxes. I change out of my warm layers and replace them with pre-chilled PJ's.

Kevin lights the lamp. The golden light below reflects a little off the boards which are both the roof and ceiling above me.

He lights the fire, feeds the animals and goes back to the van to carry in more laundry and our new gifts.

Back down the ladder, I try to take an interest in my new book. No need to talk. We are both tired, in between 'then' and 'now' and submerged in our own thoughts and feelings. Each of us quietly reorienting the dreams of long-ago Christmas with the reality of here and now.

But the cold is so not fun, so I decide to leave my husband with the radio and go to bed early. Kevin suggests heating up some of the leftovers our hosts have so kindly sent home with us, but I have had enough to eat for one day.

Well maybe, since it is still Christmas Day, I will allow myself a slice of the richly flavoured fruit cake that Kevin's Mom sent to us. I need the love as much, probably more than I crave the deliciousness.

But, what is this? Under the large up-side down metal mixing bowl, where last night I had so carefully stored the treasure, I see torn red cellophane, crumbs and scraps of cake, cherries and pineapple and currants set aside and a large amount of the cake...missing!

Kevin turns just as I call out in a half scream, half question, half angry, half disgusted tone, *"What has eaten our fruit cake?"*

Anxious that I not repeat all of the emotional storm that I experienced last night, Kevin moves quickly beside me. "Do you see it?" I am almost howling. "What could have done this? Lifted the bowl? Eaten the cake? Left the yummy cherries? Spit out the pineapple? Contaminated the whole thing?"

I almost reach out to pop a ruby cherry into my mouth, then jerk back, disgusted by the intruder who dared to rob us of our delicious Christmas fruitcake which I had intended to share with our friends. Tonight I hope a zillion mice die and their nasty little heads are smashed by the trap's mortal blow. I can't believe I am watching my own hands drop the jeweled banquet into the fire.

Unlike any other Christmas, I find my way to bed, whirling thoughts and feelings gradually become still.

Sometime later, after waking, climbing, poking, feeding the fire and snuggling back into the warmth of my multi-layered bed, I hear the scratching explorations of tonight's curious invader. I hold breathlessly still, willing it to find the bait. SNAP! A-ha! Triumphant! But then the deadly dance begins. Flappity-flap. Clickety-clack. Rustle and crash. Silence. Then again. It keeps on going. Loud and strong. Breaks of silence do not indicate the end, rather rest to struggle on and on.

"Kevin, wake up. Something is happening!"

I roll over on my tummy, reach for my glasses, click on the flashlight and aim down towards the noise.

"Ooh!" an involuntary scream pierces the scene as my eyes struggle to comprehend what I am looking at down below. "Kevin! It's BIG!"

Now I have his attention. "What?" Imagining a raccoon or bob cat, a pack-rat or weasel, he lunges over me towards the ladder.

I see large, bulging, round, white eyes. Some nocturnal prowler I cannot recognize.

"Kevin! Be careful!"

But the wild 'something' is trapped and the trap is tied to the nail in the wall. So, whatever it is, it cannot escape, no matter how it tries to twist, wrestle, fight, bite or scratch my husband.

Kevin slips his feet into his boots, hurriedly puts on his leather gloves and takes a closer look.

In the beam of the flashlight I hold above his head, he lifts the moving fur enough for us to see. It is a flying squirrel! Kevin opens the folds of skin along both sides and, since the trap snapped on its paw and did not harm it badly, he opens the door and releases it to glide into the night.

After so much pent up excitement I burst out with a cheer! "Wowie-Zowie! You are a Hero! You saved the fair maiden from the fearsome foe! Hurrah and Hurray! Look at that handsome man! He's my husband! Let the bells ring out! Let the people rejoice!"

Kevin puts more wood on the fire, climbs back to bed, settles in, mumbles something about "enough adventures for one night."

And I chuckle quietly in the pitch dark.

Christmas Day, 1978. This one I think I'll always remember!

Chapter 6
December 26, 1978
Tuesday

Do what you can
with what you have
where you are.
  —Theodore Roosevelt

When we got home last night we discovered something mysterious. Some forest dwelling creature had eaten the fruitcake that Kevin's mother had sent. I was saving it to offer to our guests today and now it is ruined!

It was under a large upside-down metal bowl to keep the mice away. But what kind of creature could have moved the bowl, lifted it up, crawled inside and back out. Worst of all, the 'cake' part of the cake was eaten but the 'fruit' part of the cake was not. Bright red cherries, tropical pineapple, yummy dates, friendly raisins and golden candied peel was licked clean, spit out and left behind. Besides the shock of being robbed, my eyes felt the sting of tears with the realization that the creature had spit out the very best part! Now, although over half of the dark, rich, moist, sweet smelling Christmas cake was left, 'whatever-it-was' had contaminated it all.

With a moaning sigh I felt it was just too much to sacrifice on my first Christmas away from home. No family... No Church... No music... No decorations... No tree... No shopping... No anything familiar... and now: the only treat that I had to look forward to, a treat I could pretend was a magic carpet to connect me to my own family, an expected enjoyment and comfort is now ruined... Denied... Gone.

Frustration, confusion, disappointment and disgust at the thieving rodent snitching my most prized possession was not a very pleasant way to go to bed. After a brief outburst and 'rant' I changed tactics and tried to look for something positive to engage my mind and heart.

"Well, the fruit tray is safe." I had put it away in a large plastic pail with a tight lid. The basket loaded with attractively arranged dried fruit, was intact. Only a creature with an opposable thumb could unsnap the lid. No raccoons. No monkeys. The pears, candied pineapple, figs, apple rings and prunes were undiscovered, unopened and undamaged.

Christmas Day had been such a whirlwind of activity. In the kitchen, Cheryl's hands raced to feed so many people. Running through the house making the sounds of constant interruptions and excitement were two small children on Christmas Day clamouring for attention. In the living room nonstop loud rock music and/or blaring sportscasters on TV bombarded the ears while three bachelors with beer draped themselves over the chesterfield. Sounds. Smells. Flashing coloured lights. All without rest. Then there was the un-holy-day hustle and bustle of chores, including me carrying my laundry through four rooms of the noisy house from the washer to the dryer out on the porch.

Thankfully, I could retreat next door to Fran and Archie's house-trailer. There was a sanctuary of peace on earth.

The day after Christmas, December 26th, is an additional national holiday in British based Canada called 'Boxing Day.' Tradition held that after the servants cleared away the empty wrappings, they had the next day off. An 'at home day' allowed both the employer and employee families time to relax and enjoy their treats. As we left their cozy home, I had turned back to invite our Christmas Day host and hostess, Fran and Archie, "Would you come to share our new home on Boxing Day?" I just wanted so much to provide the two of them with a contrasting example of how to entertain guests, provide a welcoming, calm, atmosphere, abundant generosity, uplifting topics of conversation, perhaps quiet background music, a festive tradition of reverence for the Christ and inner joy radiating from the hostess's heart which finds expression in refined manners and domestic customs.

Now I realize with a jolt: This single plate of dried fruit and Fran's own mint tea would be all I had to offer my guests. Look again. Kevin, Eleanor, Fran, Archie. That's four people. Now I count the fruit. 2-4-6-8...there are 16 pieces of fruit here. That's four each. Well, that's all there is.

Fran and Archie will understand. They know we are just starting. It will make them proud of us that we have stayed on task and achieved so much in such a short time. They will gladly watch as we develop and expand in the coming year. Their guidance has meant so much. I am just so pleased that they are willing to drive all this way to come on Boxing Day.

So, off to bed I go, planning the sequence of preparations I will have to work through before our guests arrive in the morning. Shall I attempt to bake something on the wood stove for the first time? Hmm...Seems a bit risky to feed guests an experiment.

Kevin and I have decided to be a little more systematic about keeping the fire going all night. So far the overnight cold has only been a few degrees below freezing. If I wake up in the night and catch the fire in time to feed it or if it goes out by morning, it is not a big deal. I have deliberately made use of what the Old Timers call the 'Indian Alarm Clock' method. By taking big drinks of water, 'Nature's Call' prompts me to wake up every 2-3 hours to pee. There are barely any embers left, but it is enough to catch and re-fuel.

But, tonight Kevin heard the weather report on the radio. It is a little hard to get an accurate forecast. Since our population is so small and the valley so long, there is no specific radio announcement for our area. Since the major weather pattern from the Arctic tends to slide down the prairie flat lands and seldom pushes up and over the mountains, we may or may not experience the incoming frigid blast. Since the warm, wet weather systems from the Pacific can remain locked in the shelter of the valleys, we may or may not continue with this mild, overcast, dreary-day-after-day sky. But we are content because it is so easy to keep the house warm. We cannot be sure if announcements for the larger cities in the southwest coast or the northeast prairie will provide us with the most useful information. Or, there is a third possibility. Perhaps the incoming cold front will meet the incoming moist air right overtop of us and dump a major snowfall.

The temperature may drop. We agree to take turns to keep the fire going all night. Kevin heard the forecast of -15°C for a city to the south. We are moving from 'A Wee Bit Nippy' to one of his Dad's sayings: 'There'll be Frost on the Pumpkins!' To be sure of a deep bed of coals which will certainly catch, we agree that we should take turns getting up every one-and-a-half hours.

Kevin sets the alarm clock.

If I go to bed early and he stays up to feed the fire, then I will get three hours of sleep before my first trip down the ladder.

Like leap-frog, if we alternate, a three hour sleep plus a three hour sleep plus another three hour sleep…it will be morning. It doesn't sound too hard. Right?

But, Kevin comes to bed right away. He wants to listen to the radio theatre again. I will not get any sleep before I am jerked alert by the clanging metallic ring.

Another factor I had not considered. How will I ever fall asleep while this annoyingly loud ticking measures off the precious minutes?

How can I muffle the ticking and still hear the alarm?

Under my pillow? No. It's still drummingly too loud. Under the blankets? In my sleeping-bag? No. I might bump the clock and set it off, or knock the pin and disengage the alarm.

Under the foam mattress? Yes. Now I can't hear it ticking, but I will hear the muffled alarm and I can easily reach it when the bell rings. I hope I remember how to slide the tiny peg to stop the incessant signal while I am groggy and confused.

Drifting away into sleep, I imagine my comfortable guests admiring our cabin. I make a mental note to open box number seven, to bring out the white, brand-new guest book we were given for our wedding. History will be made! Our first guests in our first house!

Suddenly. Awake. I force my warm body to exit the layers of coverings. Down the ladder. Feet into boots. Parka on. Black room bright with flashlight's beam. Open the vents. Rake orange coals together. Lay kindling. Wait. Blow. Poke. Wait. Will it light? Yes. Add fuel. Close vents. Hang up parka. Boots off. Back up the ladder. Reset clock. Push it in under Kevin's side of the mattress. Slide into the sleeping-bag.

My nest has grown cold while I was away. Back-to-back. Curl and Shiver. Hands into armpits. Pull blanket over my head. Exhale warm breath into the cocoon I am in.

Why am I so cold? What can I do to feel more comfortable? While we stayed in Howard and Opal's little camper with the big wood stove I slept in a summer T-shirt. The first night here I slept in my warm, fuzzy, thick, new flannel PJ's. Now I have long johns on, top and bottom, the same PJs and socks, too, but I can't seem to find a way to feel warm.

Sleep comes. Kevin goes. I wake for the alarm. Wake again when he leaves. Wake again when he rattles the cast iron lids and grinds the grate, thumps the wood, slides the vents. I call down the ladder to him. "Could you bring up my hat? May I use a pair of your wool socks? These nylon socks don't seem to be helping any."

He opens his side of the sleeping-bag and the whoosh of cold air hits me. I clamp my jaw so as not to scold or complain. No words can change this situation. It is what it is. Short sleep. Jangling alarm.

My turn again. While I wait for confirmation that the fire will catch the new, large wood, I count on the calendar. This is our 5th night here. There are 5 more nights in December, plus 31 January nights, plus 28 nights for February, 31 nights in March...That makes exactly 100 nights until April 1st. How many one-and-a-half hour apart trips to feed the fire every night for 100 nights with a load of four pieces of wood each time? It is an unthinkable amount of wood...and we have so little to begin with.

Let me think about this again. 7:00-8:30pm... 8:30-10:00... 10:00-11:30... 11:30-1:00am... 1:00-2:30... 2:30-4:00... 4:00-5:30... 5:30-7:00... when it begins to get light again. Wow! This is going to be hard. I wonder how the human brain reacts to that much interrupted sleep. Well, I guess we are about to find out. I am an experiment.

It was a long night, up and down the ladder to keep the fire, interrupted by the encounter with the flying squirrel. With all of that effort, it never seemed to get warm, though. When I open the door in the morning to check the red line of the thermometer, I begin to understand. As predicted, the temperature changed from −5°C to −15°C. This is a significant drop. It explains why we felt so chilly in our beds during the night. Now, with daylight slowly brightening our cabin, it will take quite an effort to make the fire roar. I leave the air vents open so the fire will blaze, not shut down to smoulder. We will have to actively chase the cold back outside.

But that means the woodpile will be used up faster.

I return to my bed to wait for warmth to spread. Through the fog of my sleep deprived brain a thought more stimulating than the alarm clock's announcement: "We are having guests today!"

Not to tour our building project as they did in October.

Actual Guests! To be welcomed into our actual home!

It is only the fifth morning in our new home. And yesterday we left for Avola as soon as we woke up. Our morning activities are not yet a smooth routine.

"I'll do the fire. You get dressed in your sleeping-bag," Kevin suggests.

I pull my clothing in to warm it up against my body before I strip off sleeping layers to add daytime layers. "Good plan," I answer. "Whoa! It feels like I stored my clothes in the refrigerator."

The dish water in the slop-water bucket on the floor has a three-inch layer of ice. But the jug of water for drinking and cooking that we had on the kitchen counter has only a thin layer of ice. Interesting. Warm air does rise. Whatever is above the height of the firebox is not as cold. But everything below the height of the firebox is below freezing. I'll have to be sure our guests leave their boots on when they come inside.

"Could you please bring in another two stumps for Fran and Archie to sit on?" I ask Kevin while I go in and out to collect snow in the water jacket for washing and in every pot I have to make tea.

"Be sure to pack down the snow," Kevin coaches me. "It will shrink down so much when it melts." Every pot I own is packed tightly with snow. I can see that the repeated trips to refill the pots will be an on-going task every day. I realize that every time I open and close the door it will spill warmth out and stir cold in.

Oatmeal is ready and we look at the clock. While I wash the dishes and sweep, Kevin brings more wood inside and we straighten up the partially unpacked boxes. I use straight pins from my sewing kit to hang up our three Christmas cards and the wall hanging that Fran made for me by tacking them onto the log walls.

I wipe off the table and spread out a red and white checkered cloth I brought from home. The lamp is so boldly brass. I am inspired to make an arrangement with the Christmas ornaments from the box Mother sent. Opening the box of wedding presents, I find the clear, glass salad bowl from my aunt in Vermont. I fill it with colourful glass spheres and tuck in little twigs of evergreen. I tie other ornaments on threads to hang in the window like sun-catchers: a silver glass bell, a white china angel, a gold glittery star. In a place of honour is my precious 'Christ Child' picture book. I look forward to sharing my treasures with these friends. They have shared so much with us.

What else can I do to ensure their comfort? I place a folded towel on their two stumps improvising a cushion to provide a little softness, a little warmth.

Four cups, four plates, four spoons, a jar of honey, the plate of dried fruit, pretty napkins and as soon as the kettle boils, I'll be ready!

Just in time, too. I hear the dog bark. Kevin whistles as a signal to me. I can hear voices along the path.

I peer out of the window, expecting to see Fran in the lead, Archie's hand on her shoulder as she guides him slowly through this unfamiliar territory. In an all white snowy world, there is nothing for his failing sight to be able to distinguish the path.

But, wait. That's not Fran. That's Red! Tall and lanky, no hat, curly hair, I recognize his long-legged stride up the path between the trees.

Who else? More men! Dark coats. Tall boots. Loud voices. What is happening?

My heart beat changes its rhythm. How many people are here? They keep coming!

I recognize Cheryl's coat. She is holding Bonnie's hand and Jim is carrying Jack. Now I see Fran and Archie. Kevin follows them all, already telling a story of our beginnings. Sam bounds along in the snow barking his announcement and declaring his authority over everyone entering.

I had everything set out for Fran and Archie and here, unexpectedly came everyone, Jim and Cheryl, the two children, Red and Marshall and Grant. Plus Kevin and I...that's eleven people! Four clean cups! One pot of hot water! Sixteen pieces of fruit! What am I going to do? There are only four stumps to sit on!

Gathering my feelings and pressing my brain to solve this impossible math problem, panicking to supply some sort of refreshment for this many people, I govern the muscles which produce a smile and open the door to greet the crowd.

"Good Morning! Welcome!"

"Look what I found," Kevin hollers from the back of the procession.

"Welcome! Welcome! Come in! Come in!"

Jostling at the doorway, the custom here is to remove one's boots. "No, no. Don't take off your boots. The floor is a little chilly," I explain.

Tromping boots, bumping coats, the space fills up, the noise is insulting to the forest. There are so many eyes, questions unanswered, raised eyebrows, shrugged shoulders. Whatever they were expecting, this isn't it.

How long must the door remain open to accommodate the entrance of eleven people? How much precious heat is wasted out of the open door? Eleven people stand shoulder to shoulder in the very small space we are so proud to call 'Home.'

"Come on, guys," Red seems to be the leader. "Let's get the wood unloaded."

And suddenly Red, Marshall, Grant, Jim and Kevin vanish.

Now Fran and Archie can sit on their new stumps. Cheryl, with one child on her lap, can sit on my stump and the other child can sit on Kevin's rather tall stump. With some measure of order I can now pour tea, offer refreshments and tell my charming stories of how we built. "Come see the loft. Here is the kitten Kevin brought me. Isn't the lamp wonderful? Thank you for the windows. Doesn't it all work out so well?"

Cheryl thought to bring goodies from her Christmas baking. I gratefully accept and pass them around. But Jack tips his cup. Cheryl's sudden scolding sounds so foreign in our quiet cottage.

The children are curious and want to move around, but there is no room, no toys. It is so chilly, they have to stay near their Mother. The kitten scampers back up the ladder and the children whine and wriggle, bringing more scoldings and shushings.

Clearly her children are not comfortable. Cheryl takes charge. "If you open the oven door and the warming oven door the place will warm up faster." She moves her stump closer to the open oven door, lifts Jack to one knee and perches Bonnie on the other.

I have always lived in houses with central heat and an electric stove. I would never have dreamed of leaving the oven turned on with the door open!

Meanwhile, Fran and I are trying to have a ladylike conversation. Archie is a little left out, can't see the features of the cabin, not part of the ladies' conversation, can't help with the children's troubles, can't keep up to the menfolk outside, can't chew the dried fruit.

And why are all of the menfolk outside?

Crash! And again: Crash!

Red has delivered his pickup truck full of firewood!

The sawmill where they work, 25 miles to the south in Vavenby, allows people to come and take lumber scraps home for firewood for free. 'Mill ends' are cut off of 2x4, 2x6, 2x8 and 2x10 inch lumber that is too long for the standard bundles.

Because our driveway is really just a parking space beside the road and does not come all the way up to the cabin, the menfolk are walking back and forth, carrying armfuls of wood. Crash! They drop the wood, forming a pile near where we will stack it up against the wall of the cabin.

The walk is not long. The work is not difficult. The gift is appreciated. But still: it is Boxing Day. A day when no one wants to work. After their usual daily wood-chopping chores at home, these guys started the day after Christmas by filling the truck with wood from Jim and Cheryl's wood shed. Wood they had already cut, loaded, delivered, unloaded, split and stacked there, and now, either their sister, Cheryl, or step-mother, Fran, had instructed them to re-load, re-deliver and now hike with this 'free' wood, to give it away to people they didn't really have a connection to…and their collective tempers were a little short.

Grant, always good-natured, a tag-along ready for whatever comes, tosses me a grin and a nod while I ask if anyone would like tea? Marshall, the straightforward one, just has the one-step-at-a-time look on his face. He'll do what he's asked and rest when it's done. Jim, Cheryl's bearded husband, works on the railroad. He is used to being outside in all weather. He is always quiet and it is hard to tell what he is thinking, enjoying or unhappy about. But one thing I know. Today is a holiday. No trains are running. Everyone is supposed to be home, warm and toasty with family, relaxing, enjoying their gifts, goodies and games. Not hauling firewood.

I am trying to play the part of the confident hostess while madly calculating a difficult math problem: I only own six wedding gift mugs and the two matching autumn cups from my brothers and sisters! That's eight. There are eleven people. Kevin and I will not have anything to drink, that makes nine people to serve. I will have to ask Cheryl to share a cup with her children!

As soon as I realized the number of guests, I have been continuously melting more snow, poking the fire over and over again to coax leaping flames to hurry the heat and bring the pot to a boil so I can refill and refill my teapot. But, for some reason I do not comprehend, there are no orange flickerings, only black murmurings grumbling in the firebox.

It all seems to be taking so long. It all seems to be going by so fast.

I can hear some muttering about working when you are a guest. Blushing and poking the fire I turn my back. How many times has Kevin helped out with the work on their property? His Mennonite background has instilled an ethic: 'First you work. Then you eat.' Wherever he goes, Kevin offers to help out with the work. It is something I respect about him. Sitting around swapping tall tales is not part of his lifestyle. Drinking beer is something he never does. Mocking comments never cross his lips.

The wood pile gets to be about waist high. It sounds like they are almost done. I hope I have enough hot water by now. I open the door to express my appreciation with every load the men deliver. Sincerely, I am enormously thankful.

Red breaks the ice, "Coffee on?"

"Oh, Red, I don't have any coffee. May I pour you some tea?"

"Is it real tea or some of them damn weeds?" he refers to his step-mother's mint, lemon balm, chamomile and other herb teas she grows, dries and serves. I can never tell if Red is friendly-teasing or he really means what he says or he is just plain rude. But, he is my friend's son, so I accept his banter as best I can.

"Herbal tea," I offer.

"Witch's brew," Red grins.

I am mortified.

The men swap stories and toss out friendly complaints and silly comments while they work. Now they want to rest.

They come into the cabin again to warm their hands. Nobody brought gloves. There is no way that this noisy crowd can even glimpse what is good about this little cabin. We are like sardines. Anyone can see the grey, untreated floor boards are shrinking, the gaps allowing frigid air to flow freely into the room. Anyone can see the tar paper in between the gaps in the roof where that lumber is shrinking, too. There are no furnishings. No electricity. No TV. No plumbing. Not even a chair to sit on.

Back outside the men drink their rapidly chilling tea and eat a couple of Cheryl's cookies and a piece of dried fruit.

In an attempt to entertain my guests, I relate the events of last night and the capture and release of the flying squirrel. But it falls kind of flat. My storytelling and gestures are a little too exaggerated. Country life is full of animal stories. This once in a lifetime experience for me is not that unusual for them.

Inside, the children are so chilled from the door being open and closed again and again. Outside, it is way too cold for the menfolk to be standing around.

The visit is over abruptly.

"Well," I sigh heavily as the voices fade away down the path and I survey the dishes, the extra stumps, the mitten left behind and try to reconcile my picture of my life with what they might have thought of my life.

It was altogether an embarrassing day. Not charming, witty, generous, or remotely how I thought I would feel as a hostess after the departure of my first guests. And I didn't even remember to open my Guest Book!

I hear the vehicles pull away while I stack dishes and dipper out of the water jacket to wash up.

New voices are heard outside and Sam starts barking.

Up the path come Karl and Annika.

What a surprise!

With all of the drinking water gone, all of the cups unwashed and no more fruit, I am again caught short as hostess. But Annika brought a dozen freshly baked muffins. So we have a more substantial treat together.

They invite us to come over on New Year's Day. I will look forward to that. They have guests coming from the Okanagan Valley who they used to pick fruit with. It will be a full house, but ever so nice to be included.

We say good-bye and I again tidy up after guests.

Well, that was that. I feel foolish and disconnected. I feel small and inexperienced. I feel foreign and embarrassed and ashamed. I feel invaded and dizzy from all the noise and voices and guessing the meaning on all of the faces.

I have such a different relationship with each person and there they were all scrambled up together. I so much wanted to make a good impression on these people who have helped us so very much. I was so inadequate and under prepared.

Guests have left. Christmas is over. I gently re-wrap the ornaments, close the box, put away my yearnings. Evening has come. Necessary chores must be finished before it is too dark to see. Although we have scooped up snow again and again all throughout this day of surprise guests, we have no water left for our own evening baths, morning dishes, tonight's cooking or drinking, so I take another turn. After all, I have been inside all day! I have to walk a little farther away from the cabin to find clean snow. So far there is only about eight inches of snow this winter. Dead leaves and twigs from the shrubbery, black hanging lichen clumps blown off by currents of wind, fallen pine needles will all be strained out of the water when I filter it through a clean dish towel, held by clothes pins over the mouth of a gallon glass jar I brought home from the restaurant.

When all of my pots are filled with packed down snow and I hear them sizzling on the stove top, I join Kevin at the wood pile.

The freshly cut wood which the menfolk delivered today looks so golden in contrast to the weathered grey logs of our cabin.

"I love the smell of all of this fresh wood," I offer Kevin a cheery greeting. "How generous of them to bring us a whole truck-full!"

Abundance this evening where this morning we had so little.

Scrap lumber ends of 2x4s, 2x6s, 2x8s and 2x10s are in random lengths as short as eight inches and as long as 30 inches. It makes an awkward pile. I estimate that there is enough wood for maybe two weeks.

"So, if we cut our own wood as we go along and supplement our daily work with this magical gift, then we can relax a little and not be so anxious about wood every day, right?"

"That's what I was thinking," Kevin nods.

"May I take a turn?" I offer. I could use the practice on something easy. If I get the muscles and coordination right on these pieces of wood which only need a light tap to split, then I will gain confidence to put more effort into each stroke and be able to deliver a more powerful blow to split larger logs.

This scrap lumber is easy to split since it is all only two inches thick. I choose 2x8 pieces because the smaller ones will fit in the stove without needing to be split. But some of the pieces are also way too long to fit in the fire.

I suggested that the guys sort the pieces that were too long into a separate pile. But they ended up just dumping armloads into a big messy pile for us to sort out later. The gift of the wood, the gift of the delivery, the gift of carrying and walking was enough. Now it is up to us how we want to stack it.

Kevin has an eye on the lumber which could be used in our home. We need book shelves, dividers in the kitchen, a kindling box and perhaps a wash stand as well as tool shelves and boxes for smaller things. He tells me his plans and I imagine our improvements.

Keeping my right hand on the splitting maul's long hickory handle, I reach for a piece of wood with my left hand, stand it up on the chopping block on the squared-off end. Now both hands grip the maul handle, left above right. Bending my knees slightly, feet shoulder width apart, I take in a deep breath. Swinging in a circle down and behind, up and around the splitting maul's wedge shaped head arcs, the weight of the head and my effort to swing it brings enough force to split the wood, bouncing each half away from the chopping block.

We need kindling, too, lots of kindling for those middle of the night restarts.

Kindling needs to be sliced into pieces as small as a broom handle. I can't stand up such small pieces and I don't need the force of the maul. I can't hold the kindling with my hand and chop with the sharp axe, nor hold the weighty maul to make precise strikes.

Kevin shows me how to manage this task requiring more precision and caution. His technique is to hold the upright wood with the left hand, choke up on the handle of the axe keeping the right hand close to the head of the axe. The right hand can better control the shorter distance, less force and deliberate direction of the blow.

With a little tap, he lodges the cutting edge of the axe into the wood. Now lifting the wood with the axe head wedged in place, he can tap, tap, tap the kindling against the chopping block which will force the wood to split in a fine, straight length following the grain. I come and take a turn. It is pleasant to use these repetitive movements and gain a much needed resource. It is satisfying to build up a supply, plan ahead, be ready. I can feel my muscles learning, the concentration of my brain relaxing and the coordination becoming a habit.

"Wood is the only fuel which warms you twice," Kevin stops for a break and offers a word of wisdom. Looking up, I meet his eyes and wait for the explanation.

"How's that?"

"Once when you cut it. Once when you burn it." It is a tid-bit of country wisdom.

Enough for now, I bring the wood and kindling I have split through the door to build a stack inside. Pausing to warm my hands over the fire, I sigh deeply. Christmas is over. How much winter lies ahead?

There has been such a significant heat exchange every time the door was opened and closed today. Even as we prepare for the evening, bringing in snow and wood, taking out slop-water and chamber pot, feeding the pets, we spend precious heat again.

It is discouraging. Like running the water in the bathtub while the plug is out. I have to deliberately close my mouth from commenting on the cold. I just want to sit on a comfy couch, pull up a colourful afghan and read a favourite book. Or maybe catch a TV show. Or lay in a hot tub of water. Or phone a friend to talk about today's ups and downs. But, no. I have to keep my coat on for a while until the ratio of warmth from the stove chases back the cold drafts we have been letting in all day.

Noticing the sky's darkness and glancing at the clock I make decisions about preparing supper.

Fran brought a housewarming gift of a dozen eggs. I still have a pot of cooked brown rice. I had intended to use the rice to bake rice pudding for supper on Christmas Eve. Somewhere I had read that it was a Scandinavian tradition to have rice pudding for Christmas Eve dinner. It seems so quaint, wholesome and filling when the next day's feasts would tantalize the children with so many treats. A simple meal for the housewife to prepare while continuing the bustle of a zillion preparations for Christmas the next day.

But, on Christmas Eve I had no brain power available to solve the problems. In my tears and gloomy frame of mind I could not think how to make even such a simple meal. Now would be a good time. Boxing Day rice pudding sounds like a good new tradition!

I crack the eggs into the rice. Scoop out a heaping spoonful of brown sugar. Estimate a cup of milk powder. A splash of vanilla, a spoon of cinnamon, a handful of raisins all stir into the mixture. I oil the casserole dish we bought on our honeymoon and pour the mixture into it.

The oven door has been open all day, since Cheryl's suggestion, allowing the heat to radiate and fill the room. Now I place the meal in the oven, close the oven door and guard the fire for about an hour while the pudding steams and the custard becomes firm, golden, hearty and warm.

Meanwhile I peel four apples and simmer them with a little sugar, more raisins and cinnamon for apple sauce topping when the rice pudding is ready.

I notice silence where there has been Kevin's steady rhythmic chopping alternating with the clatter of stacking the wood. I hear him tromp the snow off his boots and the door latch slide. The dog bounds in, anticipating supper, too. Kevin scoops the kibble into the metal pan and Sam's munching and crunching begins immediately.

I have been working in the gathering gloom of the evening, reluctant to light the lamp. Each store-bought resource is limited. We have less than a gallon of kerosene as well as several flashlight batteries and a few candles. I don't need to see much to crack an egg!

But, now Kevin lights the lamp. I look at the clock again. If we have darkness at 4:30 and stay awake until 9:00 every night, we won't have lamp oil for long.

"Sure smells good," Kevin says encouragingly.

"It will be ready soon," I reply, straining the snow-water, pouring it all into the glass jar for drinking water.

"I think it is warm enough inside now for me to have a sink bath. I know it is silly, but do you mind turning away?" I ask blushing a little. Laura Ingalls Wilder described how Ma hung a blanket up for the Saturday night baths in her 'Little House' books. One room cabins have their disadvantages.

Still so newly married, I feel more modesty than confidence. I don't look at him and he, I trust, is not looking towards me. I have had a little practice with sink baths from all of our camping. Placing the enamel washbasin on the right, cooler side of the stove top, I begin by pouring warm, clear water over my bent down head. I collect the water in the basin. Returning it to the pitcher, I then shampoo my hair. Using the same water to rinse and collecting it again in the basin, it is still clean enough for the rest of me to bathe. Top-to-bottom, I enjoy the warmth on my face, slip off my sweater and wash, dry and quickly replace it with a clean T-shirt. Repeating the sequence for my bottom half, strip, wash, dry and dress.

The wash water is poured into the slop-water bucket. I layer on more clothes, comb my hair and braid it. Step back into my boots and coat.

Now the rice pudding is ready.

"O, give thanks unto the Lord, for He is good and His mercy is forever. Amen."

When you read a book, you can't see the action or hear the tone of voices. When you watch a movie you get a better glimpse into these parts of the experience. But neither can convey the smells: dog, cat, kerosene, matches, wood smoke, boots, kindling, shampoo, soap, cinnamon, apples.

And, even if these sensations are shared, if a witness or guests enter the scene to participate in the day's events, there is still something very personal that they can't know.

Kevin and I share a bond. For four years, since that first day that we met at Winter-Fest when we were sweet sixteen, we have grown in trust and aimed in the same direction. Learning to rely on each other's judgment and decisions, built on the belief that the One Who made us is in fact Guiding us along our path, each simple action, each turning point and accomplishment, each moment, whether 'high' or 'low,' are all woven together into our story.

There is no 'I' and 'You' anymore...it is all 'We.'

Although I missed the mark entirely as a confident, gracious hostess today, although my guests saw emptiness and cold, disadvantage and lack, although there is so little to see physically and mostly dreams and imagination bring contentment to our hearts, we know what others cannot know.

'Kaden' Kevin has called our future farm from the time we were engaged. 'Twogether' Kevin wrote on all of the cards, gifts and books he gave me and also signed them with the name I gave him, 'Samuel' which means 'asked of God.'[16] Then there is the symbolic drawing he designed: the sun, the mountains, the two birds flying together, so tiny, hidden on the inner surface of our wedding rings. Somehow these securities, three words, two wedding rings and one drawing, transform this apparent poverty into plenty.

And so, here we are. We asked. He gave. What other wealth can anyone ever have?

I head up to the loft. Kevin tinkers with the radio dial. He blows out the lamp at 7:00 and we enjoy the radio theatre all snuggled and safe in the dark.

But, when the radio plays are over and I refill the stove, I can't help but revisit the day. Fran and Archie's interested, supportive comments contrasted with the joking mockery of the young men. Where I see golden dreams and satisfaction upon reaching our goal...what did they see with their eyes?

Small, dirty, no place to sit, little food, no coffee, no beer. We made our guests work. The children had nothing to do. They all left so abruptly.

I thought that I would feel more connected. But now I feel even more alone.

My head is hurting. I must get some sleep. I have to get up for the 6:00am shift at work. Is it worth the strain of interrupted sleep to set the alarm clock to get up to keep the fire going? We decide to let it go out. It is very important to be able to sleep all night. Kevin resets the time for 4:30am. I rummage around for more layers to wear and to cover us. We will get up, boil water, eat porridge and go.

A sound wakes me in the night.

I make my mind not engage in theatrics and imaginings when I hear the trap snap. How many mice are there in all of British Columbia? Sleep, Self. Stay asleep. Don't think. Just sleep.

Back to back. Spooning. Curled up tight. Is there a best way to stay warm? Is it better to have the kitten by my feet? Behind my back? In my arms near my chest? Will she stay with me or will she go find Kevin to purr beside?

4:30am. Another day has begun.

Chapter 7
December 27, 1978
Wednesday

If you do
what you always did
you will get
what you always got!
—*Albert Einstein*

Each object I touch is cold: the paper, the wood, the box of matches. There is no safe haven. The entire world and everything in it is cold, sucking heat out of my body. I am tempted to go back up the ladder to bed. Only in my sleeping- bag, piled with other layers can I womb-like rest in the comfort of warmth. But if I stay there I will gradually become so hungry.

Which is worse? Warm and hungry? Or cold and fed? If I light the fire I will have both food and heat. So I continue, moving mechanically, directing my unwilling muscles to do what needs to be done.

Last night, I planned ahead. I saved the water in the porridge pot that I got ready from the melted snow. Now it is frozen solid! I chuckle as I begin breakfast. If I write a cookbook it will say: "The first necessary ingredient for making nutritious porridge is a block of ice!"

I feel kind of sulky and sorry for myself as we drive up the highway. The headlights drill a tunnel through the winter darkness. Kevin is 'Mr. Reliable.' We are never late or rushed or pressured. I huddle in my down parka, hood framed with fur, grey, wool army blanket over my lap and legs. I can dream away the miles and think my own thoughts while he drives.

Where shall my mind wander while the miles slide by? Where can I revisit and find comforts, security, welcome, warmth?

With the closeness of Christmas still echoing in my heart, and the distance of separation still aching in my heart, I summon the sweetness of the past and compare and contrast my experiences before marriage and after moving. I follow the trail of my own decisions.

In the Church community where I lived during my teen years, 'Friday Supper' was a custom that was pleasant for all age groups to participate in. It seemed like a little piece of 'Heaven on Earth.'

Before they were excused on Friday afternoon, the students attending the Church's elementary school prepared the gymnasium. The boys set up the tables and chairs. The girls spread out the white table cloths and set each person's place with a plate, silverware, a napkin, a teacup and saucer. The children in Grades 6, 7 and 8 had babysitting jobs in the family homes in the community. High school students were invited (expected) to join with the adults to attend the meal, worship and class. On Saturday morning the high school girls would come and wash the stacks of dishes.

The women formed committees and each took turns in rotation throughout the years planning the meal for about 50 people. Hearty meals were prepared: roast beef and mashed potatoes, or baked ham and biscuits, or thick slices of turkey and sweet potato casserole, or chicken breast with creamed corn. Each committee also prepared a salad and cooked vegetable such as peas and carrots or green beans. For dessert there might be plum cobbler or apple crisp, custard with peaches or blueberry pie.

For $2.00 per person, plates were filled with the bounty of Ontario.

I remember working alongside Mother as she planned, shopped, cooked and served a fine meal. She liked to make whole wheat buns special by rolling out each piece of dough like a child makes a snake with clay. With a quick twist, she would tie the dough into a knot. It was her signature.

"Why do you take the time to add this little detail?" I asked her.

"I am adding a little love into the menu," she replied with her encouraging smile.

From that moment I wanted to follow her example when I would one day make bread for my family.

Every Friday night, everyone knows their place. Being useful to others combined with the sense of belonging is a little taste of Heaven.

The Pastor taps his spoon, 'ting-ting-ting,' on the china tea cup to silence the cheerful voices of gathered friends and in unison they all recite the traditional blessing before supper.

"O give thanks, unto the Lord, for He is good and His mercy is forever, Amen."

Now voices fill the hall while serving bowls are passed down the long tables and everyone visits with neighbours. Meat and potatoes, vegetables and salad, a cart brings dessert dishes, tea, coffee and cake.

Newcomers to the community are welcomed by Old Timers. The elderly have wisdom to share. The younger ones tell of their children's new accomplishments. Marriages link many families. The tradition to have this weekly supper has been passed along through generations. Cousins, in-laws, friends bond together during this weekly meal. The work week over, the husbands look so dignified, dressed up in their suits and ties, they sit down to dinner with their wives. The wives look forward to this opportunity to wear a favourite necklace and earrings with an especially chosen dress. They know they will have this outing at the end of a week of domestic duties. It is a hub of social intermingling, news, opinions, memories. There is a security here. All is well.

After a leisurely dinner, the ladies clear away the meal and the menfolk take down the tables.

Slow and steady, a cart carries the china plates, scraped and stacked, back to the sink. The committee cooks take the food back into the kitchen and divide up the leftovers for people to take home.

By the time the ladies return to the hall, the men have set up the chairs in rows for singing practice. Soprano, alto, tenor, bass, smiling greetings the group members rearrange themselves for the best possible practice. The traditional hymns are well known, but the four part harmony for the beautifully arranged

Psalms need review so that during worship on Sunday, voices will ring out loud and clear and strong in all four parts.

When the clock signals the time, the singing practice is over and couples move to sit together for the next feature of the evening: a short worship service. Stand for the opening of the Word. Kneel and bow heads for prayer. Seated, all are silent while the Pastor reads. Stand for the benediction.

Now the adult religion class begins. The ladies open their knitting bags and the men settle back into their chairs. The Pastor will read aloud and explain difficult passages of doctrine.

Heaven and Hell. Marriage for eternity. The inner meaning of Scripture available by decoding symbols in the ancient texts. Translations and definitions. Descriptions in journals. There is an immense amount of material to try to cover from the 40 books that were written 200 years ago by a well-educated and well respected Scandinavian man who claims to have had 26 years of daily personal experience as a Mystic in contact with the Spiritual World. The people who read these 40 books believe the author was Divinely inspired. Because the Seer's doctrine significantly re-defines Christianity, the believers have developed a Church, schools and communities set apart, so they can continue studying this new doctrine throughout their lifetimes.

A question time after the class is a moment for the men to make known their comments, observations and thoughts, while the ladies keep their heads down counting their knitting stitches or arranging their cross-stitch colours.

The cycle is orderly. Everyone knows their role. It is much like the scenes which the Seer described about life to all eternity in the beautiful cities of Heaven. Men do useful tasks for society outside of the home. Women offer their service inside of the home. Masculine and feminine traits are God-given, permanent and each have their own place in the orderly plan of the universe.

From the time steam was harnessed and the Iron Horse replaced muscle power, after history forever changed with the industrial revolution, since the agricultural era has been eclipsed by an urban lifestyle, while society significantly shifts after the coming of the automobile and air planes, the turmoil of post World War II, the 50's brings rock-and-roll, television, and the Pill, the 60's stirs up civil unrest, assassinations, rocket launching and the moon walk, the 70's shouts of equal rights, legal abortion and the Vietnam War protests, through two centuries, these small religious communities hold steady to their lifestyle, passing on values and customs, protections and prohibitions as they hope to create an environment of Heaven on Earth.

My Dad and Mother decided to move our family into the Church community in the late 1960's. They saw advantages for their five children offered by the Church school. It was a time in North America when traditions of all kinds were shifting. Miniskirts and rock music were becoming accepted. Society was experimenting with gender roles. Women were entering all kinds of careers formerly available only to men. The doors to birth control, sterility, abortion and test tube babies and other fertility treatments were thrown wide open. Divorce, desegregation, interracial marriage, were changing boundaries. Soldiers returning from the jungle brought marijuana. Other recreational drugs were making their way into social life. Eastern religions looked attractive. Clothing, symbols, foods, music, and physical exercises from the Far East became fashionable.

As if frozen time, traditions of modesty in the Church community included: girls not allowed to wear slacks to school, chaperons necessary for dating, couples not allowed to hold hands until they announced their engagement, first kiss during the wedding ceremony. The people governing and living in the Church community held firmly to traditions that were accepted as permanently defined by this 40 volume sacred text. If these books were in fact 'Holy Writ,' then the doctrines they contained were also unchanging, unquestioned and unchallenged. These assumptions were easier to live by in a community setting, easier to keep unwelcome voices silenced, easier to remain secure.

When our family moved into the Church community, I was offered my first babysitting job. I was twelve years old.

I love to babysit. I always bring toys and books and a craft or puzzle or game to play. I know lots of nursery rhymes and finger plays to teach the older ones and amuse the younger ones. *Where is Thumbkin?* or *Eensy-Weensy Spider* or maybe *B-I-N-G-O.*

The first year we lived there, while the parents went to Friday Supper, I worked for a family with three little girls. The church was right across the street and everyone knew that it was OK for the babysitter to phone if there was any sort of uncomfortable moment or urgent question. As the eldest of five in my family, I felt confident and prepared. The six-year-old girl helped me find necessary items in the cupboards, prompted me as to the correct sequence of baths, PJs, story and prayers. The four-year-old knew which tooth brush belonged to each of her sisters. The two-year-old willingly allowed me to carry and wash her, pin on her diapers, button up her nightgown and tuck her into to her crib. I was paid 25¢ an hour and worked for a little more than two hours every Friday night. I thought I would gladly work for free. It was so much fun.

The next August, before the school year started, my Mother got a phone call from another family. Since requesting a popular babysitter was first come first served, this family acted early, requesting me as their regular babysitter ahead of the others. I accepted the position. Now, as an experienced thirteen-year-old, I felt I could take on a new challenge. A new wage was agreed on by all the parents that year: 35¢ per hour. And a challenge it was. In this family, the father was a business man and the mother was Danish. Their sparsely furnished home was always squeaky clean. Every object in place. Not a speck of dust. The wooden shoes lined up at the door so Mother or Father could step out of the tidy house and into the idyllic garden for crunchy fresh vegetables. The daughter, her long wavy red hair and charming china doll complexion, was a sweetly behaved eight-year-old. Helpful and cooperative, she could read and occupy herself with quiet ladylike activities. The younger brother already had a reputation. A lively, never-stop-moving five-year-old, his 'watch me do this' gymnastics did not match the formal furniture nor the glass sculpture on the mantel piece. There were no fingerprints on the glass doors nor toys strewn about. I had to keep my wits about me to contain or at least redirect the energetic and sometimes alarming antics of this lively lad. Fortunately he had a favourite, non-whirlwind occupation. He wanted me to read aloud a large, colourful book about firemen and firetrucks, perhaps two or three times every Friday night. So, while the well-behaved daughter felt left out and lonely, the son got all of my attention so that he remained more manageable and everyone got into bed at a reasonable time.

The next year another opportunity presented itself. There was a very proper couple who had travelled to Europe, building their foreign language skills in Germany, Spain, France and Italy before returning to Canada to take positions as high school teachers and start a family. Rowdy little kids somehow arrived into this prim and proper home. While they trained me in, ironing linen tea towels, precisely folding laundry and making sure the child in the highchair did not drip, throw or spill anything, I agreed to all of their cautions, routines and schedules. But, as soon as they left, I loosened the grip of propriety on the children and we pretended and romped, explored and made noise, splashed in the bathtub and stomped up the stairs to bed.

A pattern to my child care work was developing. It seemed that when a family was rigid, I allowed more casual play. If a family was scattered, I imposed structure. Listening and watching, observational skills focused, I guided children from where they were to where their potential could take them. I drew on a growing store of songs, games, quiet and active play, language development, imagination and brought a mixture of learning-through-play to each encounter. Every year the pay increased, but it hardly mattered to me. I had found what I loved to do. Money was insignificant to the joy I had planning activities, sharing what was in my bag, guiding eager hands, meeting curious eyes.

My skills brought me more and more calls. In a few years I was even trusted with overnight babysitting for a family of four children. They knew lots of card games so it was easy enough to keep them safe, amused and on normal routines. But then, there was the cooking. Every family has their own ways to prepare food, seasonings and sauces, combinations and proportions. I was left with a menu I thought I could deal with. But when I opened the oven I had set for 350°F for an hour to roast the thin slabs of steak and smoke billowed out, I realized that I was in a bad situation. I was hired to take care of these children while all of the Church women were at a retreat! I could not phone my Mother or the Pastor's wife, nor my previous employers or even the lady I was working for. They were all at a lakeside cabin with no telephones! I tossed the steaks in the trash. I phoned my brother to please bring over a couple of boxes of macaroni dinner.

Embarrassed, but wiser, I provided child care for several families when new babies were born. 'Mother's Helper' jobs involved cooking, cleaning, laundry, fetching and all domestic duties so the postpartum mother and her infant could rest behind closed doors. Mothers were not expected to return to their normal housework for several weeks postpartum. Again and again I entered homes to learn the family's routines, laundry machine, pet care, expectations of behaviours while they welcomed a tiny new member to their family. Some jobs required me to live-in.

'Mary Poppins' they called me. The balance of fun creativity and steady reliability was enjoyable to me and of value to my employers. Eventually, I was recommended to families outside of the Church community and to families in other Church communities. The realization that each of these couples trusted me with their most precious children was an honour. I observed a spectrum of lifestyles, gained lifelong skills regarding early childhood development and learned from varied family dynamics. I learned and taught. These things fascinated me. Sweet rosy-cheeked faces, miserable too-late-to-bed whiners, stubborn resistance, boldly boisterous boys, clever show-off girls, shy 'I miss my Mommy' tears, eager to show-and-tell achievers...all of these children were 'mine' and our interactions made lasting impressions on us both.

My sister quit early. In tears she phoned Friday Supper and reported to the parents that their children were too hard to manage. My friends left babysitting as soon as they could, got their driver's licenses and found 'real jobs.' Not me. I stayed in the home, absorbing every experience, bringing new skills, shaping a disciplinary method, combining play and work, participation and learning, strengthening each child in their character qualities and asking them to cooperate. Heart, soul, mind, body: it seemed obvious to me that if each part of the child is nourished, given a challenge to reach for, encouraged and allowed to benefit from new experiences, then all will be well. Babysitting was not the kids plunked in front of the TV while I was reading a magazine or doing my homework with one eye on the clock waiting for bedtime. It was a well-rounded experience for everyone.

One memory stands out. It was my first full-time summer job. I was sixteen. A very quiet couple in a suburban home were a two pay cheque family. In the early 1970's it was a big deal for the mother to be away from home every day seeking a career. They belonged to our Church, but they lived in the suburbs, not in the Church community.

So, every morning the Dad came to drive me to their house while the Mom got ready for the day. After work, the Dad drove me home while the Mom made supper. He worked as an insurance sales man in an office with a brief case. She was the teller at a bank in a mall.

Three kids, a fenced backyard, no pets, a quiet street lined with new houses, I could see the setting was pleasant. The mother explained to me that unlimited TV, koolaide and freezies were available to appease these three while the hours passed. Or these treats could be withheld if misbehaviour needed correction. The older boy was allowed to go bicycle riding up and down the street with the neighbour kids. The younger girl poured out her bin of Barbies every day. The only scheduled item was nap-time for the two-year-old. It looked easy enough. And it was. Too easy. Cereal for breakfast. Can of soup or white sliced bread with peanut butter and jelly or macaroni dinner for lunch. Disposable diapers for convenience.

To reduce conflicts, no one had chores. To eliminate any mess for me to cleanup, no one had any craft or creative ambitions. It seemed to me that the whole family was designed to take the path of least resistance. Flat lawn. Flat day.

I had never been in a family like this. And I had never returned to the same place eight hours a day, five days a week for three months. I could multiply and add up all the sugar and food colouring in the store-bought treats and I shuddered. I couldn't tolerate the blaring TV or accept the listless bodies draped about. I pledged to make a difference and bring a healthier balance and creative 'something' to this family.

I tried to read aloud. I tried to engage them in the pictures. "I wonder what will happen next?" I tried my repertoire of nursery rhymes, finger plays, *Ring Around the Rosie*. They all looked blankly at me. It seemed like I was the entertainment. They were passive, just like when they were watching the TV. They didn't get it that I was inviting them to actively participate.

I showed them how to make a fort with the couch cushions, a tent under the table, make animal noises and set up an obstacle course so we could play circus. Nope. TV was their go-to activity.

I started to watch and listen closely. What is the goal of this two pay cheque family? What makes it worth her time to be away from home? To miss the children's activities? What do her wages pay for that mothers who stay home don't have enough money to buy? A second car, a haircut and a perm, matching shoes and purse, her workday wardrobe, the babysitter, disposable diapers and food that needed no preparation.

If the mother had stayed home, none of these things would cost any money. The kids would be better supervised. The mother would read to them, play with them, have the neighbour kids over. And everyone would have better nutrition.

I came to a double conclusion.

1. Over all: she can't be making much money.
2. I am not going to work for pay outside of the home.

My decision to be a stay at home Mom was confirmed when I worked for another family with four children: two school aged girls and twin one-year-old brothers. The children were so used to having a Nanny and cleaning lady that they did not know how to get dressed by themselves nor how to pick up their own toys. No chores were expected. I did the math, multiplying the volume of one case of disposable diapers per week times two years and made another decision for my own child rearing: cloth diapers. Those twins would fill a two car garage with waste that was not biodegradable before they were two years old.

By the time we wed, I counted 24 families I had worked for and 80 children I knew and loved. 'Mary Poppins' I was indeed.

Maybe I thought my own family was 'normal.' I wanted to be like my own Mother. She baked bread. Not always, but often enough that we knew the warmth of melting butter and honey on thick slices. She made cookies and birthday cakes and icing and pancakes from scratch. She made jam. When we lived in Ontario she had a garden, chickens and a compost heap. We kids all had chores, folding laundry, washing dishes, helping with meals, cleaning our rooms, changing our sheets. Potatoes came from the earth, then you wash them, peel them, cut and cook and eat them. No instant mashed potatoes here! This work was not drudgery, a punishment nor fetching and carrying for a lazy parent. This was work that our Mother taught us so we could practice what we needed to know in order to one day take care of our own families.

TV was only allowed on Sunday evening. After we were scrubbed and in our PJs, Mother would bring a tray upstairs with bowls of Cheerios. That was Sunday supper while we watched 'Lassie' and 'Walt Disney.' Television advertisements in the 1960's showed all sorts of new products: TV dinners, instant pudding powders, cake mix, pancake mix, store-bought jam, special brands of white bread, cold cereal, soft drinks and chewing gum with sporty actors, pretty girls and catchy slogans. But none of these items ever were in our pantry. "If no one ever ate these foods before this TV ad. Surely they are not necessary now," was my thought.

'Mother making goodies in the kitchen!' was a typical greeting to our Mother when we stepped through the door after school and breathed deeply the smells from the oven.

Besides child care, I also volunteered for events at the church by washing Friday Supper dishes, helping out at Church camp, teaching Sunday School, backstage for year-end productions and assisting with wedding preparations. I also had summer jobs outside of the Church community during the two summers before we got married. First I worked at a downtown bakery which was very enjoyable. Healthy loaves and yummy treats were freshly baked and sold to the lunchtime crowd. The next year, I worked in the kitchen of an old folks home with 160 residents. As the new girl, I was mostly doing Cinderella work: scrubbing pots, lifting loads, washing dishes with a steamy dish washing machine, pouring 160 juice glasses. My first task each morning was making nine loaves of toast. I was curious to watch the Dietitian managing low salt, diabetic, and other dietary restrictions.

While these were all interesting experiences, I returned to Nanny positions whenever the opportunity was offered.

When we arrived in Avola, I could quickly see that housecleaning and child care were not jobs people hired others to do. Most women stayed home with their children. If they needed to be away, then most often the grandparents looked after young children.

I could get a job at the motel. But cleaning was neither my interest nor skill. No matter what the wages, I'd bring a poor attitude for sure. Because I had some previous kitchen experience, the local restaurant as my only opportunity for employment while Kevin set about the task of building our cabin.

The plan at this time is for me to earn the money while Kevin builds the cabin. Later he will get a job while I stay home and keep house.

There is plenty of work for the men. His options are: work in the bush, drive truck, work in the sawmill, work on the railroad.

Out of my sentimental memories now, we arrive at the restaurant. Out of the van now, kissing Kevin good-bye. I call to him, "Be safe!"

Oh! I can hardly wait for this day to be over!

I just really do not like my waitress job. In fact, I do not like working for pay at all. How can anybody measure the worth of an hour of time? How can what I am doing for this hour be worth more or less money than how I spend a different hour? I just don't get the whole thing.

On the other hand: I have a job. There is no place else to ask and they needed me here. So, I switch over to my attitude to 'gratitude' and step towards the day.

I see Cecile, the morning cook, just unlocking the door. She is so quick with movements that show how familiar she is with the morning routine. It is still about twenty minutes before the 6:00am opening time. I snatch a moment to I run down stairs into the staff washroom and splash a little warm water on my face, cleanup a little and change into my uniform. I am so fast, but still she is way ahead of me by the time I return upstairs.

The electric lights in the dining room and kitchen seem so bright to me after four nights with only a kerosene lamp! 'Room temperature' is luxuriously warm after four days of indoor camping in our drafty cabin. The dining room looks so long and wide compared with our tiny home. Noises seem so metallic and humming and buzzing and amplified after winter wilderness silence.

Cecile has unlocked the office so I can count the float back into the till.

She has already switched on the grill and lined up her supplies the way she likes them. I flick on the coffee pot, tea kettle, heat lamps, steam table and the OPEN sign.

There are three tractor-trailer trucks in the parking lot. The long haul drivers have each left a note requesting wake up times for us to go rap on the door of their sleeper cabs.

I am so afraid of this part I have asked the cook to do it each time I am on morning shift. Me knocking on the door of a sleeping man? A truck driver? No thanks.

Pleading with Cecile, she agrees to do it. No one really wants to go back out into the cold, but I offer to get a few of her chores started to give her back the time it takes for her to do this part of my job.

I start peeling potatoes, get out a few carrots, onions and celery. Cecile plans to make chicken and vegetable soup today.

She likes to be quiet until the day gets started so I try not to start chattering about small things until she is up to her usual, cheerful self.

The first trucker comes in and I bring his coffee and write down his order.

Now I must focus, listen, pick up clues from faces and gestures, walk back and forth many times and always smile. Ever alert, I must be available for each customer's wishes.

'Close their eyes.' 'Flip 'em.' 'Over easy.' 'Dry.' 'White.' 'Extra cream.' 'Throw on an extra flapjack.' 'Hold the onion.' 'Denver.' 'Double toast.' Each person has a favourite breakfast and the variations seem endless. Much of this vocabulary I have never heard before. Surprised at my ignorance, Cecile, Gloria and Darlene often roll their eyes at my questions and confusion.

After the truckers eat and leave, the guests from the motel come down the hill. They have a more leisurely attitude, but want to be treated as if they have all the time in the world. Small talk about their trip is part of the expectation and the possibility of tips means I would be smart to make the extra effort. Now there are children and the highchair, booster seats, smaller portions, special requests and extra spills are awaiting my rapidly moving hands. I smile at the little faces, knowing they will make extra work. I also want to anticipate the needs that might arise, catching signals from the Mom. Oh, why did they choose to sit so far from the kitchen?

I barely have a moment to clear away the family's table when the locals come sauntering in.

Here come the two local men, Mike and Jerry, who often meet here in the morning for a big breakfast. They meet again near closing time when Mike is getting ready to patrol the train tracks through the night. They have all the time in the world and lots of sideways comments to make as I scurry to please the travelling customers.

Jerry is a country and western singer. Tall, heavy, wavy white hair, his big grin and bright blue eyes make contact with everyone in the room. His warm, deep voice, although not loud, carries his humour and conveys a sense of inclusion to each person he greets. Seated at a central table, he nods to me. Jerry always has ham and eggs, exactly the same order. As soon as Cecile hears his voice she starts to cook.

Mike, small for a man, shoulders hunched, is the night patrolman on the railroad. He is just getting off shift, frosty and tired from being outside most of the night, but not yet ready to sleep all day. Mike likes choices and changes, so I have to bring him a menu and wait for him to decide. Today it is French toast. They both light cigarettes and sit back to relax.

Jerry and his wife, Monica, travel most of the year singing in small town pubs and coffee houses. They come to Avola to rest and be still. While on the road they live out of suitcases, stay up all night, enjoy the glamour of wearing sparkly costumes. It is hard work to set up, load and drive their equipment from coast to coast across both USA and Canada. When they finally return to Avola, Monica becomes a recluse. It is a kind of cycle which seems to work. Public and private. Sound and silence. Many people and isolation. Avola is a tiny haven in a vast, hectic world. A fluffy white pooch is their constant companion.

Mike and his wife have a more traditional pattern of life: kids, a mobile home, payday, vacation.

Jerry is such a storyteller. He loves to be the centre of attention when the other locals come in to the restaurant for coffee. It is interesting to catch little bits of information as he recounts their life story. Monica's emigration from Europe is a chilling reality. With her mother, she swam across a river at night to escape Nazi Germany, their meagre possessions tightly gripped in a bundle over her head. Later she reached America, met, married and had a child, and still later Jerry lifted her out of a desperate situation and together they built up their travelling entertainment business, writing original songs, singing in harmony, he playing guitar, she on the drums.

Because they are both ex-military, Mike and Jerry have lots of stories to tell each other.

Mike is a Canadian veteran of the Korean War and spent much of his time in a Chinese prison camp. Harsh conditions, starving and wet, frostbite damaged his feet. People know this, but he doesn't talk about it much.

Jerry loves to expand and embellish. His American military career seems to have been mostly touring the world, sights and cities, Air Force bases and training. He loves an audience and never runs out of descriptions, humour and adventure.

I am in the kitchen, keeping my eyes and ears open for the bell that rings when the door opens, or the voices of new customers, or the sound of the chairs or boots, or the lids of the steam table clattering, or a cough from a customer standing at the till.

I have salad to prepare and fancy desserts to get ready. First I cut, plate and wrap squares, cake or other baking that Cecile has prepared. It is fun to layer brightly coloured Jell-O with whipped cream in tall parfait glasses.

It is getting to be daylight and I pause at the south-facing wall of windows to look out at the sky. Clear means cold. Overcast means warm. Cold means no snow. Warm means there could be snow. The men add their predictions.

"It's supposed to get cold in a day or two." Mike calls out. "*Real cold.*"

"How cold is *real cold*?" I ask, turning to face them. So far this winter we have had mostly 0° to −5° to −10°C and it has not felt too bad. The last two days it has been −15°C in the night, but during the daytime it always gets warmer and it is fine to work outside. Wrapped and layered I can defend myself. So I have not been concerned. If this is mountain winter weather, I can handle it.

"I heard 30° below." Mike opens the conversation.

"They have minus 42° farther north already," Jerry replies.

I figure they are stretching it and want my reaction, so I dismiss this information with a chipper reply, "That sounds a little nippy!"

"I was out in..." And they're off. The morning will be entertaining for both of them with laughter, swapping yarns and no one will know exactly how much really happened and how much embellishment makes for a good story.

There is a short pause in the flow of customers and I can get the dishwasher going, carry the desserts and salad I have been preparing out to the cooler and bring out the heavy, sloshing pot of soup to the steam table. I re-stack ten coffee filters, measuring the coffee carefully. Because I don't drink coffee, I don't know what 'good' or 'too strong' or 'too weak' really means, so I must do exactly what I have been taught without a real understanding of the consequences of a mistake.

A deliveryman arrives. He leaves his white van running near the front door while he unloads cases with the red trolley. In the lobby he jangles keys. The metal door creaks as it opens. The coin box sheds the heavy load of silver sliding quarters. He clatters and rattles, refilling the cigarette machine. He brings me rolls of quarters which I exchange for an equal value of paper money.

This is another part of my job that I dread: exchanging a handful of dollar bills for a stack of quarters for the cigarette machine. I feel like I have x-ray vision and I can see the damage each person is making to their precious life-supporting lungs. Wives will lose their husbands. Children their Mom or Dad. Teens are already trying it. Little ones watch and want to copy their parents. Women look so old with teeth yellow, skin sagging, hands stained from the tobacco. I smile and count the change. How much money does it all add up to? What a high price to pay to ruin your own health and future? The body is continually trying to cleanse itself. The smoker is constantly repeating the offensive intake. What will be the results of the two opposing forces over time?

After the neighbourhood women get the kids off to school, their dishes done and the beds made, they all come for coffee. Arriving on snowmobiles in fancy ski-suits, they fit this daily habit in between the morning chores and the afternoon soap operas. Today there is no school and some have travelled away for the holidays, so the crowd is smaller and a little different than usual.

Katy always has little Trevor with her. He is a picture. Small for four years old, he will be in kindergarten next year. He speaks with a soft lisp and his straight blond hair has recently been to the barber. He strides in wearing cowboy boots, brown brushed-denim jeans, matching vest and plaid shirt. Reaching up to give me 60¢ in coins he announces that he'll have a hot chocolate.

I bring it over with a couple of creamers to cool it off. My smile and greeting do nothing to coax conversation with the cute little boy. He is too manly and too serious.

There are only six women here today. Some order toast. Some a pastry. Maybe Cecile has something in the oven almost ready? I go ask. There will be cinnamon buns in twenty minutes. Some wait. Others go ahead with the date matrimonial cake, her specialty.

The gossip begins. I catch little bits as I return with the coffee pot, but I do not know all of the names in town nor the history that came before today's juicy details, so I can only pour and smile and leave.

The menfolk arrive. These are loggers. Massive trees have been wrestled, tamed and are now stacked on their trucks. This is their first load already, on their way to the sawmill where mighty blades will measure and slice and reduce majestic timbers to functional, marketable dimensions.

I dread the morning crowd. I have never in my life been in a place where I had to interact with workmen. Loud, in their steel-toed work boots, they have come down off the mountain from building roads and hauling logs and maintaining machinery.

On my first day of waitressing I was so nervous. 'They' all know each other, but I don't know any of 'them.' When I saw these workmen come tromping in, blue long sleeved overalls zipped up to cover their clothing, muddy boots, fingernails black with grease, curls sticking out which need a haircut under their sweaty company logo hats, I was stopped in my tracks in surprise. Who is this walking into the restaurant? I actually hurried back to the kitchen, alarm on my face to ask Cecile, "Should I ask them to leave?" They did not look dressed for restaurant dining in polite society!

These men are so unlike my Professor-ly Dad who wears shoes always polished, white shirt, striped tie, suit coat and brief case. Whether he is off to work or arriving home again, he always looks just as clean.

I had to be told that these men are not poor and shabby. These men own their own equipment. Machine operators and truck drivers are actually the 'made of money' men in our town. They laugh loudly and talk in words I do not understand. 'Skidder,' 'Feller-Buncher,' 'Cat-Skinner,' 'Chokerman,' 'Bucker,'

'D-8,' 'High-Lead.' In the springtime work comes to a stop during 'Break-up' while the snow melts and roads become deep muddy ruts. Prolonged dry weather in the summertime signals the risk of 'Fire Season' and the logging companies are shut down. When the autumn rains bring relief, great piles of branches and twisted roots are deliberately set on fire, glowing orange on the mountain sides all night long. Now that it is wintertime, equipment must be kept running all night so the engines don't lock up solid in the cold.

I can't imagine the 'feast or famine' lifestyle of these men and their families. A few months of big pay. Suddenly weeks of nothing. I can't imagine the physical effort, unforeseen dangers, working outside in the wet with clouds of mosquitoes, making decisions in the cold, nor the financial risks of maintaining all of that machinery!

I feel very uncomfortable during the weeks when I work the morning shift as I pour coffee for the men. Bending forward across the table to refill their mugs, my uniform feels so incomplete. I have never worn a dress this short in my life. The brown miniskirt rides up as I reach. The low orange v-neck becomes a focal point as I lean to serve the men sitting in the booth by the window. I feel so uncovered. So visible. I am not used to men looking at me while I walk and move and bend and reach.

The other waitress looks so cute. She is petite and confident. Her movements show that she knows the men are looking and she likes for them to notice.

I want to jump in a hole and hide.

Their on-going banter, generously embellished with cuss words is another thing I have never experienced before this. I never know if these fellows are engaging in friendly teasing, exaggerated bragging, deliberately humiliating me, or they are casually using rude and repulsive language simply because they don't have a bigger vocabulary, laughing all the while. It is impossible for me to react with anything but another embarrassing blush.

Some of the women who are already enjoying their goodies are the wives or sisters or cousins of the work men who have just arrived. Teasing and laughter show how well they know each other. There are many details of their exchanges that I do not understand as I do not know everyone here, who is married to who, who is living common-law, who is related, who is flirting with a single or married man.

As they prepare to leave, who is paying for which coffee and treat becomes all tangled up. I just blindly trust and take whatever money anyone gives me. I can't keep track of it at all. Some are running up a bill to pay at the end of the month.

Jennie comes in from her grey pickup truck. She has Cecile's youngest daughter, two-year-old Becky, and her own four-year-old Danny with her.

She greets the others and laughs about something cute the kids said or did over Christmas and then the little group moves to the back to sit at the staff table. Cecile brings some goodies and has her morning coffee break with her friend and little daughter.

Becky is so adorable. Every time she comes in I remember the first time I saw her. Picture-perfect, her thick, black, shoulder length hair, round cheeks and shy dark eyes seem the perfect opportunity for an artist to paint her portrait. My eyes drink in how beautiful she is.

Shy, she turns her head away when I try to make her smile. But Danny likes attention and while the women talk about the food Cecile will make today, the children and the news in town, I draw and ask questions and play rhymes with Danny. Becky smiles while I am not looking at her, so I know she is listening.

Too soon, the break is over and Jennie zips the kids back into their snowsuits and heads back out into the sunny day. It is bright sunshine and clear! Maybe that cold weather is coming.

I see the boss, Dave, has just settled in at the desk in his office and I knock on the door.

"I just wanted to remind you that we have finally moved into our cabin. We don't live along the highway anymore. We live two miles down an unmaintained road, with no phone, so I won't be able to tell you ahead of time if and when I can't get to work. When either the heavy snowfall or a cold spell means I can't get in, then I know my job here is over. I don't want to start and stop or make you wonder if I am coming or not. But, I do want to work as long as I can."

"OK," Dave replies. "I have a new girl waiting to come in. She is training this afternoon."

"I'm sorry I cannot be more definite," I feel embarrassed and turn to go.

Lunchtime. Menus. Orders. It is so fast. It is a blur. Cecile is great. I am the one who makes mistakes. 'Travellers' is the name of the restaurant and travellers are who we serve. Today the customers have either Christmas cheer or holiday strain on their faces from little sleep and many miles.

Look at all the dishes! The steam and soapy smell fill the kitchen and I follow the pattern of work from the smiling composure of the dining room to the back-stage hurry of the kitchen. It takes some time to get caught up. Scrape and load the plates. Push the heavy tray into the hot cavern of the stainless steel dishwasher. Out comes the flat tray of upside-down coffee cups. Wait to sort the silverware until it cools off. Out to the serving counter to replace the cups, saucers and soup bowls. Get the stack of plates back to where the cook can reach for them. Oops. Better empty the whole silverware tray to clean out the crumbs. Wipe the drips from the lids of the steam table where the soup is running low. Rearrange the dessert cooler and check to see if we need the salad freshened up.

At last. There is a lull in the early afternoon. Between meals there are fewer customers, so I look around for other places that need attention. 'Clean' is a message every guest notices within a few seconds. No one wants to lose a customer from a bad first impression.

The sun is planning to exit. The windows show all of the little children's fingerprints, tic-tac-toe patterns from where the teens played on the foggy window while waiting for the school bus, the cigarette smoke, the streaks from the last window washing. Washing windows is a pain, especially when there is no way to address the outside. But, I have to give it a try. Windex in my left hand, paper towels in my right, I make another attempt. I have to stand on the booth benches to reach the highest places.

It is time to finish up, cleanup and get ready for the next shift. But there are two regular locals who come in for coffee at this time of day. They like to sit alone, quietly.

Mr. Buis is a grey haired, muscular, slim man who has been here since the 1950's. What untold stories of his experience with the Dutch Resistance fills his memory as he relaxes in the booth by the window, looking down the valley and quietly draws on his cigarette? He came from Holland with his young wife after World War II. They raised their four children here. He built both buildings for the gas station and the restaurant. His skill as a businessman made the town grow and prosper. His wife ran the store and post office. Their well built house is white upstairs and green siding downstairs. All along the front, near the highway, there are beautiful flowerbeds overflowing with tulips and daffodils in the springtime, a fountain of colours all summer climaxing in a crown of lupins: white and pink, golden and deep, rich purple. A garage and workshop make space for his sons to do maintenance on their logging trucks. The wood heated greenhouse is nearby where these former Hollanders enjoy their gardening skills.

I feel awkward with Mr. Buis because of a mistake I made. When I was first learning the job and he came in for his daily coffee break, I brought him a bill and told him how much he owed for four cups of coffee. I stood there and waited for him to pay me. After all, even if the second cup is free, there's no way that four cups of coffee are free!

When he came to the till and I counted his change, Cecile came bustling out of the kitchen. As he walked out the door, she gasped, a shocked look on her face. "You never charge Mr. Buis for coffee! He built this place! He is like the mayor of our town! He always gets free coffee!"

I wanted to disappear into the mist!

So, today I move my muscles to produce a smile and bring the coffee pot, attempt small talk, enjoy his Dutch accent and wonder what error I will unknowingly commit today.

As soon as I am back in the kitchen the doorbell sounds. It is Blake. The second of my predictable afternoon solitary fellows slides into his usual booth. He is about seventeen and works at the gas station next door. He sits for an hour every day, the same as Mr. Buis. But instead of the free coffee that Mr. Buis is honoured to receive, or the free second cup that every other customer accepts, Blake is charged the full price for each and every cup. This is the boss's method to try to discourage him from sitting here for so long every afternoon.

He has no family. He has no friends. He has dropped out of school. He is so thin and long haired and lethargic. His one daily treat is about six cups of coffee at 1:45pm.

So, as I prepare to leave for the day, I keep count as he gets up to refill his cup while I am working in the kitchen, wiping up the washrooms, washing out the ashtrays, scrubbing the deep stainless steel kitchen sinks, refilling the coffee filters, counting the money in the till.

Here come Darlene and Gloria.

Cecile and I recount the day's events: what is finished, what is still to do. And the shift change is over. Kevin comes in to wait for me. I step downstairs to change back into my warm gear and we are outside in the fresh air, away from the meaty smell of the hot grill, the crisp brown smell of the deep fryer, the comforting smell of fresh baking and the nourishing smell of the chicken soup.

Sigh.

Home.

I'm going home.

Another package arrived in the mail today! Kevin's Mom has such good ideas! It is a set of dominoes that go all the way to double nines! My Grammie taught me how to play with her ivory dominoes. I am eager to sharpen my wits.

However, I must wait until after the fire is lit, news exchanged, spaghetti sauce simmering. Kevin and I sit together by lamplight and lay out all the pieces face up on the table. I show Kevin how to begin. The first piece has to be a double. Then the next player adds another piece. Where both pieces touch, they have to have the same number of dots. Only multiples of five get a score. You keep score with a tally: one stroke for each '5.' You can play either until all the dominoes are used, or agree to keep playing until one player has a score of 250 or until 500 is reached.

I love competitive games. Chess. Checkers. Parcheesi. Yahtzee. Cards. I like to strategize, focus, plan and win. Kevin is not familiar with this game, nor does he like the competitive spirit. When he was very young the unpleasant atmosphere of quarreling and loud voices in his home while his parents had relatives over to drink and play cards has left a mark in his memory that still hurts.

Never-the-less, there is nothing to do except go to bed or stay here by lamplight. So, we begin. "I know. To make it interesting, let's play for a challenge. Whoever wins gets to stay in bed and the loser has to light the fire in the morning."

At first we play an open hand so I can show him how to use his dominoes for the best score. Soon Kevin catches on to the game. I keep tally. It's fun to try to out-smart each other. Tricky tricks and clever come-backs make us laugh together. It's fun to play.

But, since I am leaving for work again for the 6:00am shift, there will be no fire to light in the morning. It was so cold to try to eat breakfast this morning, we will try a new plan. We're not going to use the alarm clock tonight. We're going to let the fire go out again in order to get a good night's sleep. We're going to get up and go, so losing has no penalty...this time.

I go to bed early. I add a thick, navy blue, wool sweater to my sleeping layers. I pause to tuck my top layers of clothing into the waist band of my long johns and PJ pants. I tuck the cuffs of my pants into Kevin's wool socks. No bare skin will feel the chill of the nylon sleeping-bag fabric when I move as I sleep.

It takes awhile to build my nest. Slide into our zipped-together sleeping-bag. Fluff up the additional down sleeping-bag that is opened to cover us both. Smooth out the quilt. Stack on the yellow and the green nylon blankets from our wedding.

Kevin feeds the fire. The newly delivered lumber pieces fit tightly together. Maybe the fire will last longer tonight. I can hear the metal-on-metal scraping sounds as he turns down all the dampers, drafts and vents. Creaking up the ladder he pauses to wind and set the alarm clock. He enjoys another entertaining radio play in the dark, while I try to stay asleep. Stamina for my day tomorrow is more important than entertainment now. If I have another night of broken sleep to tend the fire it will be especially difficult to be cheery with a pasted on smile at work tomorrow.

"Kevin? Does it seem cooler in here tonight?" I mumble when he joins me.

"It might be a little cooler inside. The radio said that the temperature is going to drop soon," he informs me.

"Do you think it might be the kind of wood?" trying to sound like an Old Timer. "They say different kinds of wood give off a different amounts of heat."

But I don't hear his reply. My nest is so cozy. Tucked in and curled up I love the sensation of falling asleep.

Sometime in the night an unknown sound awakens me. It's not inside, either. What could be making that loud crack? Not the clap of thunder in mid-winter? Not the sharp percussion of a gunshot? Not the metal-on-metal of a truck door slamming? Not the surprising sound of a machine backfiring?

Another crack in the distance. Another. Now closer. Irregular. "Kevin? What is that?"

We lay still and wait. "There it is again!"

"It is the cold. The temperature is dropping. I heard the weather forecast on the radio. The sap in the trees is freezing. It expands, like when water freezes in the cracks between rocks and splits rocks off the side of a cliff. The trees' veins are bursting."

Oh, well, then, I guess I'll go back to sleep. It is not a threat. It is only the trees bursting!

"But, Kevin, how cold does it have to get before tree sap freezes?"

How can he go back to sleep so quickly? 'Temperature dropping.' I wonder exactly what does that mean? I pull the sleeping-bag hood up over my head, make sure I have the kitten strategically placed to warm my feet, tuck all edges closed, wrap my arms around my chest, hunch my shoulders and borrow warmth from my husband's back.

Sleep is so important. I want to go to sleep.

Chapter 8
December 28, 1978
Thursday

It is better to light a single candle
than to curse the darkness.
—*author unknown*

The personal possession I would most like to destroy is my little wind-up travelling alarm clock. It folds away cleverly into its own brown case to slip safely into a suitcase or bump along in a backpack. When it unfolds the triple sides form a stand so I can see the face measuring off the seconds, minutes and hours.

Somehow incongruous in a log cabin, this tiny reminder of the outside world was really an instrument of torture.

In order to arrive for my waitressing shift at 6:00am at the restaurant, it is necessary to start driving at 5:30. With no shower, no electric appliances, only pitch dark to welcome the day, my husband and I decided to just slip into our clothes and start driving...well, after a quick dash to the outhouse. The plan was to have a sink bath in the staff washroom before I went upstairs to the kitchen and dining room.

And so, at 5:15 on December 28, 1978, with all my courage I reach my arm out of my warm sleeping-bag, not to wing the clanging clock across the room to smash it into unmeasured silence and leave me blissful in my dreams, but to gently press the 'off' button. With the same extended arm I reach for my clothes to pull them in and warm them with body heat before exchanging my snuggly soft pastel flannel PJs for the stiff brown polyester uniform.

Something was different. Very different. "Kevin, it's really cold!" I signalled to my still drowsy husband. What an obvious thing to say. In this tiny cabin, in the dead of winter, fire long burned out, my voice the only interruption, surrounded by silent snow, to say, "It's cold" is stating the obvious! But this was unlike anything I had yet experienced during my brief attempt at 'roughing it in the bush.'

Nudging my still unmoving husband, racing the clock, I wriggle out of my sleeping clothes into my uniform. Who invented pantyhose? I add a brown nylon turtle neck sweater under my brown polyester uniform, decide to layer first pantyhose, then my long johns and add a pair of polyester brown pants, at least until we get to town. Better put the heavy navy blue wool sweater on top of my uniform, too. With a gasp, I lunge out of the shelter of the sleeping-bag.

The cold stuns me like a bird slamming into a window. Unseen force, invisible something stops me for a moment.

"Kevin! It's really cold!" Grab the flashlight. Down the ladder. My feet on the ladder rungs tell me the ladder itself is cold. Keep moving. "I can't!" One part of my brain is screaming. "I have to!" Another part of my brain commands. Just keep going. Inside the van it will soon be warm. Shove feet into boots and arms into sleeves, shoulders hunched and voice trying not to shriek, my every sense is gathering information and all of it is announcing the same thing: "COLD!"

When I grab my parka it feels stiff and reminds me of the walk-in freezer at the restaurant. My boots are, yes, tug them and twist them, frozen to the floor! As I slide open the latch with my already chilled fingers, I stop again as my eyes check the thermometer and struggle to comprehend, "Where did the red line go?" I had seen −15°C for the past few days. But what was this? "Kevin! Is there such a thing as minus 40 degrees? How cold *is* that?"

As fast as it is humanly possible I move to the outhouse. Why am I thinking of my brother who, years ago, couldn't resist licking the snow off the metal gate as we waited for the school bus. His eyes filling with tears and flashing a signal of fear as we called, "Daddy! Come get his frozen tongue unstuck!" What dangers to bare, wet skin are possible in this cold? I decided to squat in the snow beside the path and not contact the toilet seat with a temperature colder than cold.

Kevin is up and out and striding towards the trusty van. I glance around the cabin, wrap the grey wool army blanket we use in the van around my shoulders and call the dog to jump in. The door hinges are stiff. My seat is rock-hard. My now frigid fingers move slowly and awkwardly. "Oh, please! Start soon!" I silently will the welcome heat that the van motor would soon begin to share. Fists clenched. Jaw tight. Shivers rattle my whole body.

I pull the blanket up around my face. Tense and silent and fiercely stopping any sound of complaint, I wait for the familiar sound of the Volkswagen motor firing. But Kevin, in the driver's seat, is making all of the right gestures, turning the key, pumping the gas, listening for the turning of the motor, the kick of the first firing. But he's moving in silence. Not the dreaded 'rur-rur-rur' of a motor not drawing enough fuel. Not the half-light generated by a weak battery. Not a coughing splutter of a bad fuel-air mix. Not a gasp or chug or growl. Nothing. It was like he has put the key into a block of cement. No life. No spark. No hope of wiggling a wire or tightening a knob. No remedy in a bottle or jug or spray. No replacing a fuel line or battery or any of hundreds of options to double check. 40° below is just too much.

As the reality of this present moment sets into our minds, the reality of what lies ahead for us also dawns.

Six months ago I had been waiting for this moment. Six months ago I had been a young bride, saying 'good-bye' to family, friends and all things familiar. Six months ago I was looking forward eagerly to being alone with my husband in our cabin in the mountains, cheerfully lugging water buckets and firewood. Six months ago I had a clear vision in my mind, dog and cat by my side, needlework on my lap, soup on the stove and bread in the oven. Six months ago I was funneling all of my resources, reaching towards a future golden sense of satisfaction, imagining our first winter, looking back at the work we had done together and the domestic scene we had achieved. And here it is. Three days after Christmas. All my dreams come true.

'Today is the first day of the rest of my life.'

Swing open the door. Step out into the snow. Past the wild blueberry bushes. Past the stump of the first tree Kevin felled for the new cabin. Past the waist high stack of firewood beside the door. I can hear Kevin and the dog behind me. How much will power does it take to open the door and enter a house that is 40 degrees below freezing? How much will power does it take to crawl back into a sleeping-bag which has rapidly chilled? How much self-discipline does it take to speak not a word of complaint or dread or worry or fear? How much I had wished for another hour of sleep and now that I have all day, how much I would rather be working in the warm restaurant.

How do you decide when to get up on a day when there is no time? No one else expects you to come or go. No 'should's' or 'have to's.' No difference between now or later, today or tomorrow.

My wool hat is pulled down over the back of my neck. Trying to conserve warmth inside my sleeping-bag, I peel off the ridiculous pantyhose, replace the long johns and wool socks. Strip off my uniform and switch for more efficient woolen layers.

Kevin lights the fire, hurrying to climb up to dive in beside me. I try to think of any resources we have not yet used. "Kevin? Please bring the grey wool army blanket up, too." Spreading it over both of us, I also rearrange the extra down sleeping-bag, wool-padded quilt, blankets as additional insulation. Without words, my husband's warmth at my back, I wait for sleep to cover me and dreams to return and release me from the cold.

Four hours later, the sun brightens the sky. My tummy is hungry. Nature's cycles are powerful and I wake to begin the day again. No holiday. No storybook. This is real life.

Everything I touch hurts my hands as the cold sucks warmth out of my flesh. "Concentrate, Eleanor. What can you do to make this better?" Lift the stove lid. Four hours is too long. No fire here. Crunch the paper. Lay criss-cross kindling. Add a pair of small birch pieces. Reach for the matches. Strike. Flame. Smell of sulfur. Sound of crackling. Now watch and wait. Believe that soon the flame will drive the cold away and my muscles will relax and my mind will have something else to think about.

Wearing thick down parka (which feels like gauze), hood up around my face (the equivalent of a rayon scarf), wool pants (as much help as tissue paper) pulled on overtop of the long johns and PJs (their weave seems as effective as a sieve), the wool-felt in my boots (feels as thin as newspaper) it seems impossible that my most reliable assets have become so inferior. The warmth in my feet gradually drains away. I no longer accept incoming messages from my feet to my brain. I stand pressed close to the stove. Why is it taking so long for the fire to slowly heat through the ice-cold thick cast iron?

Moving slowly, numb not only with cold, but also with the realization that this is now my life. These walls. This table. This view. This set of limitations and possibilities. I no longer look forward to a pioneer lifestyle. I am living it now.

What food is in the house? How long will it last? How much money do we have? How long will it last? How cold is it now? How long will it last? How much wood do we have now? How long will it last? And what can we do to get more?

No one knows what will happen next.

I take inventory of our food supplies. Because we have been guests, because we have been in transition moving from one place to another, because the restaurant offers variety, convenience and plenty, we have not been stocking up on food supplies. Because we have squeezed every penny and stretched every dollar to obtain building supplies, we have not looked ahead to this long-range part of the plan. The bare basics are on the shelves of the cupboard: peanut butter, honey, jam, cans of soup. In glass jars and in the food box are the items I don't want to share with the mice: beans, rice, oats, raisins. There are still a few potatoes and apples, now rock-hard. Frozen. OK, then that's what we have to eat.

I know I have lost my job. My last pay cheque will be there on the thirtieth. But, wait. My pay cheque is ten miles to the north. The food store is 45 miles to the south. How will we get there?

Soon the fire snaps and the stove itself is no longer cold to the touch. With the oven door open and the smoke beginning to draw up the chimney nicely, I can feed more and larger pieces into the firebox and move to other tasks.

One thing I can get more of: water. I take all of the pots outside and scoop snow where it is deep and clean. Pressing and packing more and more, knowing how little water is in the fluffy snow, I carry the pots back into the cabin, stomping the snow off my boots and put them on the stove. The snow stuck to the bottoms melts, hissing and spitting, steam clouding my glasses. When the water melts I will strain it through a towel, cleaning out pine needles and bark, moss, twigs, dog hair and bits of soot. Then I will measure water for porridge. When it boils, the oats will be added and soon the warm food will be in our bowls.

It is our seventh day in the cabin. My now normal routines help me step into this drastically different abnormal day.

Kevin searches for a weather forecast on the radio. He sums up the various reports announced for cities and towns throughout this central part of British Columbia. "We can expect more of the same for the foreseeable future."

My eyebrows raise for an unspoken question.

"Maybe three weeks," is his somber reply. "Good thing there is no wind. On the prairies you have to factor in the wind-chill."

That's one thing about Kevin. His attempt to make me feel better is usually a statement of something worse. He faces reality. I'd rather continue to dream.

But, today is so raw, so shocking, so solid. Rosy daydreams melt. Childhood storybooks evaporate. Today is where dreams meet reality. It is new territory for me.

Hands cupped around the warm bowl, steam rising from the food, a day begins like no other I have ever lived, knowing that many more like it will follow.

I have water for dishes now and in a few minutes the kitchen is cleaned up.

40° below is a fierce and terrible thing. Frostbite is a real possibility. Care must be taken to protect the nose, fingertips, toes and cheeks. We have scarves, which were uncomfortably too warm while we are working at minus 15°. They feel like paper when it is minus 40°. Kevin crosses his scarf over his chest, tucks his mittens into his sleeves and keeps aware of circulation in his toes. He wears a man-made fibre face mask inside his hood. I follow his example, my face almost completely covered by the wool scarf tied across my mouth. Glad for the down parka. Glad for the men's wool pants. Glad for the expensive hi-tec mittens. Glad for my strength and endurance. Alarmingly aware of the ever-fragile ratio of wood brought in and wood burned up.

"Ready?" Kevin signals and we head out to cut firewood.

Very glad to be together, we depend on the bond between us, whatever the discomforts or difficulties.

We work slow and steady and long that day. Feeling the hazards of the temperature drop we would rather be inside tomorrow. We can maybe earn a day off tomorrow by working longer today. I think of Hillary climbing Everest. He learned to step and breathe slow and steady to keep the oxygen in his blood even with the work he called his muscles to do. I do not like the way the cold bites in my lungs when I exert myself. So I develop a pace of walking and breathing which allows the icy air I breathe in to warm in the folds of the scarf over my face before it enters my lungs. I watch the gymnastics of a scampering squirrel and hear the scolding of a pair of boldly blue Steller's Jays. Cold means clear. And clear means brilliant sunshine. I draw in the sparkling snow, the blue sky, the welcome sight of the cabin and the escort of the dog back and forth all day.

The Old Timers told us that cold days are clear and sunny. To see the blue sky is a wonderful thing. The autumn months of warmer, wetter weather wrapped the mountains with mist and filled the valley with thick clouds delivering days of dreary darkness. Thankful for sunshine, I trudge out after Kevin, following the sound of the saw and his tracks in the snow. He is satisfied when he works. I carry armloads of wood to stack beside the cabin. It becomes a sort of mathematical equation. I stay home and burn wood to heat the cabin, melt the snow, cook and the woodpile gets smaller. Kevin goes out and cuts and hauls and splits and stacks wood and the pile gets bigger. We watch and calculate and estimate. Are we getting any saved up? Or is it equally balanced? Or are we burning more wood than we can collect? Will we, too soon, surrounded by a forest, run out of firewood?

I think often of the first pioneers. Now I know why the young man would go out first, away from the comforts of civilization to set things up and come back later to claim his bride. Should we have done the same? No! I wanted to share the work and the problems, the struggles and disappointments, the uncertainties and setbacks. I wanted to see and experience all of it. I did not want to be sheltered from the reality or absent from the progress, unaware of the effort, a non-participant, simply provided for, just walking into a finished home.

I also realize the reality of the race with the seasons. Like others who settled the west, there is only so much time in the spring to travel and find land, in the summer to cut and build with logs, in the fall to seal up the gaps and set up house and in the first winter to supply wood daily. There is no saved up cash, no stored up food, no stack of firewood for this first winter.

I enjoy the work of the saw and take my turn opposite Kevin. He wrestles one log into position and we get a push-pull rhythm going which cuts deep and quickly through the fragrant cedar, birch, pine and spruce logs.

Lugging the wood home is a bit more difficult. I am unsure of my footing. The six to eight inches of snow hides fallen logs, broken branches, slippery slopes, lose rocks. A trip, fall, sprain or broken bone would have serious consequences. It is two miles to the highway and then 45 miles to medical help. And now we have no vehicle. But, since the snow is not deep, by the third load my footprints have flattened a trail as I go back and forth with armloads. During this serious cold, there will not be any more snowfall. But, when the cold lets up, the snow will start to fall again. It will not always be possible to struggle with both the weight of the wood and the uncertain footing in the snow. We are using up the trees suitable for firewood near the house. As both the distance and the difficulty increase, there is more motivation to build a small sled to better carry a larger load with less effort.

The lumber scraps our guests brought on Boxing Day are an unexpected resource. There are lots of pieces that are too long for the stove. "I wonder if you could shape two long pieces of the lumber ends into sled runners?" I suggest. "If I pulled a sled full of wood I could probably move more than a single armload and it would take less effort and I could even walk faster?"

"There's a thought," Kevin replies. But, the time spent building the sled will be time not spent cutting wood! Will the ratio of the adding and subtracting of the wood pile allow for him to take the time to stop cutting?

"While you're working on the sled, I think I'll start another project," I decide.

"What's that?" Kevin asks.

"I was trying to think what to do about the cracks between the floor boards. We don't have any more moss for chinking, but I think I'll try crumbled-up paper shoved in the cracks. I can tear up the dog food bag and use up some of the newspaper I brought home from the restaurant for fire starter. If it works, we can get more paper. It's not an especially fun job with such intense cold in the house and it will take a few attempts to finish it, but I am sure it will make a difference."

Kevin draws a curved line with a pencil to prepare two sled runners and fires up the generator to power the electric skilsaw. He smooths the edges with his knife. He fits crosspieces, sides and a rope to pull the sled. It is sturdy and will hold three to four times what we can carry in our arms!

Meanwhile, I tear the three paper layers of the 50 pound dog food bag into strips. Twisting and scrunching, I can use a butter knife to shove the paper into the pencil-wide cracks. I kneel on all fours to continue the project. My fingers ache with cold. I have to keep standing up to warm by the stove.

To occupy my mind I calculate. The boards are ten inches wide. The floor is fourteen feet across and fourteen feet wide. That's about seventeen cracks. Each crack is about a quarter inch gap. If you shoved them all together that would make one fourteen foot long crack over four inches wide! If you rear-ranged it into a rectangle that would be roughly equivalent to 30 inches by 20 inches of incoming 'fresh air.' Yipes! We might as well have a wide-open window!

My fingers hurt. I can't keep going. But the air flow must be stopped. I have to keep going.

There is only so much paper. About one-third of the job is done.

"Lunch is ready!"

"The sled is ready, too!"

I get the first ride and we laugh as if there was not a care in the world as the snow sprays and my handsome husband runs, his boots tossing clumps of snow all over me!

Kevin has found a new supply of dry wood. On the landing across the road where the forest was logged off last summer, several birch logs were left. His sawing and my loading and pulling the sled gain us a great advantage as the size of the woodpile grows. It is a bit of a walk, but almost no effort to bring the wood from this place. Kevin and I pass little tid-bits of observations, a funny thought or a word of encouragement each time we meet when I return with the empty sled. We feel wealthy and gain a sense of mastery over this huge wild place in this endless frozen landscape. There is a place where we can be warm and rest. There is meaningful work to do each day.

Kevin is cutting wood faster than I can haul it away! So, as the daylight fades and I stop working to go inside and start supper, Kevin fills up the sled with a larger load. He pulls hard down from the logs, across the road, up the driveway, around the bend towards the cabin. I step out to help unload and stack.

Creaky hinge. Open the door. Inside. Thump of firewood dropping from my arms into the wood box. Tromp the snow off of my boots. Clatter of the wood stove door. Crackle of the fire. Scraping of pots dragged across the stove top. Trickle of water dripping off the steamy lid into the water. Plop of adding another scoop of snow.

I am still wearing my black felt-pack manly winter boots, my navy blue down parka, a black wool toque. I can see my breath inside. No sense removing my outdoor layers. Thick and clumsy, I start making supper.

What do vegetarians eat when it's 40° below?

I realize the value of the meat-based diet of northern peoples. Inuit live near the ocean with ready access to the fat, marrow and ocean-rich protein sources of fish and mammals. I look around at our winter reality, realizing that bears are hibernating, deer and moose will forage on the spring-ready buds on the tips of twigs or scrape down through the snow to eat dry grasses. Small mammals are sleeping and many birds have migrated. No plant foods are available for people. Anyone who made it through the winter based on living off the land would have had to store up enough food for six to seven months! We might have food for four more days.

While I wait for a pot of water to boil, I take down the calendar from the nail in the wall to look again. December, January, February, March. That's a lot of blank days on the calendar until there will be any hope of springtime returning.

Big sigh.

Really.

It is getting dark. I pick up the lamp and try to judge how much kerosene is in it. Screwing off the top, careful not to jar the tall, slender glass chimney or worse: break the fragile white mantle which sends out so much more light than the simple wick lamp. I step outside and lift the tarp off of the supply box. The jug of kerosene empties into the lamp. The lamp is not full. Less than seven evenings until there will be no more light.

The cold hurts my hands. I should have worn mittens even for this brief encounter with the fierce ever-present temperature. But I didn't want the smell of the fuel to soak into the only mittens I have.

Light the lamp. Replace the chimney. Wash my hands.

The water I dipper out from the water jacket into the white enamel dish-pan is still cold with the newly added snow still a floating iceberg. For the zillionth time today I hold my hands over the stove top in a position of begging, calling, searching, waiting for warmth to penetrate.

An arch of smooth, flat split peas splashes into the cooking pot. I struggle to chop the round ice-onion into the frying pan to brown it in oil. "It's frozen rock-hard!" I exclaim, though no one hears. Pea soup will warm our insides and replace calories and add protein to our tired muscles. A little soy sauce is stirred in for flavour. Now for the last, also frozen, carrot sliced thin. Surprised, always learning something new, I pause to look more closely at the beautiful star-burst pattern of the carrot's frozen slices. Orange. That's a colour I have not seen today.

That's it. Supper will be ready in an hour.

The rhythmic tromping of Kevin's weary boots and Sam's energetic four-footed percussion burst into the room. Sam takes up a lot of space indoors and is sent to lie down beside the door. Kevin reports that it is getting too dark to manage, but he found more wood to cut and pull over another day. I peek out to see the pile and nod, "Looks like we have more than we started with! That's a good thing." The pluses have overtaken the minuses.

Kevin removes layers. He is very aware of the damp inner layer of clothing from the sweat of work. Wearing wet clothes will wick warmth away from the body. I see steam lifting off of his shoulders as he removes the warm, damp T-shirt and replaces it with a chilly, dry one. Stacking the layers back on, he washes his hands and comes to the table.

Our enamel camping bowls, this morning full of porridge, are now full of pea soup.

We hold hands and bow our heads. "O give thanks unto the Lord, for He is Good and His Mercy is forever. Amen."

It is comforting to recite together these words I have heard and said since I was a baby. For a moment, there is no distance between us and those we love. For a moment there is no obstacle or difficulty or hardship. For a moment, like when the clouds part and the sunbeams stream down in glory, we know that we are Provided for and Protected. For a moment my heart is open and courageous and certain. For a moment I squeeze my husband's hand as I did on our wedding day and I am united with him as we begin to do what we set out to do.

I lay thick slices of bread on the stove top to toast and bring them with honey for dessert.

"How about another round of dominoes?"

It is barely 5:30 and the day is done.

Pitch dark outside, I consider a trip to the outhouse. But it is ridiculous to bare any skin at this temperature. The chamber pot will be used night and day while this impossible cold lasts.

"Kevin, I've been thinking. On Saturday it will be payday. How will we get to town for my pay cheque?" Those picturesque winding forested roadways, those smooth highway miles suddenly seem ominous. The little village of Avola, smoke stacks puffing, signalling the comfort of homes nestled amongst the snowy mountains seem very, very far away.

"We'll have to hitchhike."

I raise my eyebrows, alarmed. I have never done such a thing. My Dad and his friends used to thumb a ride back in the

1940's. It was what people did. Not everyone had a car. Young men got a lift in to town. People travelled across the country to see America.

But these days it is considered dangerous. Women go missing. Bodies are found in the ditch. Rape and beatings, kidnapping and murder are real. For women.

"We will be together. We will be OK."

"After we have the pay cheque, how will we get to Clearwater for food? How will we get the load back home?" I don't want to whine. But I just don't see what will happen without our own vehicle.

"We'll walk to the highway, hitchhike to Avola, walk to Fran and Archie's, ask them for a ride to Clearwater. There has been no more snow since she came on Boxing Day, so her car will be OK to drive us back into our place. It was only two days ago. She said we could ask her for help. Then we'll be all set. No worries."

Sounds like an endurance test to me, I think inside my head. Out loud I point out, "We have no way of signalling her. She might leave for town before we get there?"

"We'll leave early in the morning to catch a ride. We'll phone Fran from the restaurant when you pick up your pay cheque."

OK. That means we have one more day here first. I'd better plan our shopping list carefully.

"Kevin, will you ask about working on the railroad? Now that you're finished building the cabin?" I groan inside, thinking of being alone in the wilderness while he's gone for the day. But no money would be bad, too. My income is done. Now we switch. I stay home and he goes out to earn.

"Of course. But not much will have changed since last week." There's Kevin's reality again. "We really can't predict when I will get a job."

"Cheryl said that the Road Master hires new guys often."
There I go, dreaming again.

"He fires them pretty fast, too, if they are late, drunk or he
thinks they might be using drugs," Kevin's practical reply.

"If they did hire you and you could start right away, how
would you get to work with no vehicle?" my future imaginings.

"We'll have to solve that problem if and when it arrives."

A story retold in my family comes to mind. Sleepwalking, my
seven-year-old brother was confused and crying. When Mother
coaxed him to tell her what was so troubling he explained his
dilemma, sobbing. "I can't get a job...if I don't have a car! But
I can't buy a car...if I don't have a job!"

"Do you think we should just stay in town now? Stay with
Fran and Archie again? or someplace else?" my imagination is
zipping about searching for an easy way out.

"No. We've gotten this far. We aren't going backwards.
I didn't build this house so we would not live in it." Kevin
speaks between spoonfuls of soup. "We're here now. We made
it. This cold won't last. The guys say it stays cold for a week or
so and then goes back up to only minus 20°. That's not so bad.
We can do it."

Well! At least I know what he's thinking.

"Dominoes?" he invites.

"It is too cold to sit at the table. My feet are freezing inside
my boots," I sulk. It's not fun to be cold anymore. But then
I think of the prize. If I win, and I think I can, then I get to stay in
bed tomorrow morning. So, I try. A few more minutes of cold
now in trade for a few more minutes of warmth later. Seems
like a good deal.

"Take your boot-liners out to dry," Kevin coaches as I get
ready for bed.

I hang them on a nail behind the stove.

He steps out to load in more wood. The cold slices into the cabin and I gasp and brace myself and hurry up into the loft. Warm air rises. There is a difference between the freezing cold floor, the air at the height of the fire and the up-in-the-loft, right-above-the-stove, almost-warm air. But still. There is no insulation in our cabin. Cracks between the floor boards draw in frigid air. Cracks between the ceiling boards show the inside surface of the black tar paper. The only really warm place is inside my own clothes and under these layers of bedding.

Last night, I couldn't get warm enough. The temperature dropped while we were asleep. Now I know. Now I can get prepared, physically and strategically to defend myself from the every-hungry cold. Long johns top and bottom I have been wearing day and night since we moved in, flannel PJs, wool sweater. Last night I added a wool toque and a pair of Kevin's wool socks.

We leave the bedding folded open to air out all day. It seems strange to make the bed this way, but the moisture needs to escape. So every night the routine nest-building is repeated. Actually, I am learning that there is a lot of repetition in this lifestyle.

Our winter-weight Polar-Guard™ sleeping-bags are zipped together. Last night I made use of the drawstring hood feature which kept the moving air away from my head and neck. Now I will tuck in my waistband, my ankles. The cold air is too harsh to let any skin show. On top of our sleeping-bags again I spread out Kevin's down sleeping-bag and the woolen quilt, and three blankets.

"I need another pair of your socks. Will you please pass up the kitten?" I call down.

The kitten burrows down, purring, glad to have my warmth added to her own and I feel likewise. What a difference it makes to have a small furry friend.

And a few minutes later, "Will you please pass up my parka?"

A head appears up the ladder and he hands me the coat which I spread over top of the pile. I feel like a hamster burrowed into my nest. Shivering until the cocoon warms up from my body heat, I tuck my head inside the blankets and my exhaled warm breath is captured and conserved. Curled up tight. Arms across my chest. Chin tucked low. Blankets up high. Hands in fists. Head covered. Only my nose is poking out for air. It seems possible that I will become warm enough to sleep.

Kevin pokes his head up again. "Time for our show," he announces. "Listen to this."

He puts the radio near my head on the boards near the edge of the loft. He blows out the lamp and by flashlight, he climbs up, opens the sleeping-bag with a knife-like slice of cold, and scooches in to settle for the night.

'Sears Radio Theatre.' It must be 8:00pm. Monday is a western. Tuesday is Comedy. Wednesday is Mystery. Thursday is Romance. Friday is Adventure.

"Today is Thursday, right?' Kevin likes to be the host. "I wonder what it will be about?"

I was asleep. I'm awake now.

And so, another routine is added to our daily life in the woods: kindling and wood, melting snow for water, feeding the animals and making our meals, trips to dump the slop-water bucket and the pee-pot, after supper dominoes game, go to bed early to save lamp oil, but enjoy the entertainment in the dark while tightly secure in our wrappings, all night up and down the ladder to feed the fire. That's the plan.

The radio play is a real treat. Sound effects coax the imagination to fill in details. Dramatic voices give the listener the hint of facial expressions. Narrator describes the setting. Music sets the mood.

The advertisements are also fun to listen to. It is different from TV. There is so much more of the message that has to be conveyed with only the voice. Social friendliness is conveyed as two women compare their problem with the solution the product offers. Warmth is coupled with persuasion as the narrator emphasizes the benefits of using the product. A man's voice states some scientific facts. A woman's voice shares her satisfaction with the product. The narrator offers guarantees and information as to where the product can be purchased. A jingle, tune, rhyme or slogan plants the product name in the listener's brain. The shopper will remember the message when he or she sees the label.

Before the show ends, there is an announcement to "stay tuned for the next hour" for the nightly murder mystery.

I bravely offer to feed the fire.

When I get back, Kevin has dozed off.

The murder mystery has begun. I am wide awake!

Spooky sounds, creaky doors, gun shots, screams, running footsteps, a telephone ringing, a siren, theme music fill my mind with scary images and alarming possibilities. My heart is racing. My secluded cottage feels dangerously isolated.

How will I calm my mind enough to actually sleep?

The next hour after the murder mystery is a church service. I listen to the choir. The hymn is familiar. The Bible text restores a sense of security. The droning voice of the preacher causes me to drift away. My heart rate slows and my imagination calms and begin to sleep. No. Not yet. It has been over two hours since the fire was fed. I brace myself for the plunge and slide out of the sleeping-bag. Push the flashlight button. Back down the ladder. Poke the coals. Shove in first small, then large pieces of wood. Pause to hear the fire catch. Shut all the vents and chimney damper. Scurry back up the ladder. Oh, how I hope the bedding still holds some of my hard-won warmth.

Set the alarm clock for one-and-a-half hours. I scrunch in, readjusting the layers, tucking in all gaps, pressing my back up against my husband's. Seek sleep. Don't count anything. Not money. Not days. Not water. Not wood. Not food. Not miles. Not hours. Just sleep.

One-and-a-half hours tick by and the alarm clock shocks the brain. Nudge Kevin. "It's your turn." I doze off. No movement. Doze off. Jerk awake. I go down. Yipes. It is cold. The coals are so small. I need my parka, but it's up in the loft. I pull on Kevin's coat and my boot-liners. I pull the coals together. Slide open the vents. Turn the damper open. Birch bark, shredded, criss-cross kindling, little wood slabs of the lumber. Wait. Breathe in. Breathe out. Wait. Blow. Poke. Wait. There it goes. Snap! Snap! Carefully stack on more fuel. Wait. Yes, it is going to catch. Slide closed the air vents, turn shut the damper. Out of the boot-liners and coat. Yipes again. Up. In. Reset the alarm.

Next time, it *is* his turn!

How many one-and-a-half-hours are there in one night?

No. I don't want my brain to start all of this math again. I just want to find the pathway to sleep. It seems that the more exhausted I get from night after night of broken sleep, the harder it is so be quiet and still in my mind.

I went to bed at 5:30pm. Kevin fed the fire and came up at 7:00. The radio plays go from 8:00-9:00. I added fuel and then listened to the mystery from 9:00-10:00. The preacher started at 10:00. I fed the fire at about 10:30. Now is 12:30am, next 2:00am, then 3:30am, 5:00am and it will still be pitch dark at 6:30m and it will be getting light at 8:00am. Ugh. That is a lot of waking and sleeping. A lot of ladders and kindling. A lot of shivering and burrowing. A lot of effort and not much reward. But the alternative is horrifying. We can't let the cold take over every single object in our house. Every sock and towel. Every onion and carrot. My hairbrush and tooth paste. The box of matches. If every item is colder than a walk-in freezer. How can we possibly survive?

No. We have to keep it up. Tomorrow I can nap. One good thing. Let me think of one good thing. The sky is clear when the weather is this cold. The sun will shine and the blue sky will be splendid. One more good thing: no mice tonight. I guess they are staying warmly tucked into their nests, too.

Chapter 9
December 29, 1978
Friday

If you love someone, set them free.
If they come back they're yours.
If they don't, they never were.
—*Richard Bach*

What is that horrible, annoying, metallic, clanging noise?

I struggle up and out with effort. The door I must push open is so heavy as I attempt to climb up out of the comforting world of sleep and enter the harsh world of awake. It is so hard to move. Dreams are so much more real and pleasant than this unreal, ever-pressing cold. I need a crow bar to open my eyes.

It's the alarm clock. Doing what I told it to do. Interrupting. Clamouring. Insistent. Unrelenting.

I can't find the wires that signal my limbs to move. I can't figure out the complexity of arranging my muscles to shed the sleeping-bag, locate the flashlight, balance my weight on the ladder.

The cold is too terrible. What good does it do to keep the fire going anyway? I can't feel any warmth rising up into the loft.

"Kevin…" nudge, nudge, "Kevin…can you do it this time?"

Big sigh. Long pause. I doze off into bliss. Jerk awake with a jolt.

If I don't feed the coals which willingly ignite the newly placed wood, if I wait until there is only ash, the shivering additional time it will take to relight, stand and wait, blow and protect a brand-new fire will be worse than the plunge into the vicious chill for a quick renewal now.

OK. OK. Here I go.

Will power. Focus. This is the lesser of two evils. I push back the layers of coverings, a little clumsily. 'Accidentally-on-purpose' I meanly shift so that my exit will blast my unmoving husband with the frigid air.

Yes, the coals are orangely glowing. Yes, the kindling will catch. Yes, the snapping sap signals a healthy start. Yes, larger pieces fit tightly. Yes, shut sliders to reduce air and extend the life of the flame.

One good thing. One luxury I can look forward to: Kevin has to get up first in the morning. I won the dominoes game last night. Oh, yes I did! As darkness smothered the day, I was moody and grumpy, but Kevin suggested a round of dominoes and the game cheered me up. At first I found it hard to concentrate. I think that the lack of sleep is eroding my nerves. But, the sense of competition boiled up and the motivation of the prize helped me focus. The agreed upon prize is more time in bed for the Victorious while the Defeated attends to the bubbling breakfast.

Reset the clock. Tuck it under the mattress. Shiver until body heat saturates the layers. The only warm place is in dreamland.

Jangling again. Kevin's turn. I'm awake anyways. But at least I can stay wrapped. Is there anything else I can do to shield myself from this cold? It is seeping between gaps, drilling through the layers. Mentally I inventory what other resources I might have.

Kevin crawls back up into the loft. "Shine the light for me," I command. Swiftly, losing heat, I open a box at the foot of the bed under the eaves. There it is. I pull off the heavy navy blue wool sweater, pull on the dark green wool turtle neck sweater, replace the thick blue layer. Now my neck has insulation. Wool feels good.

Spooning, we help each other regain the warmth that was lost in the quest for fire.

The clock says it is morning, although the sun is too lazy to make an appearance.

I gotta pee. So, although I won the privilege of sleeping longer, I forfeit my prize to Nature's Call.

Tugging my down parka on, slipping my feet into the boot-liners which may as well have been imported from a distant ice-locked planet, I am stunned to realize that I will need to set the enamel chamber pot on the stove top to melt it enough to release the pee-sicle so I can dump it in the outhouse!

Seriously? Every daily habit has become part of an obstacle course as the cold rips away normalcy and replaces it with problems to solve. And the problem solving part of my brain is foggy, exhausted, depleted, dull.

Grey dawn makes it possible to see inside without the lamp.

I whip through morning chores quickly so I can return and stand beside the stove and drink in the lovely heat. "You'd think I'd know by now," I mutter to myself, but it comes as a surprise that everything I touch is cold. The hand full of cat food I grab in my fist and trickle into her bowl is bitingly cold. The scoop in the dog food bag shocks my grip with cold. Each piece of firewood sucks the warmth out of my fingers. My boots inject cold into my already rapidly chilling feet. Mittens deliver cold. I fumble with the sliding door handle. The morning air slaps my face, pierces through my layers, stabs my lungs.

The thermometer howls with laughter. The red mercury is shriveled into the bulb. Still 40° below.

Now I'm mad. It's not my turn. I won the game. Now I feel sorry for myself. Why do I have to do this? Clamping my jaw shut against shivers rattling and revengeful unspoken words, I scoop all of the pots full of snow. The world is one big repetitive to-do list. An endless cycle of necessary movement. There's no way out.

Back inside, the snow on the bottom of each pot sizzles into steam on the cast iron stove top. Mittens off, I hold my hands open as close to the flames as I dare. My legs feel the heat penetrating my layers. Unzipped, I hold my coat winged open, collecting heat. My front half is warmer, my back half is still cold. Turning my back to the heat source, I need to cross my arms and tuck my hands into my armpits inside my closed-again coat to conserve the heat they absorbed from the fire.

Now I notice the water jar on the counter top less than three feet away from the all-night fire. It is frozen solid.

This is awful. I can hardly stand this. Food, shelter and clothing are life's essentials. I have all of that. I have safety and clean water and fresh air and soon I'll have sunshine. But what good are any of them if everything you touch is frozen like a rock?

Before it gets too hot and shatters the glass, I strain the melted snow-water through the towel, then pour it into the porridge pot. Lift the stove lid to place the pot directly over the flame. Stir in handfuls of oats.

Kevin is still asleep. I eat. Standing. I bend forward over the stove top to catch the rising heat on my face. Fill the stove with wood again. Shut it down. There's no point standing here. There is only one place I can hope to be warm. Back to bed.

"I left your porridge in the warming oven. I need to sleep. Please keep the fire going. Please don't wake me." I am blunt. I am so sleep deprived. My head hurts.

Distantly aware, noises tell me what is happening down the ladder. Spoon clinking on bowl: Kevin is eating. Clattering iron: Kevin is loading wood on the fire. Tromping floor: Kevin has his boots on. Creaking hinge: Kevin is going outside. Yelping dog: Kevin is dragging the sled. Rhythmic grating: Kevin is sawing more wood.

I sleep. Deep. No alarm clock. Safe. Oh, how I hope I can refill my brain with what-ever-it-makes while I sleep.

It must be after 10:00. I know because the sun has finally climbed up and over the mountain to shine bright and bold into the south facing windows of our cabin. I am awake. Why? I hear a steady, rhythmic, thumping softness. The cabin shudders with weight thrown against it. What is happening?

Sliding out and down, I see Kevin through the window. He is shoveling snow against the house, filling in the empty space between the lowest log and the earth. Now the arctic delivery of air will stop flowing under the floor. The air will be still, trapped. Less heat will escape from the cabin through the cracks between the floor boards. Less frosty air will enter our dwelling place.

Grateful for his idea and effort, I am also annoyed and offended that my sleep has been robbed yet again. What is happening to my brain by this continuously shattered sleep? Didn't I read somewhere that the REM cycle of dreams must be experienced and that breaking it brings serious consequences? Oh, my head hurts.

Poke the fire. Feed the fire. Gear on. I shuffle outside to help, at least a little. Bleary eyed, grim faced, I bend and lift to scoop more snow. I bend and lift to stack more wood. I can't keep up any cheerful banter. It's already too hard to make my muscles move. I can't be expected to multitask a conversation, too. I don't remember how to make a smile. I used to smile. A long time ago.

More snow for water. More wood for fire. Lunch? A can of soup is easiest.

The can is cold. The can opener is cold. The soup in the can is frozen. I have to dig it out with a fork. The fork is cold. Red shards of crystallized tomato soup swim and soften and melt in the used-to-be-snow water. Stirring. Waiting. Leaning in, my face is soaking up heat above the steaming soup. Warm the bowls, otherwise they will zap the heat from the food.

Kevin is enthused, telling me about his morning accomplishments. He was tinkering with the van, trying to pump some kind of life back into the engine. Was it the battery? spark-plugs? fuel line? He tried the what's-its and wiggled the thing-y.

He tested the something-or-other and attempted to correct the do-dad. He likes me to praise him and admire his skill, strength and plans. He wants me to say, "Good for you" and "That's nice" and "Wow" and "You're so clever."

My left elbow is on the table. My heavy forehead is supported by my left hand. In my right hand, the spoon is a challenging weight. "Kevin, I can't understand what you are talking about." My eyes lift to make contact with his, but he seems so far away.

Discouraged. He is silent.

Disgruntled. I feel a wave of self-pity engulf me. Blocking my mouth from uttering any words, miserable thoughts swirl inside, but are not spoken. "Sure. You're the hero. Clever mechanic. Big muscles. Braving the wilderness. Important 'Man' work. You can fix things and make things and drive machinery and get the wood and be the 'Mountain Man'. I get to be the 'Little Lady' and stay inside and feed the fire and melt the snow and stir the soup. Nobody gives me a trophy. Nobody thinks what I do is important. Nobody brags. 'Guess what I did today? I melted snow so we could have water to drink.'"

I tell myself, "Don't say it. Don't start. You don't really think like that." Where are these nasty thoughts coming from? Like insects swarming around me, I swat them back.

But, invisible, they keep attacking. "Sheesh! Men get paid for the work they do. I'll never get paid for the work I do in a day." Men's roles. Women's roles. Really? I have to fight this battle now?

Slop through the dish washing. Melt more snow. Feed the fire. Stand and breathe in warm air. Hold my hands over the heat.

"I'm going back to bed," my eyes down, without touching him, I slide past him sitting at the table on his stump to get to the ladder.

My body is still. But my mind keeps racing.

Tomorrow is payday. I worked six days for eight hours at $2.57 per hour. My pay cheque will be $123.36. We have almost no supplies. Every penny has gone into building, driving back and forth to work and start-up essentials, like buying a kerosene lamp. Since we have been moving from place-to-place, we have not stocked up on food. We have been guests. We have been provided for.

Without the van, how are we even going to get to town to get the pay cheque? The temperature is a very significant factor. It is two miles to the highway. It is not too far to walk. But is it safe to do so? Frostbite is a real threat. And, even if our moving muscles keep us warm enough, how long will we stand still beside the highway waiting to get a ride? Is it a fair trade: frostbite for food? I have never, ever hitchhiked. I am terrified, knowing that women go missing.

Supposing we get a safe ride and we get north ten miles to Avola for my pay cheque, supposing Fran and Archie are willing to give us a ride the 45 miles south to Clearwater to cash the cheque and buy groceries and north again 45 miles to return with our load? $123.36. Can we buy everything we need with $123.36? Can we carry everything that we buy? It's a two mile hike! I'm tired already!

And once we arrive safely home with supplies, after a summer of camping and solving the problem of keeping food cold enough, after those first few nights in the cabin solving the problem of keeping the mice out of our food, now we will have to deal with food that is frozen rock-hard right inside our house!

And here's a dreadful thought: since the fire will be out while we're gone for the entire day, by the time we get home every single item in our whole house will be the same fierce temperature inside and out.

And the unspoken biggest question: What's next? My job is over. After this pay cheque is gone there is no more money. None. Zero. Kevin has just now finished building the cabin. As thankful as I am to God's Omnipotent Providence for this perfect timing, there is still the reality that he has not applied for a job or interviewed anywhere. And, even if a successful job opportunity was within reach, he has no way to travel to it.

$123.36. It has to last for an unknown amount of time. Like a shear drop-off, we stand at the edge of a cliff. That's all we have. That's all there is.

How did we get to this situation? Why are we doing this? Shall we stay? Maybe after only seven nights and seven days we should give up, go to another town, get a job, rent an apartment and begin again in the spring?

Laughter sounds in my head. Mocking faces of my co-workers at the restaurant. Relatives with eyebrows raised. I remember just before our wedding, when Kevin was one day later than expected from his canoe trip, his sister-in-law said, "Maybe he's not coming." Like he would 'leave me at the altar.' Really? I can hear the echo of my own Dad saying, "I just don't want you to come begging back to my door." Then there were those days when Kevin seemed paralyzed this autumn while he was supposed to be building. He couldn't get away from the voices of the men he worked with in the factory. "You'll never make it" and "You'll be back" and "We'll save your locker" and other comments less worth repeating.

Why do people doubt us?

Quitting. They all think we're going to give up and quit. Well, maybe we won't quit. We could just step aside for awhile.

It would be a logical and sensible thing to do. We just have to say, "Oops. We got a little ahead of ourselves." We could pause without quitting. Couldn't we? Or: We could stay here just to 'prove it' to 'everyone.' But, why would we keep going when it is unendurable and there are three more weeks of 40° below and three more months of snowy chill? And who is 'everyone?' And ...

Why do we need to 'prove' anything?

Unable to sleep and dizzy with inner-conflict I push away the layers of bedding and descend to attempt to open a logical discussion with my husband. Quietly.

"Kevin, what if we go back to town? We don't have to stay here. No one is forcing us to endure this." He's likely been debating the same question in his own head.

But, he's already fought this battle. And, he's already won. He has more determination to stay. His own comfort is not a weight on the balance. The thermometer is not the deciding factor. His dream has a deeper purpose than my 'Little House on the Prairie' visions where every TV episode presents a conflict which is resolved within one hour. Cue the music. Camera zooms in to smiles and hugs. Wipe your eyes from the tears of joy. All is well. Pa and Ma can overcome their challenges.

Kevin's motivation comes from the example of his Dad. As a young man, Harold's desire was 'Go West.' He wanted to scale mountains. Go hunting and fishing. See Alaska. Ride the rails and enjoy scenic Canada. Harold wanted to achieve a lifestyle which steps away from the roar of engines, the smoke of factories, the pace of the city, the pressure of conformity, the heavy load of debt, the ticking of the clock, the foreman always watching, the bombardment of advertising from the consumer society. His aim was a life based on self-reliance, practical skills, lasting values and inner courage. He had a farm boy's upbringing. He knew what he was capable of.

But, circumstances dictated otherwise. Kevin's parents were married just as the 'Call to Arms' sounded for Canadian men to come to England's aid. Married in uniform, Harold and Adele had only two weeks together before he left on the Queen Mary. He did not return for years, until the end of World War II. Her employment was in the city. When he returned, their first child arrived very soon. A second son lived only a few days. Kevin's healthy birth was a treasure to both of them. Factory jobs were steady. Setting his ambition aside, putting family first, Harold was a dutiful provider, walking to work in a factory year after year.

Teaching his son both outdoor know-how and those lessons of values which are interwoven in the Father-Son bond, Kevin heard his Father describe his goals. But then, a stroke. Harold's life was suddenly torn away after lying in the hospital, unconscious, for three days. Kevin was only thirteen years old.

This great loss is fueling Kevin's pledge to accomplish what his Father had to set aside. Unwavering, a little thing like 40° below zero will not deter him from his mission.

The sun has set over the steeply walled mountain. There is not much more daylight before the shroud of darkness claims the land.

"Not in Avola," I rush ahead. "We've already asked Fran and Archie for so much. I don't want to be a parasite. We could go to the city. We could both get jobs. We could pay rent. We could take the bus to work." I coax aloud. Unspoken the message: "We could be like everybody else."

He lowers his head to his folded arms on the table. No reply.

"My pay cheque might be enough for a bus ticket back east?"

Persuasion is not something I have mastered.

Debate is not something Kevin participates in.

There is no place for me to go as the daylight fades except to retreat to my sleeping-bag again.

Kevin struggles silently in the circle of lamplight on the table.

I struggle silently in my cocoon.

The bare facts: We have a post office box number. We have a roof and walls. We have a dog and a cat. We have a VW van that does not run. We have (if we can go get it) $123.36. We have wedding rings and the vow they represent: 'To love, honour, comfort, and cleave unto you alone that we may dwell together in the holy state of marriage according to the ordinance of our God,' forever.

The raw despair is too much to dwell on. The strain is inescapable. I cannot leave. I have to get out of here.

Imagination, richly detailed, provides me with an escape. I can go anywhere I want to go. I can relive any experience I want to return to. I can revisit all of the people who love me. I can march down the corridor of time and observe my own motivation.

Expanding and savouring, I recall each place I have lived. The winding, hilly, tree lined, narrow roads in Pennsylvania, security and family ties, the wealth of the Church I have been raised in. The sense of belonging is powerful and nourishing.

The canyon-like ever-climbing highway in Colorado, leading to the property which has been in my Dad's family for three generations, the rustic cabin he brought us to, the architect designed house he had built. Dad's academic accomplishments and Mother's creative ideas provided for our family's needs. The sense of satisfaction is what I am seeking.

The Spanish moss and suburban street in Florida, swimming in the ocean and searching for treasures along the sandy beach, we experienced one year without winter. The sense of family togetherness and exploring is at the heart of my dream.

The Church community in Ontario where neighbours shared beliefs, music, celebrations, cousins, school events, life events. The sense of abundance and connection was ever present.

What exactly was my motivation for permanently severing these bonds, walking away from this cornucopia of pleasant experiences? Why would I trade all of that for this rugged hardship, agonizing isolation, unending endurance test?

Maybe I am crazy. Maybe I should have stayed in the 'women's role' that the Church expected of me. But the pressure was unbearable. Smiling, nodding, I felt like a bird with wings bound tightly. I could sense the road up ahead with a sign reading, 'This is driving me mad.'

Maybe I can't help it. Maybe it's inevitable and I'll end up in the 'Loony Bin.' After all, people say traits run in the family. "You look so much like your Aunt Madeline," I have heard since I was very small. "You are so smart like your Aunt Madeline," they coach my Mother to allow me, like her, to skip two grades. But what became of her?

Shuddering, I try to shut the door before the nightmarish stories of attempted treatments for my (is she bipolar? is she schizophrenic?) Aunt rush in to frighten me. It was the 1950's and 1960's. New treatments to try. Mismanaged medications. Therapy gone wrong. Electric shock to her head. Hospital corridors. Children boarding with relatives. Whispers. That look in people's eyes when her name is mentioned. Police. Wailing. Fear. Laughing. Confusion. Loyalty and innocence stripped away leaving wreckage from the storm.

Is it happening to me? Am I crazy? Will I go crazy? Do I have a choice? Will insanity come and overtake me? How can I tell if it is happening? Can I pull myself back from the brink?

Leaving reality behind has a certain attraction. Anything but this.

Sleep deprivation, now there's a real situation.

Losing her marbles. Nut case. Fruit cake. Off her rocker. The lights are on but nobody's home.

I'm so scared.

I don't know what to do. No matter which way I turn in my mind, which pathway I take, each leads to an impossible riddle, an unresolveable conflict, more confusion.

Sucking swamp, impenetrable jungle, scorching desert, hazardous rock slide.

I'm so alone.

I can't seem to tell the difference between clear, solid logic and swirling, quicksand insanity.

Stumbling in the fog.

Trapped in a maze.

Pushing through a deep snow drift.

Slipping up a sand dune.

The effort to keep going is exhausting.

The energy I spend brings me no closer to a safe haven.

I can't remember what or where is the goal.

I feel lost at sea. Is there a life raft or anchor that I can cling to? A lighthouse that can warn and guide me?

"God? Help me."

More spiraling doubts. More conflicting voices. Is God real? Can He really see, hear, help and guide me? I have always believed. I have never doubted. Now that I am in difficulty, do I walk away from Him? Has He turned His back on me? Do I give up because, for the first time in my life, I am experiencing discomfort?

Where dreams meet reality I wander, gathering clues, linking details, piecing fragments into a whole.

Back and back in time I focus my mind. There have been so many times I thought I was following the Lord's guidance. Details fit together that I had no way of constructing, no way to foresee outcomes, tiny prompts I followed. How did I feel sure of that then? How can I discern God's guidance now? Stay. Or. Go.

> One thing have I desired of the Lord that will I seek after,
> that I may dwell in the house of the Lord all the days of my life,
> to behold the beauty of the Lord and to inquire in His temple.[17]

My Father recited these words when he led family worship in my childhood. Kevin and I had these words printed on our engagement announcement. This focal point underscores our decisions, nourishes us when forces seem to derail our pledge. 'One thing' gives direction to our future.

What else am I sure of? What core of certainty can I cling to? What unshakable foundation can I solidly stand on? Memory verses from elementary school begin to spill into my mind. Nourishment? Mocking? Central? Distant?

> Thou shalt love the Lord thy God
> with all thy heart, with all thy soul,
> with all thy mind and with all thy strength.
> This is the First Commandment
> and the Second is like unto it.
> Thou shalt love thy neighbour as thyself.[18]

If God is only in church, He has no Presence here. I have no hope. If God is real, then there must be a way He can reach me here. If there is no God, then this would be a good time for me to say, 'Me First' and walk away from any promise I spoke, any pledge I ever made.

> What doeth the Lord require of thee, but to do justly, and to love mercy, and to walk humbly with thy God.[19]

Does He require suffering? What if I turn away and 'walk' without Him?

> I am come that you may have life, and have it more abundantly.[20]

Well, that would not be this.

> Ask, and it shall be given you;
> Seek and ye shall find;
> Knock and it shall be opened unto you.[21]

Yes, I have certainly asked. I asked for exactly this: husband, mountains, cabin. And I was given exactly this: husband, mountains, cabin...and 40 below. Six days ago I was bounding with joy and overflowing with thanksgiving. I was astonished to recount how every door seemed to burst open, every obstacle seemed to melt away, every challenge seemed to be Provided for, everything I was searching for I found. What was I thinking? That there would be no difficulty? No hardship?

> As for me and my house, we will serve the Lord.[22]

Yes, I want to, but how can I do that curled up in a ball, battling unseen enemies, hearing vicious laughter.

> These three things I pray
> Day by day...
> To see Thee more clearly,
> Love Thee more dearly,
> Follow Thee more nearly.[23]

I believe these. At least I did yesterday. But none of them, like a math question, tell me 'the' answer. Stay. Or. Go. Where do I see the Lord more clearly?

"Please, God, show me which direction!" I'm moaning deep inside.

Some of the Psalms record this moaning. Perhaps I am in territory that others have experienced. Perhaps this is not mental illness rearing its ugly head. Perhaps this is part of 'The Journey.'

'The Lord is my Shepherd...'[24] I am indeed the Little Lost Lamb. He is looking for me. I am looking for Him. Is this what the Shepherd provides? Is this what I accept? Or do I take action?

Perhaps my steady, reliable husband has a more clear sense of direction.

Down the ladder, tears welling up, spilling over, carefully controlled gasps. "Kevin. Please. Can we go?"

He turns to me, deeply sincere, eyes steady, his voice identical to the precious "I do" he spoke only six months ago. "You may go where ever you go, for as long as you need to go. I am not going to stop you. I will be here. This is where I live. This is my home. I will stay."

A strange howling cry escapes my throat, collapsing to the floor, buckled over, head down. I gasp and sob a begging sound. I let out a long anguished moan. Each of three long breaths expressing bottled up anxiety and fear and anger and longing and grief and desperation and dread.

Then, spent, a sudden shudder like thunder. Total silence. Time stands still. I see in myself the 'sin' of the first wife, luring Adam to be less than who God made him to be. "Just this one little adjustment to the Plan."

I am Eve. I think I have a better idea than God. "I really like the Garden You gave me, but, no, thanks, God. You have Your

Way, I have mine. I'd rather listen to the present doubts then the past certainty."

I have tempted my husband. Tested his resolve. Eclipsed his calling. I have tried to influence him to turn away, to be less than who God has called him to be. And. I have nearly broken the same in myself...attempted to be less than what God has called me to be.

Suddenly still. Silent. In shock.

They were kicked out of the Garden. Shall I stay in mine?

The only oasis, my bed.

In a blinding flash I face 'alone.' Here we are: two people in the same environment, eating the same food, breathing the same air, sleeping in the same bed, both physically feeling the harsh, penetrating chill. Together. But, our experiences are vastly different.

The naked truth of existence: "I am alone."

'Alone' is how we are born. 'Alone' is how we each die, and in fact, although linked with bonds of love, 'alone' is how we, in essence, are. However, 'by myself' is not the direction I want to go. I will not abandon my husband. I will not sabotage the dream. I will not take all the money and leave. I will not hitch-hike, homeless. I will not go back to live in the too-small trailer with Fran and Archie. I will not go begging to my Dad. I will not seek asylum within the Church community.

With x-ray vision I see myself. I can't go back east to my former life, either, and for my own reasons. There is something back there that is too terrible to live with. Something worse than 40° below. It will be hard to endure 100 more days of winter. But there are two unendurable things back there which I will not return to.

The first unendurable thing came to my attention within four months of attending Church school. When my Dad moved us to Canada in 1969, the enveloping warmth of the Church community was blissful. But the Pastor taught something in religion class that Christmas unlike anything I had ever heard before. By the definition of the Seer (who claims to have spoken to Mary in Heaven face-to-face), Mary was not the pure vessel, like the Ark of the Covenant in the Holiest place in the Tabernacle, through which God could enter time and space to dwell among us. According to the writings of the Seer, and thus the teachings of this new Church, Mary was a source of contagion! Through her, the Pastor explained, her Son would be contaminated by 'hereditary evil' which He would gradually overcome and become Divine by 'putting off what He had received from His Mother.'

What does this mean? Every Christmas card depicting the Madonna and Child is false? Her sweet face and gentle hands are actually foul? Jesus came to earth for the purpose of rejecting what Mary gave Him? If we are to follow Him, then are we to pull away from our own Mothers? Who can you rely on if you cannot trust your own Mother?

I was only twelve years old. Something quiet and fierce formed deep inside me. "This is not true."

But, there was no place for me to turn. Surrounded by parents, neighbours, school and Church which all agree, where could I go for consideration, for confirmation? At that time and in that place it was forbidden to consult other forms of Christianity.

I could see that the entire structure of who Jesus was hinged on what happened in Mary's womb. God, mankind, sin, salvation, history, the hereafter, text, prayer, song, cultures all pivot on the definition of this moment. What was being asked of her? What did her "Yes" mean?

I was so young, yet, I vowed to read and ask and listen and question and continue searching for a satisfactory truth. And when I find truth, like clear, free-flowing water, I will share it with others.

But wait. This solemn solitary pledge brought me to the second unendurable thing.

"I want to be a Minister," I told my Pastor.

"No, the Seer wrote that a woman cannot be a Minister," was his immediate reply.

I cannot change my gender. He cannot change the Text.

The pain caused by my ever-earnestly-seeking to 'serve God' and the impossibility of doing so simply because I am a girl was the fuel driving my decision to put a continent between me and my former Church community.

Why?

Latin words.

200 years ago the Seer, who claims to have been in contact with the Spiritual World daily for 26 years, wrote 40 books which are the foundation upon which this Church was organized. The Church community around me considers these writings to be a new Divine Revelation.

One sentence, actually a fragment of a sentence, penned in his Spiritual Diary, seen by members of this new Church as Sacred Writ, declares that the intellect of a woman who preaches becomes 'crazed' although she may still seem in outward appearance to be normal.

No one would want a crazy clergy. Therefore, no women shall be ordained.

Could Latin words, written over 200 years ago, in a diary, hold this Taboo power over me? Feigning ignorance, while I was fifteen years old and the only volunteer to teach Grade 5

Sunday School, I disregarded the ban on women reading aloud from the Bible and boldly strode forward bringing stories to life through songs, activities and art projects.

Meanwhile, I read the New Testament for myself to prepare for the Sunday School lessons and I noticed one thing. There are no parentheses in Jesus' instructions.

Follow me and I will make you fishers of men[25]

...(but not the women)...

Go ye therefore and teach all nations[26]

...(but not the women)...

Let your light shine[27]

...(but not the women)...

No! It seems to me that this barricade preventing women from becoming educated, equipped and encouraged to share the Good News is a structure that people have put there, not what Jesus Himself ordained.

The Seer mentioned that he had seen a woman in Hell who had been a preacher during her life on earth. But, that doesn't make sense. People don't go to Hell because of their career path? They go to Hell because they deliberately turn away from the Lord, insist on staying that way and refuse to repent and accept the forgiveness He pours out for everyone continually.

How could I ever return to live in a culture which has this suspicious view of me? Is a woman who desires to serve the Lord with heart, soul, mind and strength through reading the Word of God aloud a Divine 'No-No'? Ordination, a paid position, a voice reaching out, a voice calling others to come in... how could this be 'crazed?'

It is a terrifying conflict.

I am so young. I am so sincere. I am torn. "I can't. I have to."

The Pastor dismissed me without a pause to attempt to comprehend the 'calling' I tried to explain. The God he understood had declared a wall forbidding me to read the Word of God aloud to others, learn how to listen and counsel using its Wisdom, banishing potential for females in any meaningful role in the organization of the Church...it was all too much to either overcome or accept.

They see a woman speaking as crazy. But, not speaking is what will make me crazy.

So, in order to serve the Lord, I left the Church.

And this is where it has gotten me. Exiled. Not on a boat adrift like Noah. Not jailed in Egypt like Joseph the dream interpreter. Not wandering in a hot desert like the Children of Israel. Not homeless refugees like Mary and Joseph leaving Bethlehem.[28] But, outcast, in the Frozen North.

What does this agony have to do with worship? This pit of doom have to do with angelic heights? This 'alone' have to do with the One?

Now my eyes are opened. I see what I have never seen, although it was there all of the time. These Bible 'heroes' (and heroines) are named and their stories recorded precisely because they believed God was still with them even when their lives got impossibly difficult.

"I was talking to God and He said 'build a boat.' So, I did. But look at me now: 40 days and 40 nights of rain...and now these 150 days of the doldrums. How do I know it was actually God?"

"I had a dream that God would put me in a position of leadership. But look at me now: I'm in prison accused of a crime I did not do. Maybe the dream was meaningless?"

"I saw a burning bush. My rod parted the sea. I thought I heard God's Commands. All of these people expect me to lead them. But look at me now: we keep wandering in circles year after year."

"I heard an angel declaring my Child to be the Son of God. But look at me now: sleeping in a stinky barn. Maybe it was an illusion?"

Although none of them mentioned being this cold, they all had a length of time when darkness and disconnect might have filled them with fear and a sense of abandonment. However, it *was* God speaking. They each said, "Yes." Then it got hard. They all had to wait. They kept reminding themselves: 'He *did* promise.' And then, at last, in an unexpected way: He gave what He spoke. He finished what He started. Although for a period of time they did not see any evidence, they did continue to believe. God gave a Message. He will continue to Provide.

Like the deep groaning rumble as the earth rearranges her layers, a heavy cornerstone shifts in my mind. Maybe this pain is more to the point than the pretty Sunday School pictures. Maybe this is the 'Narrow Way.'[29] Maybe Jesus Himself stood in this place. Can you believe when you cannot see? Can you obey when you cannot hear? Can you finish the assignment you were called to do? Can you stay on the Path? When others laugh and shake their heads and its all upstream can you keep going?

Maybe the answer is, 'No thanks. I quit.'

Maybe the answer is, 'Not by myself. Only with You. I still believe You are near me. I can't see. You can. I have no strength. You do. Please, help me.'

At an irreversible turning point my mouth silently forms, "Yes" and I stand with the others in a place of belief that my Maker will Give and Provide.

Down to face my husband. Red-eyed, but quietly calm, I speak deliberately.

"I will stay. I want to stay. You are my home."

Seeking calories to fuel our bodies, I fry pancakes for supper deeply in oil, pouring melted honey on top. I need to shine a flashlight into the pan to see if they are crisp and ready. My husband's hands are warm as we bow our heads asking a blessing on our home, food and decision. I soak in all the heat from the golden food, sun-drenched, colony-gathered honey, calming mint tea.

Quickly back up to curl and breathe slowly, deeply, relax and try to release tense muscles, I remember another point of view which captures accurately what I meant when I said, "I want to be a minister." Surely, not a crime against the Almighty. Surely not rebellion from such a young, innocent heart. Surely not toppling the mind into insanity.

I can be a Bodhisattva.[30]

When I was in public high school World Religions class, I read this description from Buddhism. I thought, "This is what I meant when I said I wanted to be a minister."

Three companions are journeying through a seemingly endless desert. Exhausted, dry, at last they see a beautiful golden city up ahead. Hurrying, eagerly they search all around it. The walls are high. There seems to be no entrance.

The first of the travellers climbs up on the shoulders of his friends, looks inside, yells 'Eureka' and jumps inside.

The second climbs up and disappears over the wall.

The third, with great effort, climbs the wall and sees a garden, fountains, beauty, abundance.

But, instead of entering this wonderful place, the person jumps back down, returns across the desert and tells others how to find their way.

This is the Bodhisattva.

Dictionary definition: Bodhisattva. noun. Buddhism. 'An enlightened being who, out of compassion, forgoes Nirvana in order to save others.'

Perhaps, although I cannot see what, when or how, there is something I need to live through here that will one day be meaningful to others.

But it is not 'Nirvana' I will be sharing.

Distilled from thousands of years of individual's experiences and hundreds of pages of ancient text, the kernel, the whole point of the Bible is this. And this I not only believe, I now have experienced: "Emmanuel. God is with us."

I am one of the ones who was lost. I am one of the ones who is found. I am one of the ones who wants to share this message.

Same night-time routines. Same radio. Same fire. Same alarm clock. Same impossible cold. Same resources. New resolve.

Chapter 10
December 30, 1978
Saturday

Undertake difficult tasks
by approaching
what is easy in them.
Do great deeds
by focusing
on their minute aspects.
—*Tao*

We have to eat before we go.

Although the fire was kept smouldering all night, the outdoor temperature is still -40°C.

A scoop of snow melts, boils, oatmeal is ready.

By lamplight we bundle up, scarves around our faces, wearing empty backpacks. Kevin locks the door.

"Stay!" I point Sam to his bedding of straw under the cabin. Ember is much too small to stay outside.

No moon. Only starlight sparkles, reflecting off the snow. We need the flashlight for the pathway, but when we get to the road the wheel ruts in the snow are darker so we can walk, each on our own side, with only shimmering night sky light.

At first I keep looking back. What if Sam follows us? We have never left him. He comes with us everywhere. He could easily catch up. What would we do? Go back? Bring him along?

But he doesn't.

I shudder to think of him with such minimal shelter for a whole day. He has a thick undercoat, a bushy tail, four years of experience. Still, I can't let myself think of it.

Rhythmic trudging for two miles is the only sound in the silence. There's nothing really to say. Our tightly tucked in hats, hoods and scarves muffle our voices and block our ears.

"You OK?" Kevin pauses to look at me by flash-light face-to-face.

"Yup!" I answer.

I tuck my chin down into my scarf, but my glasses keep fogging up. I want to breathe in through the folds of the scarf to warm the air a little before the bitter cold shocks the inside of my lungs. But, when I exhale, if my warm breath travels up in front of my glasses, the moisture fogs and immediately freezes to the lenses. After I make adjustments, another problem becomes evident. The cold air makes my eyes water. The steam from my tears is enough to form a layer of ice inside my glasses which blocks my vision. I don't want to keep stopping to fumble in my pocket for a tissue to clean my glasses bare-handed, so I wipe them with my mittens, glad I did not spill kerosene on them when I filled the lamp.

Above the closely standing, snow laden, tall evergreen trees, slowly, blue replaces black. Such a beautiful blue. The stars twinkle every colour like crystals refracting rainbows. They have been doing what they have been doing forever and ever. I have never done what I am doing now: walking through winter wilderness silently hopeful for the day ahead.

I have pulled each solitary thumb into each mitten to be kept warm with my other fingers, making a fist, keeping my arms close to my body, my face down in the scarf. Every little bit helps.

There is no wind, thankfully. My body is getting warmed from the work and fills the folds and layers of my clothing. I have tied the parka drawstrings tightly at my waist so that my movements do not, like billows, pump frigid air in and out of my coat. Through the boots, thick felt liners, two layers of wool socks, my toes are getting cold. But I know they are OK. As long as they hurt I know they are not numb. The backpack acts as a shield insulating my torso.

Good progress and no misadventures, we round the bend, cross the bridge, seek the highway.

So, now to break the 'Taboo.' I am going to attempt hitch-hiking. Without my husband at my side, I would never, ever take the risk to do this alone.

Morning has arrived. We can see their headlights. They can see our bundled shapes. But who would even consider stopping for strangers headed north in the middle of nowhere on such an early morning?

I am afraid of all the drivers. But, surely, they are all afraid of us.

Transport trucks roar by in both directions. Pickup trucks with business logos motor past. Company policy does not allow any of them to pick up extra passengers.

A jeep travelling south boasts a huge rack of moose antlers strapped to the roof top.

A family van swishes by. No room there.

Wide gaps of silence stretch between vehicles. Summertime tourists are gone. Autumn hunters have returned home. Workers have days off for the holidays. Christmas families have already arrived at their destinations. Anyone who lives here would be going south if they were shopping in town or the city further on. We need to go north.

I pace and move to stay warm. My feet start to send warning messages I need to pay attention to.

A huge, classy motor home slides along the pavement. It looks out of context in December. Leaping into my heart: Jealousy. Really? Your wealth and luxury cannot reach out to my obvious poverty and elemental need?

I battle my hard, cold heart, seeking a return to an attitude of Trust.

The scrunching of tires in snow. Lights stop. The window rolls down and a friendly voice calls out a word of welcome. "How far are you headed?"

"Just a few miles. To Avola."

"Hop in."

It is amazing how much warmth is inside the cab of a pickup truck. I scooch into the centre. Kevin tosses the empty pack frames into the snowy pickup box. The driver has heard there were people living on this logging road. People say we are hippies, but not dangerous!

Tension from the waiting, from the cold, from the need, from the anxiety begins to relax. The menfolk make conversation. This is the warmest I have been for three days.

Daylight. Warmth. Transportation. Things are looking up. The streetlights in town are still on. The restaurant sign blinks red 'O-P-E-N' letters looming large and high above the brightly lit dining room. I am both eagerly anticipating familiar faces and dreading curious questions and fault-finding eyes.

I am an outsider now. No longer a uniformed employee. Whatever inconvenience my absence caused the others, this is the reality and I have to live with the consequences.

Warm! Layers removed. The coat rack in the lobby is cloaked with my cast offs. Dark blue down parka, brown corduroy vest, navy wool sweater, dark green wool turtle neck, red wool vest, toque, scarf, mittens. Kevin waits for me by the door. I slide out of my boots and brace myself to face my boss.

I round the corner to see my former co-workers busy with the bustle of morning routines. They have never seen me except in the 'I'm just like you' brown miniskirt, polyester uniform. Now I wear thick rough men's work clothes. My hair, usually pulled back into a smooth, tidy braid, is now static electric hair every-which-way. My hippy alpaca wool sweater signals 'alternative lifestyle.' The too-big-for-me grey men's wool socks flap like duck feet. I hope my pink rose bud long johns are not showing under the cuffs of my black men's wool pants.

As they say: I look 'bushed.'

"Is Dave in?" I ask the waitress, as if I'd never met her before.

"In the office." It is payday. He's got paperwork to focus on.

Awkwardly, I ask. Hunched over the adding machine, he calculates.

$2.57 per hour, multiplied by my hours for two weeks, minus two days, plus holiday pay, plus severance pay for four months work. It's more than I thought, but the very last money we will see for an unknown amount of time. $180.00 even. The good news is: we don't need building supplies and without the van, we no longer need to buy gas or insurance. This will all be for food.

I force myself to make eye contact and stand up straight, exchanging pleasantries, "Happy New Year." My employment here is over.

Now I compel my feet to take me back through the kitchen and dining room where the cook, waitress, teenagers and neighbours are watching me. I force my face, stiffly masked, to not show how deeply emotional the last few days have been. I feel like I am looking through the wrong end of binoculars. They seem tiny and far away.

I will not see, talk to, or know about daily life with these people again until springtime. This warm cheery place, these yummy smells and abundant food, everything clean, everything safe, it is all in my past starting now. Three days ago I didn't want it. Now it looks like a luxury cruise ship stocked with every physical comfort in abundance. Now I am drifting way out to sea on my life raft.

Jerry (ham and eggs) and Mike (pancakes and bacon) are enjoying their coffee, cigarettes and breakfast near the entry-way. "How's it goin' out there?" Jerry's question is genuine.

"Oh, I'll bet they know how to keep warm!" Mike's wink-wink, sideways grin and dancing eyes imply an invasion of our privacy.

I blush.

With so many layers of clothing necessary day and night, there has been none of the 'keeping warm' that they are suggesting. I hear their laughter while I drop a coin in the pay-phone.

As we guessed, Fran and Archie are just getting their day started. He's out to the barn milking the goats and gathering the eggs, feeding and watering the animals. She's in the kitchen perking coffee, brewing tea, measuring oats, buttering toast, scrambling eggs.

"We'll keep the food warm," Fran invites us for a hearty meal.

I am nearly skipping down the gravel road. Knowing that hospitality is ahead, my spirits are greatly lifted. Wispy mare's tails clouds are tinted pink. The sky is infinitely, softly blue. The eastern mountain ridge hides the steadily climbing sun. The rays have reached the topmost tips of the western slopes and gradually bright white light will fill the valley.

Strong steady strides shrink the distance. My thoughts elevate. All the pioneers did this, I coach myself. I am following in the footsteps of my ancestors. Less blizzardly wind than Laura Ingalls Wilder wrote about in 'The Long Cold Winter.' No cannibalism like the Donner Party. No one is forcing me. I am choosing this myself. Struggle and hardship and endurance are part of life. Right?

No, wait. Not in my family tree! For seven generations on my Father's side of the family tree there were academics: clergy and professors, authors and translators, proof readers and newspaper columnists. These people lived in Baltimore and Boston. None of them had covered wagons. None of them had dirt under their fingernails. None of them ever broke a sweat.

My Mother's parents were emigrants from Europe after the Great War, entering America through Ellis Island. For generations they have found ways to earn a living working for well-to-do families. Cooking, cleaning, laundry and child care provides a satisfactory income from the wealthy. Tending fields and flocks and herds for established farmers, their families never set out for new horizons. No pioneers there, either. For the first time I realize: I have no background in these skills at all.

Dizzy again, I hesitate. "What am I doing?"

Besides that, unlike the pioneers, it is also obvious that everyone around me is not sharing this experience, knowledge and know-how, purpose and drive, courage and cooperation. We are doubly foreigners. We are from the eastern city consumer culture entering this western resource based economy. We are also from the modern world of electricity, telephones and technological conveniences attempting to return to the old-time, primitive way of life.

No wonder everyone thinks we're nuts.

Sunbeams stream into the kitchen as Fran answers the door. She is wearing the royal blue checkered apron I made her for Christmas! Her blue eyes twinkle and her familiar grandmotherly chuckle combined with her gentle hug feels wonderful. Fran insists we enjoy a second breakfast, I greedily pour goat's cream on my steaming porridge, slather butter on my warm toast and scoop deeply into the jar of home grown strawberry jam.

It's the same breakfast menu we were given when we first arrived and camped in their yard back in August. The continuity and abundance strike me anew. The first time I tasted goat's milk it seemed to me that it tasted like the hay and grasses the animals were eating. I also had to stop myself from expressing distaste when I removed a short, stiff, tan goat's hair from the tip of my tongue. Glancing at the others, I realized, I sure am a city girl. The reality of the source of food from animals is so far removed when you buy a carton of milk in the store. Bruises on apples. Bugs on greens. Dirt on potatoes. A twig or leaf or grass or hair in the milk. No harm. This is the real thing.

Archie heads out to unplug the block heater and start the car. It has to run for at least twenty minutes to heat up the lubricants before putting the engine in gear. Fran, so ladylike, crosses a blue, decorative scarf around her neck and holds it in place with a sparkling blue broach. Her sweater is that familiar royal blue and I notice how she deliberately dresses to feature her blue eyes.

No need for all of our extra layers in her warm vehicle, although she carries wool blankets and an old sleeping-bag in the back in case of a delay. I have removed my inner layers of long johns, wool sweaters, double socks. I stuff these and Kevin's extra outdoor layers into one sweater, like a bag. It will make a big, fat pillow in the back seat.

It is 10:00. Our harsh pre-dawn exit from the cabin is in sharp contrast to these leisurely preparations with 'all the comforts of home.' Fran and Archie have been married a long time. Their habits dovetail and their to-do list is second nature. Like well rehearsed choreography each knows the other's patterns and they efficiently cooperate.

And we're off. No need to apologize for the intrusion. Fran knows what it is like to ask for help and the importance of generous neighbours. During the years she lived as a widow with four small children, her bartering and garden, favours exchanged and community interactions were the economy which made her welfare cheque stretch across their many needs. She has assured us many times since we arrived four months ago, that we may ask for unmet needs on one condition: that we 'Pay it Forward.' After we're established she asked us to pledge to continue the tradition to volunteer and lend, give generously and keep a look out for others who need a boost. Agreed.

Buckled in, toasty warm, in seconds we retrace the roadway we just walked on. Turning south onto the highway, the brilliant sun pierces our eyes. In minutes we pass by the place we stood begging for a ride. The pavement is bare. Snow removal crews dealt with the earlier snowfall when the temperature was 'warmer.' Since there is no snowfall when it is this bitter cold, the highway is clear and we can travel with both good visibility and no slippery surfaces. Warmer temperatures mean fog in the valley. Warmer temperatures mean snow melting into puddles by day and black ice at night. But, not today. Today all is well.

Fran drives her sky blue, perky, small station wagon. She points out landmarks, narrating local history, answers our questions.

Archie is up front. His eyesight is nearly gone and he depends on her for many things. His hands know a lifetime of skills he can no longer use. At home, he returns items he frequently needs to the same place. His back-and-forth to the barn every day is possible by following the snow banks. His TV viewing is mostly listening to the news. Their marriage is such a partnership. Their years together are an example I want to pay attention to and strive towards.

Kevin and I are happy in the back seat. It is so pleasant to be comfortable and safe, spending time with people. I send out a silent message to who ever invented heaters in cars. "Thank-you." We share our news of recent days.

At 11:00 we arrive in Clearwater.

A routine begins which will reach many years into the future. First stop: the Credit Union. Then all the errands, first on one side of town, then the other to be efficient with gas. Last: the grocery store. It is an hour's drive to return home. In summer we have to protect food that needs refrigeration from spoiling in the heat. In winter, we have to protect the delicate vegetables from frost damage.

While the others wait in the car, the motor running to keep the heater blowing, I step in to the Credit Union to cash the cheques: my pay cheque and the additional holiday and severance cheque, a $20 cheque which is a monthly gift from Kevin's Mom, and the $100 Christmas cheque from my Dad.

Time stands still as the cashier counts the $20 bills out onto the counter. For a moment, outside of time, I feel paralyzed. Here is more money than I have had since we left Ontario. Here is enough money to take me back to Ontario.

Is this realization an inspiration? Or a temptation?

They say your whole life flashes before you when you know you are going to die. I have seen my past. I am standing on the brink of my own future. Whichever choice I make right now, the other possibility will die.

Here is a very real opportunity. A pivotal turning point.

I could buy food and stay.

I could buy a bus ticket and go.

The Greyhound will pass through here in three hours. This is my chance. My only chance. My mind is racing as I imagine the prairies whipping by, the city inviting, my family welcoming. Then, like the sound of squealing tires in a movie, I screech on the brakes. No. Wait.

All in an instant I see a vivid flashback.

My Dad's face looms up before my eyes.

Sitting behind his office desk at the university, typewriter, books, stacks of papers, he had summoned me, shortly before the wedding, for a rather strained interview. He systematically doused cold water on each part of my dream.

He didn't like it one bit when I decided to quit my university education. After all, because he worked there, my tuition was only $600 per year! With 'Women's Lib' and women demanding to enter every kind of career, he wanted me to choose a professional path and achieve great things in the academic world.

"You'll be cutting yourself off from an income. It's such a terrible waste of your education. I'd hate for you to come knocking on my door, children in tow, begging for help, realizing that you should have finished your degree."

He even set up an appointment for me with a fellow economics professor at the university, a well-established female just down the hall from his office. Her suit, title and status did not impress me favourably. No, thanks. This is not a role model for me.

"Why would you want to work so hard for the food you need?" Daddy puzzled.

"If I am thirsty, I want to go get a bucket of water. If I am hungry, I want to go dig up some potatoes. If I am cold I want go to light a fire." Gesturing I add, "I don't want to be in debt for the car I drive to go to work way over there to earn the money I need to buy food to bring back home way over here. I don't want to spend my whole pay cheque on my appearance and for someone else to look after my kids and clean my house! It makes no sense to us to live in a house that it will take us 30 years to pay for! By then our kids will be grown and gone! It all seems so alarming to me."

Daddy shook his head and sighed, like he was talking to a moron. "It is no longer necessary to dig in the dirt for potatoes."

I don't remember how we got on the topic of birth control. Maybe he was worried about starving, raggedy, barefoot, scrawny children popping out every nine months.

I explained confidently. "Daddy, we went to the birth control clinic on the university campus and we understand all of the options. Blockades and chemically tampering with hormones are not acceptable to us. We have learned how to observe and chart the ovulation cycle." The conclusion seemed so obvious to me. "We choose to abstain during the days of fertility."

"What?" Now he frowned, his face showed shock and disbelief. "But Kevin is a virile young man in the prime of his..." He gestured where no words will do. "You can't really expect him to...wait?"

"We have been waiting for four years. I thought virginity was highly valued in our Church? I thought you'd be proud of me, of us?" I'm confused.

Embarrassed, I take a moment to gather my thoughts. "I hope you can understand that there is nothing more important to us in our marriage than the self-discipline of living by our ideals." I can sense Kevin's strong character encouraging me to stand up for our values. "We don't want to believe one thing and do the opposite. There are larger issues here."

"Let me try to explain," I continue. "The Earth is our Mother. People have been treating Her so badly. In our own small microcosm we do not want to re-create what is happening to the whole planet. For example: Look at this abundantly fertile farmland here in southern Ontario. How horrible is it to 'pave paradise and put up a parking lot'? We keep pouring slabs of concrete blockading this valuable soil! And then there are all of the chemicals. Kill this. Destroy that. Slow down. Speed up. Chemicals strong enough to change the force of Nature seem very harsh. Will we make the Earth uninhabitable? Will we deliberately destroy life? That makes no sense."

"We do not want to treat the Earth this way and so we believe a husband will not expect to treat his wife's body this way, either." Will he understand and accept my logic? "The best way to take care of the Earth is to understand and respect Her cycles and participate in Her gifts. That is how my husband and I intend to live, too."

Daddy's eyebrows came down in a frown. "Ideals are all very fine, but you can't actually live by them."

"I wish you could hear me, Daddy," my voice low. I am trying to share something precious to me. "Waiting is part of having. Waiting is part of every cycle in Nature. We can certainly wait a few days out of every month. It is part of the gift my husband has to give me and I to him."

He let out a long sigh. He shook his head and gave up.

"Daddy?" I am almost whispering now. "Don't you have anything positive to say to me?"

Somehow, I had always imagined that 'The Father' gives 'The Daughter' some kind of a 'Blessing' as she approaches her wedding day. Whatever words are spoken, the message would be "I'm Proud of You."

But, he just threw up his hands to dismiss me like I was totally beyond hope.

So, as the cashier smiles and courteously waits, just as my mother taught me, I calmly count back the $20 bills.

20-40-60-80-100

20-40-60-80-200

20-40-60-80-300

It is the heaviest weight I have ever held in my hand.

I thought I answered this question last night?

Must I re-fight this battle? Re-evaluate the pros and cons? Re-balance the scales?

For $300 I can buy a bus ticket back to civilization, warmth, familiarity.

For $300 I will shatter my marriage vows.

For $300 I can walk away from my husband and add my voice to the mockers who laugh at his dream.

For $300 I can rip away from him the gift his father gave him, the dream 'go west' and smash the goal he has dedicated to his father, this life we have just begun.

For $300 I can admit defeat.

For $300 my Dad will say, "I told you so" when he picks me up at the bus depot.

For $300 I will forever abandon this domestic, 'do-it-yourself' dream, re-enter the career path and accept '9-to-5,' a mortgage, the suburbs and keep running on the hamster wheel looking for all of the latest trends and status symbols.

For $300 I will be mute about the inconsistencies and hazards of the Church I was raised in, muffle my mind, swallow what seems unacceptable and put my head down and knit with the other respectable women.

For $300 I can forget all about this unpleasant ripple momentarily interrupting my otherwise predictable 'normal' life.

For $300 I will blot out the possibility of having Kevin to be the father of my children.

For $300 I can throw all of the gifts God has given me back in His face, all the tiny details, all the prompts and guidance and signals in my past, all the help and hopes and hints for the future.

Pro: For $300 I can be warm this winter.

Con: For $300 I can stop being me.

Decision: The price is too high.

I hear my own words which I have said again and again since we announced our engagement: *"I'm going to get married, go out west, build a log cabin, have a bunch of kids, teach them about the Lord, volunteer in my community...and then write a book about it."*

If I decide right now, today, to walk away from my husband after a mere six months, how will my book read? What would there be worth writing about? 'After four years of planning, we got married. We went out west and built our cabin in four months. We slept there for seven nights...and then I quit and went 'home to Mother,' married a music teacher and took the kids to Disney Land."

Nope. I don't want a role in that story.

Turning abruptly, I walk mechanically out of this heated, secure institution and into the jolt of shocking cold and the insecurity of personal freedom. Physically: I reclaim my place in the car. Internally: I reclaim my life, my husband, my dream, my reality, my hardship, my future.

The others continue their conversation, unaware of my struggle, turning point and victory.

Next stop: the hardware store which houses the Sears catalogue pick up desk. My snow pants and skates have arrived. Hurrah. This is how I spend $50 of my Dad's gift. Kevin did not choose anything. We agree to add what's left to our budget for food and necessities. A five-gallon can of kerosene will last a long while. Flashlight batteries are essential. Everything else is put on hold.

We cross town to the grocery store.

I have admired Fran and Cheryl's root cellar and freezers. The whole garden is stored safely for many months of meals. Jars and jars of gem-like jams line up in rows on shelves. Pickles and relish, chutney and pie filling show their texture and hold tempting flavours. Peaches and apricots, cherries and pears harvested further south save brilliant sunshine in their jars in this damp, dark, earth-sheltered basement. Baskets of carrots and potatoes, squash and pumpkins, beets and turnips will offer variety to the family. Braids of garlic and onions bring warmth to otherwise bland recipes. Apples and plums, herbs and teas preserved in the dehydrator yield their nourishment. Boxes of bags inside long, white freezers store up greens and beans, peas and corn. Venison, goat and home butchered chickens, fish and even some rabbits are in the freezer providing protein to this hunting and farming three-generation family.

This is what Kevin and I are aiming for. I have books about this. I have no experience with this kind of 'from garden to storage to table' small-scale farming.

I have seen other neighbours who have storage shelves in their entry way, groaning with the weight of both store-bought and home canned foods. A good sized freezer is standard equipment for these rural families who have both hunters providing for them and income for store-bought goodies but who live so far from town they can't be sure when the weather might block them from a trip to the store.

How could it be that we have nothing saved for this first year? We have been married for six months. The first month we slept at my parents' house and Kevin's Mom's place. The next month we were on the road, camping and day-to-day shopping for food. For two months we relied heavily on Fran and Archie. The month or so at Glen's we prepared our own meals, knowing we weren't going to stay long. Last payday, since we realized we would be in our own place soon, we started to store up non-perishables and write a list of necessities. So, this is the first time in my life I have ever planned a shopping trip like this.

We are not looking for payday treats. We need to focus on nutrition, cost, storage limitations and the fact that a few hours after we reach home, every single item will be frozen solid.

How much does it cost?
How heavy is it to carry?
How much nutrition is it?
Can we use it many ways?
What can I make from scratch?
Can I reuse the container?
What will happen when it freezes?
No meat.
No monosodium glutamate.
No food colouring.
Dog food. Cat food.
Do we have enough
left over from last payday?
What if we run out?
Fresh.
Canned.
Frozen.
Dry.

The list I made is mostly raw materials. I will use these ingredients to do baking and make meals from scratch.

Twenty pounds of whole wheat flour, five pounds of oats, two pounds of corn meal, yeast, baking soda, baking powder, cinnamon, brown sugar, molasses, bran, raisins, butter. That covers breakfasts and baking.

Eggs, peanut butter, cheese, sardines, tuna. That takes care of protein.

In the bulk food store we scoop out staples for our vegetarian meals: kidney beans, pinto beans, lentils, split peas, brown rice, barley.

"What about milk?" Kevin hoists the three litre jug.

"It will be frozen solid. We won't be able to get it out of the spout."

"How about these bags?" Three one litre bags of milk are sold together in a strong carrying bag. An orange pitcher made to fit one floppy bag securely is for sale. With a snip of scissors, the pouring spout is formed. Without refrigeration while we were camping, we didn't buy milk. Now it is too cold. Kevin looks disappointed.

"We'll buy milk powder." Remembering how unpleasant it is to drink, Kevin frowns. I hurry to explain. "We'll buy plain yogurt. I can use it to make more yogurt with the milk powder. Fran gave us homemade jam to stir in. Yum!"

Honey we already have in a five-gallon bucket. Soy sauce, oil, shortening, Italian herbs, garlic, onions add flavour to whatever I make with the proteins. We already have salt and pepper.

As Kevin pushes the grocery cart while I select the items and cross off the list, we are learning, too.

"Kevin, look at this small bottle we usually buy. If we buy this gallon can of ketchup we will pay twice as much for four times the amount."

Potatoes, apples, carrots I know will freeze, but as long as they go straight from frozen to cooked, they will be a different consistency, but not spoiled. One sweet potato, too, it's a favourite.

The biggest box of pasta, a case of canned tomatoes, one case each of canned tomato soup and of mushroom soup rounds out our supplies.

We have to buy 24 rolls of toilet paper. We can't run out of that. Toothpaste we can ration. Other toiletries are luxuries and are not even on the list. Laundry soap is unnecessary. Dish soap we have already.

It is a big load.

Everything is placed onto the black conveyor. The cashier punches in all of the numbers, hitting the '+' key again and again. Everything is added up. I count out the precious, finite cash.

We load it all into our backpacks, estimating the weight, more for him, less for me. Lots of tourists come through the store in the summer months. There is nothing unusual to see a young outdoorsy couple with backpacks leaving the grocery store. But, I feel eyes wondering where we are going at 40° below?

There's money left. It has no use at all if I take it back to the cabin. There is no place to buy food in Avola and no transportation to return to Clearwater. We might as well spend it all. Kevin goes back for a 50 pound bag of dog food. The cat will eat this if we run out of cat food.

Mentally, I run through the list again. If I have missed anything essential, there is no way to return. Cocoa. I can bake cookies and cakes and mix cocoa with the milk powder to stir up hot drinks if we have this one splurge.

Still a few dollars left.

I circle the store again asking myself, "What will we have for supper tonight? Feels like a good day for a celebration."

Fresh fish, fresh broccoli, two bananas we will eat before they freeze. How will we live without fresh greens? An idea pops into my head: alfalfa sprouts. In the bulk food area I dig out three scoops of the tiny brown seeds and pour them into a bag. If I can keep them continuously damp and above freezing, we can have greens.

With a sigh of relief we survey our wealth as we load up the car.

Then Fran has a surprise. It is 1:00pm and she parks in front of the department store and coaxes us in to the lunch counter! I'm a little embarrassed accepting even more generosity. We all order golden crisp grilled cheese sandwiches, creamy tomato soup and a slice of lemon meringue pie. Fran and Archie carefully divide evenly an order of French fries. I don't want any, but Kevin orders some. "I just want one or two." I slyly smile and reach for a few tasty samples from Kevin's plate. Dipped in ketchup, the crunchy gold and tangy red are irresistible.

Room temperature in these stores, as well as indoor plumbing has been much appreciated today. Warm. Full. Cared for. Bliss.

The tic-tic-tic of Fran's left signal light sounds while we wait at the intersection to turn north and re-enter the highway traffic.

It is 2:00pm. The southbound Greyhound intercepts us.

My heart reaches out, yearning, then snaps back inside my chest. I have already decided. I am here. To stay.

How is it possible that God is not too busy running the entire Universe to arrange for me to experience this moment so precisely?

Someone really does see every single sparrow that falls. The hairs of my head really are numbered.[31]

Two roads diverged through the snowy woods. And today, I am committed to take the road less travelled.[32]

Exhausted from broken sleep, from inner battles, from countless decisions, I lean against the pillow of clothing and sleep on the return trip.

By the time we get home the sun is behind the mountain, but darkness will not be complete for more than an hour. Good-byes are brief as the cold bites into our faces while we unload. Fran and Archie are so much living the life I'd like to live someday with a grown family, comfort and security, character qualities to admire, a respected place in the community and the contentment of their partnership. A toot of the car horn and I wave as they drive out of sight.

"Kevin, do you know what she just did?" I ask as I turn back towards him.

"What's that?" Kevin shoulders his pack, then turns to help me lift and adjust mine.

"She lived out the example Jesus expected of His followers:

> For I was an hungered, and ye gave me meat:
> I was thirsty, and ye gave me drink:
> I was a stranger, and ye took me in:
> Naked, and ye clothed me:
> I was sick, and ye visited me:
> I was in prison, and ye came unto me...
> Inasmuch as ye have done it
> unto one of the least of these my brethren,
> ye have done it unto me.[33]

"Wow! She did almost every single one of those for us!" Kevin agrees.

"I want to be like her when I grow up," I pledge. Standing still, a flash of realization comes over me. Without one single doctrinal debate, recitation of a Scripture text, flipping pages to prove a point, she has done precisely what Jesus requested of His followers. This kindly 'little old lady' has demonstrated to me a clear, living example of the answer at the core of the quest I have been on. 'I want to be a minister.' I want to offer nourishing instruction, calming rest, soothing comfort, a listening welcome and a word of encouragement to others who I meet along the Path on Life's Journey.

Up the trail Kevin leads the way.

"Sam! Come!" Bounding and barking, here he comes down the snowy slope. I have a new appreciation for the loyalty of 'Man's Best Friend' as we retrace this morning's footprints and step towards our cabin.

My load is lighter. I bend to pet and admire and speak encouragement to Sam.

I unpack while Kevin returns for the dog food, kerosene and other heavy and bulky items.

"I'm going to bring in more wood," he announces. Each sled full makes a difference to our first-more-then-less wood pile. There is still day light and not much he can do to help me in the small kitchen space.

"We can go back tomorrow. We've already done so much today," I suggest.

"I'll do it." And he turns to go.

I start the fire. My layers of outdoor clothes will still be needed for hours indoors. I slide on my new snow pants and realize I need to write a thank-you note to my Dad.

Opening each pocket of the backpacks, I make decisions about how to store the food. When we first moved in, Kevin brought the big food box in from the van. The paper and plastic sacks of flour, sugar, oats can go in there. The potatoes, carrots, onions, apples fit, too. I'll have to watch. I hope the mice can't climb in?

Into a large plastic bucket with a tight fitting lid I put the ten pound bag of brown rice. I refuse to share any with despicable mice! Into a gallon glass jar from the restaurant I stack up the smaller bags of beans and grains. The canned goods go on the shelves. No refrigeration is available for the eggs, yogurt and cheese, but that doesn't matter. The whole house is colder than the inside of a freezer.

I open the oven door and the warming oven door, too, allowing all of the metal surfaces to give off their glowing heat. Slowly warmth chases cold out of the house. The energy stored in the wood is released through flickering flames. Warmth we need to stay alive is pushing the boundary, differentiating 'in here' from 'out there.'

Kevin works quickly. One load. Then more. I hear him clattering the pieces of wood onto the pile.

"Supper's ready in ten minutes!" I call out when I go out to scoop more snow.

"I'll get one more load!" he calls back over his shoulder. But I see he is not wearing his face mask.

Fish is frying. Potatoes are frying. Lots of oil in the pan to bring much needed calories into our hard working, chilly bodies. Broccoli is simmering. I put the plates in the warming oven.

It is such a good supper in the circle of the lamplight. I feel like a champion who reached the mountain top. For a few family minutes we enjoy the scampering kitten. One of the paper bags has become a plaything to pounce on and hide in. Kevin makes a wad of paper tied with a thread for her to chase. I forgot how much entertainment it is to watch the antics of a cat. We laugh. We exchange glances. There is no iceberg between us now.

It seems unusual for Kevin to go to bed first. Now it's up to me to prepare the kindling, fill the wood box, blow out the lamp on the table, hold the alarm clock in the flashlight beam, turn the tiny dial on the back to set the time, push over the little white pin to 'alarm on,' wind the clock and be sure to also wind the alarm bell one-quarter turn. No need for a long jangle. One short 'ring' is enough.

A few hours of fire this evening cannot overcome the hours of no fire all day. Up in the loft, my North Pole pillow and South Pole mattress offer no comfort. I cover my head completely with blankets, my exhaled breath the only way to warm my wrappings. It is so physical. My stomach holds warm food. My heart pumps warm blood. I wonder if I can join the bears in hibernation.

"Kevin, I didn't notice you coughing before. Are you OK?" The exertion of pulling the sled in haste without the shelter of his face mask caused the arctic air to chill him deep inside. The Old Timers would say, 'He's frosted his lungs.'

He coughed, tossing and turning in the night. His warmth began to feel hot and I knew he had a fever.

With so many hours of darkness, so many sleeping and waking cycles, so much emptiness and so few distractions, there's lots of time during the night to think back over the day. I feel like I have climbed up onto a plateau. I can look around me. Down below I see my own life path. I can see the rounded, fruitful hills of my childhood. I can see the swamps of self-doubt and hear the cackling laughter of those who wanted to drag me down. I rejected the rigidly blocked out streets of conformity and chose the rugged footpath of self-discovery. Accompanied by my trustworthy husband, we have made explorations. Thorny branches thrashing in the recent inner storm nearly swept me, terrified, off the edge. But, I endured the struggle and have come to this place to pause. Difficulties ahead are hidden in mist. But, I am not afraid.

Sleeping, never failing, unshaken, my husband, friend, fellow traveller is unaware of my musings. I wish there was someone who could see me up here on this plateau, give a speech of congratulation, witness me as I plant a flag of victory.

Music. Inside. As it so often happens to me. Can I catch it? I hold very still. I scarcely breathe. Can I bring it forward until it is recognizable?

Yes. Now I know. I can hear it: *To Dream the Impossible Dream* with its compelling rhythm, increasing determination, crescendo of courage.[34] And, in contrast to the suddenly painful flashback this morning of the interview with my Father, now I can hear him singing, filling the house with this heartfelt pledge as he tucks us children into bed. He *did* give me direction. Perhaps that day in his office he couldn't sense it anymore, but I know that in my earliest childhood memories he gave me this concept of vision, this hunger for a noble life quest. And so, with his voice resounding in my mind, I rededicate, come into alignment, celebrate.

Impossible? Unbearable? Too weary? Hopeless? Yes, I certainly have come to those places. But the quest, the possibility, the reaching, the ideal, it is so worth continuing to strive for. Yes, I am willing to endure. Darkness surrounds me, yet, I still believe in the light!

My Daddy's voice, loud, strong, bold, clear, certain, determined. Yes, his songs to us at bedtime are so embedded in my heart that I cannot stumble or stay defeated for long. Stored up in my mind are the shields to protect me. Stored up in my mind are the truths to cut through lies and confusion. Stored up in my mind are the tools to continue building. Stored up in my mind is a map directing me confidently ahead.

Chapter 11
December 31, 1978
Sunday

I am only one
and yet I am one.
I can not do everything
and yet
I can do something.
　　　—Helen Keller

How fragile the link between health and daily bread. How terrible the thought that the man could be laid up sick and the woman would have to carry the full load of work to survive.

Facts are like puzzle pieces. In the pre-dawn hours I turn them this way and that, trying to solve the problems.

Kevin can't work today.

Wow, I never imagined this.

It is still so very cold.

There is no way we can both can take a day off.

My work: make fire, melt snow, make food, feed the dog and cat.

Plus his work: saw and load, pull and split, chop and stack.

I'll be busy all day.

The hazard of the cold to fingers and toes, to nose and cheeks, and the lungs will caution me as I move about.

We stay in bed until daylight slowly begins. The black sky becomes darkest blue, soon a splendid rich blue, then finally light enough to see indoors. This saves lamp oil, something we certainly do not want to run out of.

I rattle the stove lids and begin the preparation of the fire, water, food.

Strategy. I will need to pay attention all day to my every decision and move. What if we both get sick?

While the water comes to a boil, I get dressed as near to the stove as I can without scorching any unmentionable places.

Without removing the layers I have been sleeping in, the white with pink rosebuds cotton waffle-weave long johns and the green daisy flannel PJ pants, I pull on the black men's wool pants and my brand-new nylon snow pants. Four layers should guard against frostbite.

On top I have the long johns top, my favourite thin red wool pullover, the dark green wool turtle neck and the dark blue thick wool pullover. Three layers of wool and I am still uncomfortable inside my house!

I need two pairs of Kevin's grey wool socks, my boots and parka, too.

I savour the cinnamon sprinkled on top of the hot porridge, brown sugar and butter melting into the valleys, raisins on top of the hills. Hot food, deliciousness, these keep me warm, too. I don't want to pester him or wake him, but I will need to keep climbing the ladder to check and see how Kevin is doing. And what if he gets worse? How will I go for help? "Dear Lord in Heaven, please-oh-please reach into his body and make things right as soon as You can."

Kevin comes down the ladder looking pale and weak. Even when he talks a little, quietly, it triggers more coughing.

He is uninterested in the porridge and never drinks a hot drink, so I leave him a jar of water to drink and start out into the forest.

Breakfast complete, I wrap a wool scarf over my face. I zip up my down parka. The hood is trimmed with wolf fur which does not form frost from the steam of my breathing. My mittens have two special man-made fibre layers: the soft, fuzzy, red Thinsulite TM liner and the strong nylon royal blue exterior. Bulky and stiff and carefully tucked in, I brave myself to address the day.

Even with so many layers, the cold seeps in. My shoulders hunch up. My head is tucked down. I pull my thumb into the hand part of my mitten. I keep my arms close to my body, saving my own warmth as much as I can. Marching slowly, without rushing in-breaths of the dangerous cold, each daily task becomes a risky problem to solve.

Down the path, past the solitary van, through the close growing brush, across the road to the flat, wide-open landing where the loggers left a small stack of birch for us to use, up against the steep rise of the mountain, I pull the empty sled. Dark trees, bright snow, blinding sunshine, when I stop the swish of my snow pants, the crunch of my footsteps, the sound of my own breath, there is deep, empty silence.

In all of that unmarked snow I suddenly feel the childhood urge to turn, fall back into the softness and make a snow angel. Nobody in the whole world knows where I am right now. I am a spec.

Millions of mountains, trillions of trees, zillions of snow-flakes, and one person. Alone. I feel like I'm shrinking even smaller. The only person on earth who needs me is Kevin and he could survive without me, I'm sure. Everyone else in the entire world is continuing their day without me. I wonder if it matters that I even exist? Maybe there is no 'God'? Maybe there is no 'Plan'?

Now I'm a spec spinning in a void.

If there is no 'God' and I do exist, then it wouldn't matter what I do, or why. There would be no 'life after death' and no motivation to 'do unto others.' It would all be about 'me.' What 'I want' would be my only concern. In fact, 'I' would be 'God'!

Now I'm a giant, stomping across the mountains, looting, hoarding, greedy. Eat drink and be merry!

Spinning spec? Trampling giant? Intolerable! I suddenly snap back into my self. Upright, I fling open my arms and take a stand. Even if those seeking 'proof' say 'there is no God' I cannot believe that. It is too crushing to be more alone than I am right now. I would rather live my life believing there is 'Someone.' I would rather dedicate my life to a Purpose that is larger than 'me.' I would rather be part of the long line of people who trust in a Guide.

And so, the monotonous work that must be done is part of a whole. Back and forth with the saw and the loads, in and out of the cabin with emptying and filling, it is not meaningless repetition, it is necessary for life and life is of value, so each task is of value.

There is not very much wood left from the sawing we did a few days ago. I collect one load and pull the sled back up to the cabin. To the north of the cabin, I scout around for logs left from building that I can cut into lengths. I wrestle and roll and stack some log lengths so they will be easier to find when more snow falls. Discouraged, after a few false starts I realize that the bucksaw Kevin likes using is too long and flexible for me to use alone. The shorter bow saw will be better for me. Back to the house, I decide to attempt to split the rounds we already have into sizes that will fit into the stove.

Inside, I pause to both warm my hands and add snow to the pots of water melting on the stove top. I might as well get ahead on that at least. No sink bath today. No washing of hair. I can still see my breath inside. The house is not getting warm enough to even attempt removing any layers of clothing!

Outside, I notice how different each kind of wood is. With the borrowed chain saw Kevin had been able to cut the firewood we needed though the autumn months. The pine logs are very knotty and tough to split. Poplar is kind of wrapped as the tree follows the sun and spirals the wood fibres. Cedar shingles off with very little effort. Birch thwacks apart and provides the longest and hottest fire and the longest lasting coals. Spruce and fir, which are hard for me to tell apart, are a mid-value wood to burn. Most of the lumber mill ends that Red and the guys brought are spruce. I split them smaller to save Kevin the time and effort and make lots of 'cookin' sticks' as we call the small wood that burns hotter to bring the oven up to the right temperature for baking.

I love the smell of each kind of wood. Piney sap, aromatic cedar, musty poplar. I love the colour of wood. The birch is so blond. The cedar so orange-red. The others so golden. I wish I had the skill to build all of my furnishings and gifts and turn bowls on a lathe. I wish I could make crafty wooden things to sell.

The lift of the six pound splitting maul is still new to me, not too hard, just the amount of work that feels satisfying. But, new to me, I miss the mark, strike again and again. Where an experienced person would deliver a blow with accuracy and split with one or two hits. I deliver six strikes to manage a split.

Kevin can split while holding the maul on either side. I use a baseball bat, badminton racquet and golf clubs on my right side, but swing a hockey stick and the splitting maul on my left side. Kevin taught me how to chop wood while we were camping this summer. Standing with feet apart, knees slightly bent, test the distance from the chopping block with a slow, circular swing, back, up, around and down. When the distance is right, the blow will travel straight down through the wood to be split. For safety sake, this stance will direct the force so that any error will bring the blade straight down into the chopping block or the ground. Bending the knees delivers the maximum force and prevents the direction of the sharp metal from reaching the worker's legs or feet.

I know how. But, I'm still new. I'm cautious. I sure don't want to get hurt. But we really need as much of this wood cut as possible. So, I keep at it, a little timidly, but gaining confidence, until the pile of uncut rounds begins to shrink and the neat stack of split wood begins to grow.

I do know how to use the smaller, light weight axe to chop kindling. Cedar makes the best kindling. There are lots of log ends from the cedar Kevin used to build our cabin. He left some small piles of stove-length wood stacked here and there in the woods. Maybe I can find them and bring some on the sled?

Sam bounds eagerly ahead of me, sniffing rabbit tracks. The trail is a dent in the snow. Yes, here is light weight cedar I can manage.

The sled ran so smoothly on the landing, road, driveway and path, but is harder to pull on this narrow trail. The wood is tossed off and the twisted and unseen obstacles tease my judgment as I struggle, ever mindful not to breathe deeply and join Kevin in bed with painfully frosted lungs.

Inside to warm my hands and bring more snow. The big water pot is getting full. Handfuls of kidney beans splash into the pot. I like to cook a lot of one thing and then use it in different ways to start the next few meals. Baked beans, casserole, soup will all be possible when these beans are tender. Outside for another round of splitting. Inside to fill the wood box. Stuff wood in the stove.

The 'day off' we had been anticipating as a well-deserved change and rest, was for Kevin, a long day of broken sleep, feverish restlessness and painful coughing. I tried to keep up his spirits, offering tea, music, a back rub or something good to eat. I worried about how sick he really was and what to do? Should he be going to a doctor?

Outside to gather more wood. Inside to burn more wood. I tried to keep the house warm and not be too stingy while I wondered if we were burning more than I was bringing in. If Kevin cannot work for several days, will I be able to cut and haul enough to keep up? It had taken both of us to get a little bit ahead. "Please, Lord, Please, Lord," keeps running through my head all day.

I can't stay outside very long, but I mustn't stay inside very long, either.

It is noon. Anticipating a yummy lunch with our new, complete inventory of groceries, the sense of well-being is larger than the numb sensations from my toes. The beans are the base for soup. With a fork I chip frozen tomato soup out of the can. Carefully, I chop slices off of a frozen carrot and somehow cut up a rock-hard onion and dice a glacial potato. I chisel a chunk of frozen ketchup out of the gallon can. I saw the hard frozen bread which Cheryl brought with the bread knife and lay the slices on the stove to toast. The frozen jam melts, seeping into the toast. The mint tea from Fran warms me doubly, in my tummy and in my heart.

Kevin is down sitting at the table. He wants to, but decides against doing any work today. Reading a how-to book, wearing his boots and dark green down parka indoors, he will mind the fire for a few hours and try to catch the news and a weather forecast for tomorrow on the radio.

I hang my snow-crusted pants up on the nail behind the stove to dry, stripping down to bare skin because the knees and the seat of my pants got soaked. Glancing back, I see that Kevin is still reading. I quickly wrap a towel around my waist while I find another pair of dry sweat pants. My feet are sending sensations of extreme alarm up from the icy floor. New wool socks replace the damp ones. I tug the damp felt boot-liners out of the boots and hang them up to dry behind the stove. Hurriedly, I climb up the ladder to the loft. When I crawl back into my sleeping-bag, I expect it to be instantly comfortable and warm. Forgetting that 'warm' is not a word that I can use today, I gasp at the frigid nylon wherever it touches my skin.

Curled up, attempting to relax my clenched tight muscles, believing that I will soon be warm, these nights of broken sleep while we try to keep the fire going can be eased a little if I can get a good, solid nap. Stretching a wool hat over my head, I wait, exhaling into my own sleeping-bag to circulate the air warmed by my own body. Ah! The kitten pushes into the bedding and I hold her against my chest. Her tiny body adds soothing purrs to my slowly improving warmth.

I hear Kevin feed the fire, tromp to the door in his boots, slide the latch and head outside to try to start the van again. Just as I am falling asleep, I hear his boots on the step. No need to ask. I have not heard the all-important 'vrooom.' The van motor is definitely dead.

And yet, sleep is hard to find. I can't help letting my mind wander down the path of tomorrow...What are we going to do? And yesterday...Was there any other way we should have gone along the path that led here?

When I was younger, I had two re-occurring dreams. I still have them from time to time. They are always the same, yet with new variations. I am neither afraid, nor resisting these seemingly real experiences. I can remember sights and colours, sounds and feelings, sequences and efforts, yet I seldom retell them. It seems private and like an assignment or cause I must face alone. There is a kind of comfort or promise or security that this same message comes again and again. Perhaps this is the time in real life when parts of the dream are coming true?

The first re-occurring dream began while I lived in Colorado. It must have been when I was about eight or nine years old.

It starts in a garden or walkway. I see a small door up ahead and pause to test the latch, open it and find myself in another world. Or perhaps I am following a brick pathway, or a maze of some kind. Once I was swimming and dipped down through an opening, along a passageway and up out of the water and into a new place.

As each dream began it was made known to me (there was no one there that I could see or hear) that I was to experience many things, testing my endurance. Then I would be guided away to another, more pleasant place.

Endurance indeed!

First I was bundled up with layers of woolly white and furry brown coats, placed in a heated orangey-glowing room while fast percussive music was played. It made me dance. Sweating and exhausted I was released into the next room. In contrast, this was a chilled blue-grey-green room. Each layer was magically removed until I was only covered by a thin cloth, with a frigid, flat, black stone slab as a bed. With instructions to not move to create body warmth, I had to endure the cold, spread out flat, with nothing to protect me. Rusty, dusty and dim, the next room held a bed of prickly dry brown thistles and nasty long piercing thorns for me to lie on.

Again and again, these dreams came at intervals several months apart. Each variation of unpleasant experiences tested my endurance: carrying heavy weights, looking down from dizzying heights, long days of hunger, interruptions causing sleeplessness, pressure pushing me down, bright lights piercing my eyes, impenetrable darkness surrounding me, agonizing thirst, bombarding loudness, the pressure of silence, harsh wind, standing without rest, a small space without movement.

In these dreams, over time, I experienced deprivation of many kinds, and all in isolation. I made no sound, my throat holding back sighs, moans, whining. Only my breath and the muscles of my clenched jaw and fists and also my heaving, gasping rib cage indicated the strain.

Each time I awoke with a gasp, returning to the reality of my comfortable childhood home. No threats in sight. No deprivations or tests required of me. Thankful and appreciative of my parents' provision, I became aware that other children in other places and times did have to live in fear, endure circumstances of neglect, suffer daily hardship and step towards an unknown future.

When I was several years older, the endurance dreams finally came to a conclusion. Exhausted yet strong, alone yet brave, spent yet confident, alert yet unafraid, the tests were over. The second part of the same story began. After the endurance tests, a new passageway opened to more rooms. This time there was soft music, sweet smells, welcoming colours and abundance.

The first room was a luxurious bathing room featuring a huge tub filled with warm, sparkling, deep water, a cheerful fountain trickling into it. A table held an assortment of perfumes to add to the water. Afterwards, wrapped in a fluffy white robe, I was allowed to sample lotions and creams set out in pretty glass bottles. I experienced pampering massage, elegant grooming and pleasurable gentleness.

Next were the hair dressers. Regal arrangements of heaped up hair. Long ringlet curls. Jewels and flowers, veils and hats. So many experiments and alternatives were available.

Then a room filled with cabinets and displays of jewelry. Oh, that was an enjoyable dream! Hallways of cases of glittering gold and silver settings. Tiaras encrusted with gems. Broaches and bracelets with twinkling facets. Heavy, thick bands and airy, light spirals. Emeralds as deeply green as a mossy forest floor. Sapphires stunning the eye like the velvet blue of evening sky. Rubies piercing red. Rainbows pressed underground into shimmering opals. Jade swirling the colour of frothy rivers. Turquoise, smooth, cool, bold and calling to the imagination. Cut diamonds. Round pearls. Crystallized amethyst. Rose quartz. Slabs of carnelian. Droplets of amber. Spheres of tiger's eye. My eyes tried to gather and store the brilliance and diversity.

On to the corridors of capes, rivers of gowns, shelves laden with shoes, arrangements of hats and endless gloves and ribbons and belts and sashes. The entire collection was available for me to select a wardrobe with plenty of time to discover, explore, rearrange and select an outfit to take with me.

After many dreams and the final selection was complete, a wide doorway opened to a splendid garden. Richly coloured borders and huge ferns lined a smooth green lawn. A carriage pulled by prancing white horses met me at the stairway leading to a wide curved driveway. I was given the understanding that I would be meeting a man who had also endured much testing, selected clothing, shield, sword and cape.

I never saw my Prince Charming in the dreams. I was left to imagine the happy ending.

Is it possible that this dream has begun in real life? Is the reality of this unthinkable cold, dark, isolation and limitations the beginning of my endurance tasks? Shall I overcome this challenge and later find a chapter of life filled with blessings and plenty?

Remembering, I certainly sense my own courage while I was in the dream experience. Why not claim that courage right now in real life? This is the fourth day of bitter cold. Nasty, wretched, inescapable cold. Yet, I am learning how to manage. Even if this cold snap does last for three weeks. I am already one-fifth of the way through. I cannot keep the whole house warm, but I can keep my own body warm enough. This is the tenth day in our 'dream home.' Primitive, not at all like reading about it in a book or watching actors on a movie set. Yet, I am learning how to manage. Even if this icy endurance test of winter months lasts 100 days, I am already one-tenth of the way through it. And, the days really are getting longer.

Perhaps the dream was a message in a bottle. Or a time capsule sending me information I would need later. Now.

The meaning of the second re-occurring dream is a little harder to discern.

It began after I had lived in Ontario for a while. I was a teenager and the dreams have continued as I have grown to adulthood. There seems to be neither an explanation to the initial cause nor what triggers it now.

"I have to get out of here!" is the entire dream. Running, scurrying footsteps, looking back, long corridors, 'exit' signs, doorways, stairways, up and down, left and right, cement block walls. There are no other people, only me frantically running with dread to be caught, taken back, closed in again. Down long hallways, pushing through heavy double doors, just as I glimpse the out-of-doors...the dream instantly ends. Gasping, heart pounding, fear filled, I cannot in my waking life discover the 'something' that I am fleeing. And I never reach the way out.

So, I wonder, as I wait for warmth. Have I left behind the 'something' that I have been trying to flee? Or am I within the dreaded 'something' now?

"There's no way out," is certainly how I have been feeling since this cold began. Yet, I have decided to stay. The places I have come from I do not want to return to. Coming 'here' is my way out of 'there.'

Strange how I am completely alone in the dreams. Strange how I cannot see the ending. Strange how just at the turning point the dreams end. Strange how there's no one to tell me what to do.

I just don't know. I wonder if I will ever know? Does anyone know what dreams really mean?

"I can't. I have to." This certainly seems to be a re-occurring theme for me.

Sigh. No way to be sure.

Sleep. Please, give me sleep.

An incongruous sense of security and comfort wraps around me as I begin to slide into the sleep I need so much.

I nap for over two hours. Waking up when I'm finished a sleep cycle is so different from being interrupted by that pesty bell. Kevin has been keeping the fire stoked. "It felt warm in here while the sunshine was slanting in through the window," he observes. "This catalogue of wood working tools is getting me inspired for indoor projects." He is still wearing his down parka as he sits on his stump.

"I haven't heard you coughing so much," I stand and feel his forehead. "You're not so hot now," I smile down at him.

But he returns to the loft. I stir the pot of soup. There is enough to reheat for supper.

Besides nourishment for my body, I need something satisfying for my heart, mind and soul. I look through the stack of unpacked boxes and open the box labeled 'Memories 2.' It has the poems, notebooks, cards and gifts Kevin made for me and I made for him. Here it is, the spiral bound notebook in which I copied out quotations, glued in photographs of nature from magazine pictures and calendars, wrote out Bible verses and collected songs to strengthen us on our way.[39]

If there is beauty in the character
There will be harmony in the home.
If there is harmony in the home
There will be order in the nation.
If there is order in the nation
There will be peace in the world.
      Confucius

The longest journey is the journey inwards.
Dag Hammarskjold

A contented man
is one who enjoys the scenery
along the detours.
unknown

Whatever you can do,
or dream you can,
begin it.
Boldness has genius,
power and magic in it.
Johann Wolfgang vonGoethe

An unexamined life is not worth living.
Socrates

There is only one way to avoid criticism:
Do nothing,
Say nothing,
and Be nothing.
Aristotle

Don't point a finger.
Lend a hand.
unknown

In the middle of difficulty lies opportunity.
Einstein

We can easily forgive
a child who is afraid of the dark;
the real tragedy of life is
when men are afraid of the light.
Plato

To live a creative life,
we must lose our fear
of being wrong.
Joseph Chilton Pearce

All life is an experiment.
The more experiments you make
the better.
Ralph Waldo Emerson

Success is 1% inspiration
and 99% perspiration.
Thomas Edison

The person
who says it cannot be done
should not interrupt
the person who is doing it.
Chinese Proverb

Turn your face to the sunshine
and you cannot see the shadow.
Helen Keller

It does not matter how slowly you go
as long as you do not stop.
Confucius

Believe you can and you're halfway there.
Theodore Roosevelt

When people who are perceptive   have feelings of compassion
they know   that they are being alerted by the Lord   to offer help.
Swedenborg

Two shall be born the whole wide world apart.
And these two over unknown seas
to unknown lands shall bend each wandering step
to this one end,
that one day out of darkness they shall meet
and read life's meaning in each other's eyes.
Susan Mar Spading

We can only appreciate the miracle of sunrise
if we have waited in darkness.
unknown

Fall seven times and stand up eight.
Japanese Proverb

Troubles are often the tools
by which God fashions us for better things.
Henry Ward Beecher

Our lives begin to end
the day we become silent
about things that matter.
Martin Luther King Jr.

Life is not easy for any of us.
But what of that?
We must have perseverance
and above all,
confidence in ourselves.
We must believe
that we are gifted for something,
and that this thing,
at whatever cost,
must be attained.
Marie Curie

How wonderful it is
that nobody need wait
a single moment
before starting to improve the world.
Anne Frank

Friendship is the comfort,
the inexpressible comfort of feeling safe with a person,
having neither to weight thoughts nor measure words,
but pouring them all right out, just as they are,
chaff and grain together
certain that a faithful hand will take and sift them
keep what is worth keeping and then,
with the breath of kindness, blow the rest away.
Dinah Maria Mu lock Craig

What comfort! What courage! Others have been on this part of the Journey! Milestones have been left by others for me to follow.

I need this notebook near me. I unpack and start a collection of books to keep handy on the corner of the table. Just seeing them there, I can regain balance between the difficulties and the potential.

While it is still light, I roll my stump over beside the open oven door and I take up a sewing project. Today is New Year's Eve and a perfect time to begin something meaningful. Several weeks ago, I found a purple butterfly embroidery the size of my palm at the thrift store. I have decided to sew it onto the cargo pocket on the left side of my down parka. A symbol of hope, cycles, springtime, this visual reminder, near my heart, will help me have the stamina to make it through these winter months. Under the snow, somehow still alive through this cold, there are cocoons, eggs, seedlings, buds waiting. I, too, will have to wait. But new life will come.

I very much like the repetitive work of hand sewing. My hands are busy, but my mind can travel. I feel unusually peaceful today. It's strange. The conditions and tasks are the same: frigid cold, on-going firewood, more melting of snow and identical days forecast ahead. Yet, the 'Yes' I gave in my hour of darkness brought a kind of light and warmth inside me. I would rather believe that 'Someone' sees, cares and provides for me than cast away 'faith' and face this situation 'on my own.' And this gift of quiet calm and trust confirms to me that 'Someone' really does exist. 'Wonderful Counsellor' is one of His names. And surely, He is the 'Prince of Peace.'[35] I will still have to concentrate on not complaining and work with effort to do daily tasks, but the confusing turmoil of bombarding doubts is banished and a Guard is in place to protect me.

I round the edges of the butterfly's wings, listening to the coaching and comfort of thoughts which come and nourish my tired mind, heart and soul. With this Gift comes another realization. I do not have a larger community now to volunteer in and interact with. At this present time and place, I only have my husband. It is here, in the home, that I can seek ways to serve the Lord. And so, I have come full circle. Not confined to the home by the rules someone else wrote, but accepting this temporary limitation as yet another stage upon which to enact my dedication to follow the Two Great Commandments: 'Love God and Love your neighbour.' Enough. Satisfied. Pledged. 'Yes.' Not because someone made me do it. Not to follow the rules. Not 'Look at me! I'm so good!' But as a gift returned to the Giver. Sacred acts in tiny things.

"Hello the house!"

Who could that be? Sam bounds out, all wagging and dancing as he recognizes Howard, arrived from the city. I beckon him inside, pleased to see a familiar face. No, his wife, Opal, didn't come this time. He just drove up for the day to make a delivery and see if we got moved in and how we are surviving in the cold.

And, he has a surprise!

Bundled up again, I follow him back down the path to his little blue pick-up truck. He told me to bring the sled. I cannot imagine what he might be bringing us?

Wonder of wonders! It is a small heater wood stove! A miracle! And Howard is the angel delivering it! The heater firebox will hold four times as much firewood as the cook stove. Rapidly calculating, I realize that it could mean perhaps six hours of sleep!

That is, if we can install it. But, look. He thought of everything. Pulling back the rest of the blue tarp, I can see the necessary chimney pipes. Two long straight black tubes, an elbow to turn this short chimney towards the existing cook stove chimney and also the 'T' piece we will need to join the two chimneys together.

I cannot contain my joy! Hugs and grins. My loud "Thank-you" keeps bursting out over and over again.

Together we lift the metal box down and tug the sled up the slope. I call to Kevin to "Come and see!" There is a great stamping of boots and greetings and appreciation.

Howard is so pleased that we have accomplished what we set out to do. His message of congratulations is a balm after these days of self-doubt. Showing him details of construction, telling stories of challenges overcome, bragging a little, descriptions convey our effort and activities.

Generous and thoughtful, there is more. Opal sent along a large cast iron frying pan, a used muffin tin, four bread pans and a pair of cookie sheets. Now I can bake!

Too short our time together, he wants to head home and drive as many miles as he can while it is still daylight. "Please tell Opal how much we thank you!"

"Happy New Year!" voices echo across the valley.

And this kindly old man is off.

Tomorrow I will attempt to bake bread, although it might be a challenge for the yeast to rise in such a cold environment. Tomorrow we will have warm muffins and toasty granola. "Tomorrow." What a wonderful word. I have pleasant plans for tomorrow!

"Something is so much more than nothing." A new motto pops into my head.

Tomorrow Kevin will set up the new stove, measure then cut the metal chimney, struggle with matching the pieces, careful not to make a mistake. Tomorrow we will have a heater! Tomorrow night I will float in blissful sleep. When this stove is set up, there will be no more alarm clock jangling every one-and-a-half-hours!

Light is fading outside, but a bright future fills our home.

There is a noise outside again. I hear a motor. I see head lights. Did Howard come back? I hear clattering wood. I step towards the road just in time to see a familiar pickup truck pulling away.

"Kevin! Red brought us another load of lumber ends!"

The grumpy guy gets the generosity award after all!

Supper's ready.

Suppertime soup satisfies the body. Friendly companion-ship satisfies the heart. Improvements and plans satisfy the mind. Trust while moving ahead satisfies the soul.

After eating, we usually blow out the lamp.

But I don't want to go to bed yet. It's New Year's Eve!

It seems like there should be some feast to celebrate.

I begin to prepare food from our supplies. Since everything we bought is raw ingredients and not packaged prepared food, there are extra steps to take before a meal will be ready. I prepare pancake mix, measuring the dry ingredients, cutting in the shortening. I stir milk powder into water, adding four scoops of yogurt, stirring vigorously. The jar of liquid is set in the warming oven over night. The yogurt will be ready in about eight hours. I cover alfalfa seeds with water to soak overnight, preparing them to sprout.

Mixing and measuring, estimating and planning, pouring and stirring, the smells bring me hope. The work is a shield against hunger. My creativity is eager.

"What can I do with what I have?"

This is my new philosophy of life. Redirect my mind: Don't wish for things I cannot have. Inventory: flour, sugar, eggs, shortening, cinnamon, raisins. Bowls, spoons, measuring cups and my new cookie pans. Yes! I can make crispy, sweet cookies. We will have a treat to both celebrate this moment and to keep our minds off of these recent problems.

First step: Cream shortening with sugar. Mother taught me how. I have done this many times. But, wait. The butter knife I use, anticipating an easy gesture to dip out the smooth white substance won't even make a dent. Apparently shortening gets hard when it is frozen. Not to worry, I can pry enough out and heat it slowly in a pot. The knife is bent, but the shortening is in the pot.

Melted now, I pour the shortening into the mixing bowl, wooden spoon at the ready.

OK, back to the task. Add brown sugar. Oh. I forgot. Since the temperature was well below freezing in our cabin last night, all of the ingredients will be as if I had stored them, not on a room-temperature pantry shelf, but in the deep-freeze. The sugar looks and pours the same, but when added to the melted shortening instantly makes the mixture rock-hard again!

OK. I can solve this problem, no need to fuss. I'll whistle while I work and melt them together. I dump the chunk of sugary-shortening back into a sauce pan. This should work. Warm it up. But not too hot. I still want to cream the mixture. I place the pot on the far right stove top where it is farthest from the flame. I stir and watch so the mixture does not heat the sugar to become crystallized candy.

Back on track now. I can do this. Here we go. Now it is something like the right consistency. What's next? Add an egg. What's this? The eggs are frozen! Like little yellow and white golf balls! How shall I heat up an egg in the mixture without cooking it? No one wants scrambled egg cookies? Reluctantly, I peel the egg shell off of the frozen sticky egg. Now, drop it in the mixture and try to wait patiently for the egg to melt. Do eggs melt? I can't walk away or sit down. I must watch the fire, the pot and the egg.

Hurray! Now it is all stirred in. Looks a little funny, but this is what I have. Scoop the nearly ready cookie dough back into the bowl. Cheery now, domestic, accomplishing the task, preparing home-baked goodies for my Hubby. Yes, this is grand.

Here come the dry ingredients: flour, baking powder and cinnamon...ugh! You'd have thought I would know by now! Instantly hard. The sub-zero flour makes it impossible to stir. Back into the pot, back on the stove. Stir. Watch. Wait. Hope. There are no instructions for this. I am an explorer entering unknown territory.

Grease the pans. Now spoonfuls of dough, looking so orderly and predictable, all lined up.

Hmm. I have no way of accurately controlling the temperature inside the oven, but here goes. I'll have to open the door to look frequently to prevent burning.

What kind of science experiment is this? Well, they sure smell good while they're baking. That's a good sign. The anticipation is wonderful. I boil water for tea.

"Everything's ready!" I call my Hubby away from wishing over his tools catalogue.

Oh! How disappointing! Not culinary gems, these are hard, rocky, grey blobs! Well, looks like we'll dip these never-again cookies in the tea to make them palatable. A sigh. A smile. We share.

At least we'll have a story to tell about our first New Year's Eve.

The cold still presses in. This day is done.

Seeking physical comfort more than social company, I return to my sleeping-bag, arranging the wool quilt, down sleeping-bag, layers. It does not seem so dreadful tonight. I have come to accept this. The entire house is not going to be 'warm.' The only really warm place is inside my own clothes and under these layers of bedding.

Kevin joins me. He's feeling a little better. I am so relieved. No radio play on the weekend. We talk together for a few precious moments.

"Happy New Year, Husband," I croon, marking the moment. "I'm so glad I picked you."

"I'm so glad I found you," he replies, warm arms wrapping me, comforting.

Our wedding day is in the past. Our marriage is withstanding our challenges. Something new is around the bend.

"Remember when I told you my idea of marriage?" I want to share a stirring of renewed inspiration with my husband after these days of trial. "I realized that when you pick up a smooth pebble at the beach, sanded by waves and beautiful in its roundness, it used to be a split off, jagged rock, sharply edged from the mountain top. Tumbling and rolling, it has journeyed down the creeks and rivers to be shaped and softened. The sheared off rock seems harsh. But the smooth rock seems lovely." My hands are gesturing the breaking, tumbling, smoothing.

"That's how I see marriage. We start out rough and uncomfortable. But as we bump and jostle and roll and turn, we shape each other, gradually becoming pleasant and fitting together and the inner beauty can be seen." In the dark, I turn my face towards his. "That's what I think we are doing. That's why I want to keep on the Journey with you. I like how you change me. I want you to be the one to influence me."

"Me, too," his words softly spoken as he slips away from this day, through the passage way of sleep into the New Year.

But, poetry is not reality.

It is another night of broken sleep, of repetition, of fire keeping. Waiting for flames.

The patterns and pieces and pathways lead to this place and time. Resources and experiences, turning toward and turning away from, tiny adjustments and giant strides have brought me here.

Is it a deep cave with no way out?
Is it a tunnel which will lead to brightness?
Is it the great 'alone' that philosophers and monks deliberately choose?

It is the doorway to insanity?
It is the sacred 'Narrow Way?'

The firelight dances.

Close the drafts and damper to reduce the air intake, yet keep the coals glowing, Harness the fire to serve a useful purpose: to heat, light, provide food and safety. I will also learn how to harness my gifts for a useful purpose. I don't know for who, when, what or how I will be of service to others just yet. But this, too, will be given to me.

I turn to return. Up. Sleep. Wake. Down.

The next time I descend this ladder, it will be after midnight. It will be the New Year.

But there will be nothing new. Only more cold. Only more dark. Only more alone. Only more waiting.

On my way down the ladder the flashlight beam catches on the only ornamental object on the grey walls of the cabin.

A gift from Fran on Christmas Day, I had set it aside as a sentimental rhyme. I had tacked this small banner on the wall as the only available decoration. Now I look again.

> Great is the power of might and mind,
> but only love can make us kind
> and all we are and hope to be
> is empty pride and vanity.
> If love is not a part of all,
> the greatest man is very small.
> *Helen Steiner Rice*

I pull out the tacks. I will carry it back up the ladder in my hand, tuck it under my pillow, memorize the words. Balm for the heart, this simple clue serves as an antidote to the poisonous fears I have been wrestling with.

Like a beacon from a lighthouse tower
this simple message cuts a shaft of light
through the confusing storm,
simplifies the complex thrashing debates,
warns of the hazardous rocks of clashing doctrine,
overpowers the swirling waves of despair
to become a quieting stillness.

Like a steady straight beam of light this message
guides my heart and mind to clarity,
shows the way to the ship's safe harbor,
welcomes the weary traveller to a calm haven,
offers the possibility of rest to the wrestling captain.

Physically, I must still endure the cold for many more days.
Mentally, I must still solve many unforeseen problems.
Emotionally, I must continue in uncomfortable isolation.
Socially, I have rejected the impoverishment of plenty
and accepted the challenges of voluntary simplicity.

But spiritually, I have come out of the swirling storm,
crossed the godforsaken desert,
faced my fears
and found the nourishment of the oasis.

And it was there all of the time,
Available to all,
Given by the Creator,
Shared amongst His children, invisible, intangible,
motivating every act, beyond language, above creed,
threading its way into every heart.

I have been reduced to the bare minimum. Physical needs scarcely met, sleeplessness eroding the mind, few resources, unknown future, what is there to hold on to and be sure of? Love. Primary. Central. Enduring. Constant. But, I am not capable of this kind of unshakable love. I waver. I doubt. I crumble. Love does not come from inside me. Love must be stronger than I am. What is Love's Source? From where does this endless Fountain flow? How can I reach this Summit and draw on this unlimited wealth?

Maybe all of the scrolls and Sacred Texts can also be reduced to their bare minimum.

In the beginning God created the heavens and earth[36]...

In the beginning was the Word...and the Word became flesh and dwelt among us[37]...

God is not far, far away, perfect and aloof. God is not found only in a church, however ornamented and grand. God is not captured in a book, however true and wise. God is not a complex debate. God is not a fairy-tale from dreamland. God is real.

God made me. On purpose. He loves me. He sees me. He knows what I need. I can call to Him. He will comfort me.

In pictures, the Good Shepherd searches for the little lamb[38] braving storms and deserts and rocks and thorns. But now I know that He can also travel through bleak, icy darkness searching for me. I am not abandoned.

I am not alone. I am loved by Someone. I have Someone to love. And Love brings the One who loves and the one who is loved together.

Something is happening.
Something is happening inside me.
Something better than a new day
or a new year.
Something better than a pay cheque
or a present in the mail.
Something better than obeying the rules
or being 'nice' or being 'right.'
Something better than being first
or getting an 'A' or winning the game.

I look again at the quotation. 'Kind'... that's it!

Careful not to drop the wood, careful not to slam the metal lids, I can feed the fire quietly and be kind to my sleeping husband.

Up the ladder, clutching the wisdom-rich banner, I can burrow into my sleeping layers without whooshing in cold air and be kind to my generous husband.

Reset the alarm clock, slide the banner under my pillow, wrap my arm over the shoulders of my hard working husband. Kind. I can be kind.

Something is happening: 'Kindness' is making me warm!

"Kevin?"
"hmmm?"
"I can hear your heart beat."
"That's a good thing."

If you enjoyed *10 Days in December*
...where dreams meet reality...
watch for future titles Eleanor Deckert is working on:

10 Days in January
...1 husband...
...2 brothers...3 sons...4 Dads...

10 Days in February ...I'd rather be someplace else...

10 Days in March ...and then I'll volunteer...

10 Days in April ...high hopes and a detour with cancer...

10 Days in May ...plant a seed and watch it grow...

10 Days in June ...one thousand dollars...

10 Days in July ...first fruits...

10 Days in August ...so many good-byes...

10 Days in September ...learning...teaching...

10 Days in October ...glad, sad, mad, scared...

10 Days in November ...infant, sister, maiden, bride, wife, mother, daughter, single, widow, crone...

10 More Days in December ...family...community...

Endnotes

[1] Chapter 1: You can read the original 'Natural Life' magazine on-line. www.naturallifemagazine.com/7810/NLO15 Our ad is on page 67, bottom left.

[2] During the 1970's and 80's Canada was making the shift from British units of measurements to metric. During these years it was common for Canadians to use both British and metric in conversation.

[3] Psalm 128, lyrics used with permission, Lori Odhner©1978

[4] 'Hansel and Gretel' is in the public domain.

[5] During the 1970's and 80's Canada was making the shift from British units of measurements to metric. During these years it was common for Canadians to use both British and metric in conversation.

temperature comparing British and metric:
    212°F - 100°C = water boils
    98°F - 37°C = body temperature
    72°F - 20°C = room temperature
    60°F - 15°C = nice for a picnic
    32°F - 0°C = water freezes
    a few degrees above or below freezing = 'Mild'

17°F - -10°C = 'Right Balmy' or 'Brisk' or
'Bracing' or 'A Little Chilly'
5°F - -15°C = 'Frost on the Pumpkins'
0°F - -20°C = 'Starting to get *Real Cold*'
-40°F - -40°C = 'How cold *is* that?'

[6] 'Somewhere' from 'West Side Story', hear the whole song on youtube.

[7] Thanksgiving is the second Sunday in October in Canada.

[8] Sears Radio Theatre programs are available on the web.

[9] Matthew 6:33

All quotes from the Bible are from the King James translation which is in the public domain.

[10] Matthew 28:19

[11] Luke 1:48

[12] John 2:41

[13] Keekwillie is also called a 'pit house' with interesting photos on the web.

[14] poem used with permission "Remember This" from "The Poems and Prayers of Helen Steiner Rice" by Helen Steiner Rice©2004   Used by permission of Revell, a division of Baker Publishing Group.

[15] song public domain

[16] 1 Samuel, 1:20

[17] Psalm 27:4

[18] Mark 12: 30-31

[19] Micah 6:8

[20] John 10:10

[21] Matthew 7:7

[22] Joshua 24:15

[23] commonly thought to be the prayer of Richard, Bishop of Chichester

[24] Psalm 23

[25] Matthew 4:19

[26] Matthew 28:19

[27] Matthew 5:16

[28] Noah, Genesis 6-9

Joseph, Genesis 37, 39-50

Children of Israel, Exodus and further

Mary and Joseph, Luke 2 and Matthew 1,2

[29] Matthew 7:14

[30] Bodhisattva definition
    http://www.merriam-webster.com/dictionary/bodhisattva

[31] Matthew 10:29

[32] Robert Frost

[33] Matthew 25: 35-36, 40

[34] 'Impossible Dream' from 'Man of La Mancha' music by Mitch Leigh and lyrics by Joe Darion Hear the whole song on youtube.

[35] Isaiah 9:6

[36] Genesis 1:1

[37] John 1:1, 14

[38] Luke 15: 3-7

[39] To the best of my knowledge, all of the following quotations are in the public domain.

Invitation to Book Club participants who read 10 Days in December

Questions are included based on Eleanor Deckert's *Seven Predictable Patterns* ® for the purpose of stimulating discussions similar to the seminars Eleanor has developed.

"What were you thinking?"
"How do you do that?"
"Where do you get all your ideas?"

People ask Eleanor these questions when she tells about the choices she's made, the creative volunteer projects she is involved in and her homeschooling experiences. *Seven Predictable Patterns* ® offers a way to bring to awareness seven patterns found re-occurring in Nature and use them as patterns to address everyday problem solving, stimulate creative solutions, open communication and 'see' more clearly how to untangle challenging situations.

In business since 1995, with speaking tours through Canada and the USA, her seminars are presented to parents, educators, professionals and volunteers.

Seven Predictable Patterns ®
are seven patterns found re-occurring in Nature

Questions to stimulate discussion

#1

IN & OUT
OPPOSITES

... in Nature: up/down, on/off, wet/dry, empty/full ...

1a) What opposites did Eleanor experience
- as a waitress - in the cabin?

b) Does one have more value than the other?
Or are they two necessary parts of a whole?
Breathe IN. Breathe OUT. Notice the balance.

c) In what ways do you experience the Pattern of OPPOSITES?
- at work - at home?

#2

#2 CIRCLE-CENTRE-CYCLE

... in Nature: day, seasons, life cycle ...

2a) Describe Eleanor's daily cycle
- on a work day - after the cold snap?

b) What have we learned about Eleanor's life cycle?
Infancy, childhood, youth, adult, old age are all part of this Pattern.

c) Describe your daily cycle.
Where are you in your life cycle?

d) The central purpose does not change while the cycle unfolds (sun centre of solar system).
How does Eleanor's purpose give her courage through the difficult parts of her life cycle?
Can you identify your purpose for a specific task?
Can you sense your life's purpose?

#3

HEART
SPIRIT
MIND
BODY

... in Nature: our selves: emotional-social-family
spiritual-sacred-motivation
intellectual-problem solving-logic
physical-tangible-earth

3a) Before moving out west, what resources did Eleanor have to provide for each part of herself?

b) As she begins to live in the cabin, what does she lack?
   How does her awareness of this Pattern
   - cause her pain? - help her cope?

c) What resources do you have that benefit each part of yourself?

#4

TENDING THE FIRE

... in Nature: tending a fire...

4a) Eleanor describes the steps to light the fire, use the stove and the mistakes she makes.

She comes to see this as a metaphor for learning new things:
Begin (coals or a match)
Careful preparation (lay the kindling criss-cross)
Stimulate (blow, poke, monitor the air flow)
Add challenges (add larger pieces of wood)
Commit to tending the fire because the purpose is important
Achieve goal (food, water, warmth)

b) What other new skills has she had to learn using this Pattern?
Begin, prepare, stimulate, add challenge, commit, focus on the purpose, achieve the goal.

c) Is there anything in your experience of learning that is similar?

#5

NEED
NICE
NEVER

... in Nature: essential-enjoyable-dangerous...

5a) While working as a waitress, Eleanor notices that what she provides each customer is something they need, enjoy, or is something unhealthy.

b) When she describes her childhood and friendship with Kevin, what do we learn about her values?

c) How do the NEED - NICE and NEVER factors motivate Eleanor to go west?

d) On December 30, while shopping, what decisions does she make?

e) In what ways do you make decisions based on the Pattern NEED - NICE - NEVER?

#6

P
L
>D
A
N

POSSIBILITIES
LIMITATIONS
DECISION
ACTION
NEXT TIME

... in Nature: variations (same flower: many colours)...

6a) What limitations does Kevin face as he begins to build the cabin?
   What possibilities does he realize?

b) How do Kevin and Eleanor work through this decision making process to solve the problem of the severe cold?

c) On December 31, while baking the cookies, how does Eleanor experience this Pattern?

#7

DECKERT'S INDEX
SPIRIT - BODY
MIND - HEART
PAST-PRESENT - FUTURE

... in Nature: 3-dimensions ...
SPIRIT - BODY the up-and-down line
MIND - HEART the side-to-side line
PAST - PRESENT - FUTURE the back-to-front line

7a) From a very young age, Eleanor is aware that she is moving through time. How do you think this shapes her decisions and actions as a young girl?

b) In the present, she is very aware of her past and her future. How does this help or hinder her when difficulties arise?

c) How do the PHYSICAL objects she brought from the past in her 21 boxes become resources for her? What resources did she bring for her HEART-SPIRIT-MIND?

d) In what ways have you been aware of your past and future while in the present? Does this clarify or complicate the situation?

e) On the last page, after so much confusion and heart-ache, how do the whispered words between Kevin and Eleanor bring tranquility and orient them in the 3 dimensions of this Pattern?

Seven Predictable Patterns ®
www.eleanordeckert.com

Eleanor's seminars have been presented in:

Vancouver	Seattle
Calgary	Los Angeles
Courtney	Colorado Springs
Clearwater	Tucson
Barriere	St. Paul
Kitchener	Cincinnati
Burlington	Glenview
Elmira	Oak Arbor
Guelph	Kempton
Blue River	Bryn Athyn
Vavenby	Brooklyn
Avola	Philadelphia

What Readers Are Saying

Excellent. Just the kind of book I like to read.

—Mel, Heritatge Society, Kamloops, BC

A gem! A beautiful, poetic piece. Vivid pictures: one can see all the sights, smell the smells, feel the cold.

—Harmony, Librarian, Kamloops, BC

Eleanor is willingly baring her soul - her struggles and triumphs, the devastating sadness, the incredible moments of joy. A perceptive, sensitive, eloquent author!

—Anne, Author, Clearwater, BC

It amazes me how significant each moment is to you...your idealism, Kevin's incredible quiet sturdiness, resourcefulness, patience, resolve. You two really did this; found a piece of land in such a remote place, built a cabin in a few months with one man, an ax and a saw, moved in on the winter solstice. Thank you for writing this to share the reality of it all with the rest of us.....as we stand on a subway car crowded with such a multitude of strangers under the streets of Manhattan.....

—David, Architect, Manhattan, NY

You have described this place so perfectly! What a treasure your book is. Keep writing!

—Tammy, Care of Elderly, Vernon, BC

Four generations in our family have read '10 Days in December.' Looking forward to your next book.

—Kim, formerly of Avola, BC